handbook

for women

travellers

handbook for women travellers

Maggie & Gemma Moss

PIATKUS

First published in Great Britain
in 1987 by Judy Piatkus (Publishers) Ltd of
5 Windmill Street, London W1

Reprinted 1987
Reprinted 1990
Reprinted 1991
Revised edition 1995

**The moral right of
the authors has been
asserted**

*A catalogue record for this
book is available from
the British Library*

ISBN 0-7499-1439-4

Designed by Sue Ryall
Illustrations by Madeleine David
Data manipulation by Professional Data Bureau, London SW17
Printed and bound in Great Britain by
Mackays of Chatham PLC

For both Hannah and Ellen, with love and
best wishes for happy travelling, now and in the
future.

Contents

Authors' Note

Although you will find two 'voices' in this book, we have used the first person singular throughout. 'I' seemed more appropriate than 'we' for two people drawing for the most part on separate experiences of travelling; mostly in South America and the States (Gemma), or in Asia (Maggie). 'I' can therefore be either one of us.

ACKNOWLEDGEMENTS

We are indebted to the following for contributing their experience and advice: Susie Andrews, Ruth Angrove, Hilary Arundale, Geraldine Atkinson, Dena Attar, Christine Ayre, Carol Bailey, Jill Bailey, Kathlyn Bateman, Heather Booth, Susan Brown, E. Burtenshaw, Marjorie Byers, Vanessa Carson, Sue Castle, Jenny Cole, Phillipa Cubison, Nicky Cundy, Anne Hill-Smith, Melanie Challis, Michele Davies, Mary Dempsey, Jan Dryden, Sue Duffen, Ruth Ennals, Virginia Epstein, Natalie Fedecko, Elizabeth Ann Fish, Henrietta

Fitch, Christine Ford, Margaret Ford, Jill Garlick, Maggie Gillard, Sue Goldhawk, Lil Goodman, Jo Green, Linda Harris, P. Haslem, Mary Hawkins, Maggie Helliwell, Jenny Hierons, G. Hoggard, Jude Howell, Susie Iyadurai, Ruth Jarman, Carole Jasilek, Sue Jenner, Elizabeth Keates, Brenda Keatley, Bridget Keel, Jackie Keeley, Susan Kirk, Nelica La Gro, D. and L. Lawrence, Maria Lehmann, Susan Lewis, Karen Lewton, Sue Lloyd, Denise London, Brigid McGettigan, Monica Matthews, Valerie Millard, J. Miller, Anne Mitchell, Jill Moss, Barbara Neave, Zelie Norton, Sue Oakley, Caroline O'Brien Gore, Hilary Openshaw, J. E. Packham, Hilary Parritt, Hilary Pearson, Anne Pendlebury, Hilary Plass, Cecilia Platts, Finola Poyntz, Angela Raffle, Jill Reynolds, Roxanne Rowles, Christine Rawley, Ruth Rennals, Marcia Scott, E. Sharpe, Lucy Shepherd, Stephanie Simmonds, Jean Sinclair, Therese Sloan, Cathy Smith, Pip Smith, Shelley Somani, Megan Standage, Judith Stirrat, Elizabeth Jane Taylor, Katherine Towneley, Julia Vellacott, Susan Vickerman, E. J. Waddington, Jane Wainwright, Desiree Walker, Stephanie Wallis, Meg Wanless, Mrs. Virginia Watkins, Tamsin Watts, Alex Webber, Liz Wells, Annie Wood, Hazel Woodcock, Linda Wright, Seonaid Wright, Pat Yale, Sue Yates, Silvie Zovianoff-Zovak Ambrosoli.

Special thanks: to Basil and Rachel Moss, and to Mike Manson and Mike Chisholm for all their support, encouragement and patience — not to mention meals, cups of tea, and babysitting; to Voluntary Service Overseas — for their help and information, and for allowing us to attend their briefing sessions for new volunteers; to the Youth Hostel Association; to Polly Davies of Marco Polo Travel Advisory Service; to Dr Ant Goode; to Hetty Thistlethwaite for her support and advice and to Madeleine David for the illustrations which enliven our text.

Introduction

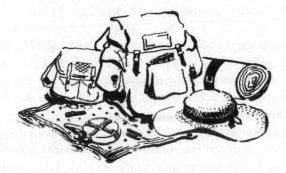

It wasn't until we set off to travel outside Europe for the first time that either of us realised how 'invisible' women are in the average guide book. Apart from a couple of sentences in the 'What to Take' section (on tampons and contraceptives), if women are mentioned at all, it's usually to warn them of the 'problems' they will face.

This handbook is an attempt to redress the balance. We don't aim to tell you country by country where to stay, what to see, or even how to get there — there are plenty of excellent books that do just that. What we do set out to do is direct the sort of general information all travellers want towards women with their special needs and interests. In addition we want to convince you that, contrary to expectation, women can travel safely, successfully and joyfully throughout the whole world.

And, if you've not already been before, we hope to encourage you to step outside the package tour to become an independent traveller and discover for yourself the fun and excitement that comes from making your own travel plans, taking control of your own arrangements, and travelling amongst local people without the cocoon of the tour party or the tourist hotel.

What can women travellers expect? Like the many women who contributed to this book you will bring back memories of times and places, of the people you meet, of incidents sad and funny to be savoured and shared at home. We'd like to start out with some memorable experiences quoted at length — the rest of the book will be using quotes to illustrate points in the text.

In the 1980s Karen Lewton visited North East Africa:

'At dawn on the second day, the train waits at Abu Hamad, the last village before the desert. You can wash under the pumps and stock up with fruit and vegetables in the little market under the trees, which smells of charcoal fires, and coffee and henna. More people will invite you for breakfast. The morning light, there on the edge of the desert, is a breathtaking pure gold. Then the desert is crossed — a day of mirages and camel trains and bones and derailed rolling stock, lying beside the track. There are ten little round stations across the desert, each with a single vulture perched on its roof.'

More recently, in China, Jude Howell met pilgrims at Emei Shan:

'Tiny shrivelled old ladies, leaning heavily on walking sticks carved with dragons and flowers, heave their shrunken bound feet up the muddy steps worked laboriously out of the mountainside. They dress traditionally — navy blue jackets fastened at the side with figure of eight loops, baggy trousers flapping an inch above the ankles, dark cloth shoes on their miniature stumps, and a knot of stalky black hair wound tightly at the back. Their cheeks are akin to the wrinkled shell of a walnut, their foreheads ploughed with ridges, their eyes, black as pitch, look purposefully ahead.

It was on the second night I had a closer encounter with these intriguing pilgrims ... the door creaked open and in came five elderly women, the youngest of whom was probably 70. They were shouting and laughing and soon flopped down on the two remaining beds. They each peeled off one layer of clothing leaving them with at least three woollen jumpers and vests to guard against the damp cold. Soon they were digging out their cigarettes and lighting up. My Chinese was limited, but a few words sufficed, and soon we were huddled up on the bed, munching dry biscuits and sipping hot water. I will never forget their resilience and warmth, their unbounding curiosity and their sheer determination.'

And Meg Wanless went to Sefrou (Morocco) with a boyfriend:

'Friendly Moroccans persisted in telling us Sefrou was "nice", in the meantime rolling their eyes in a way which suggested that it wasn't. The hotel was incredibly cheap — also incredibly hard to find. The "patron" was a small tubby and middle-aged Moroccan who looked more French than North African, whom we immediately (and privately!) christened "woolly pully" on the strength of his sporting a curious grey knitted garment which stretched over his paunch like a drum skin, and whose hem ended about two inches above his knee caps. The gardener was an ancient Arab, of fourscore years. On romantic moments in the garden, balmed by the scent of orange and lemon blossom, mingled with garlic and rancid fat from the kitchen, when we thought we were alone, he would mysteriously leap out of the bushes in front of us and present me with a rose.'

However, travelling brings with it more than just memories. Particularly if you are visiting non-Westernized countries for the first time it can be a challenging process as well as fun. For many people accepting and responding to this challenge is one of the most rewarding parts of their travels. To start with there is the challenge of trying to come to some real understanding of the country you are visiting (rather than just passively watching other people's lives through the windows of a tour bus). As Sue Yates found, exploring and re-assessing our misconceptions about other people and other societies when faced with the reality is exciting, sometimes painful, never dull:

'At the beginning all I knew about the people I was staying with was through the stereotyped images of starving children, and women burdened with hard work. All that the media considered "newsworthy" were the floods and famines, the sweat, dirt and poverty. The most common way of looking at Indian people was to see them as the abstract starving millions — to feel sorry for them, but know nothing about them. Before setting off I began to gather up information, to try to piece together what was behind the stereotypes.

But when I arrived, the picture I'd sketched out was shattered and my preconceptions had to be packed back into my rucksack. From the beginning I felt very intensely that something was changing inside me and I wouldn't be able to see things in the same light any more. I remember rushing off to write in my diary, to try and relieve the pressure against my head by letting some of my feelings out onto paper in an attempt to understand. The whole experience of being with people who had such completely different approaches to the way I lived overwhelmed me.'

Then there is the challenge of responding, of deciding how we should behave in countries where customs and traditions are very different from our own. Unfortunately as long haul travel becomes increasingly popular more and more travellers have stories to tell of places spoilt by being 'discovered' by tour operators, and of relationships between local people and travellers soured by the bad behaviour of visitors.

'We were away a year, and everywhere we met local people upset and angered by travellers who had desecrated temples and shrines by taking photographs, touching statues, smoking or not taking their shoes off. We met people whose hospitality had been abused, and others dismayed and upset by the scanty holiday wear people had on. Local people dress very modestly, they don't like to show bare legs let alone bosoms, but we saw several Westerners sunbathing topless. We even found villages where travellers aren't welcome anymore and many times we felt ashamed of our fellow countrymen. I know few visitors deliberately set out to offend local people, but far too many simply take it for granted that their ideas of how to behave will be acceptable everywhere, without stopping to think that, like guests back home, we should sometimes keep a check on what we do.'

Jill Bailey

This book gives many suggestions about how women can travel sensitively and with awareness wherever they go, and we hope that *all* travellers, male and female, will adopt the Travellers' Code (P. 271). By showing you are prepared to fit in with local ideas during your trip, *you* will have a better time, *local people* will have a better time, and so will those women travellers following after you.

All travellers share these challenges, but for women there is the additional one of travelling in what is still predominantly a man's world. For some this can be daunting indeed, but as many, many women have found, the rewards for going are immense:

'Even as relatively "liberated" Western women, we still have many conditioned fears to overcome — fear of independence, lack of confidence about our ability to cope on our own, fear of taking risks, plunging into adventure. You make the first step towards overcoming these fears by deciding to travel, and once on the road you are suddenly confronted with them and travelling can become a sort of test. But once you work all this through and find you can cope, these disadvantages of being a female traveller can be worked round to be a source of reward. I came back wondering, amidst a confused hotch-potch of impressions, what I'd gained from my experiences and suddenly thought "Hell, I *did* it". As a woman you can tell yourself you've really done something.'

Roxanne Rowles

Over 100 women travellers have contributed to this book; between us we have travelled in 105 different countries — through Africa, Asia and Europe, around China, and the Eastern Bloc, in the Middle East and Far East and down the Americas. We have travelled with women friends, husbands, partners, sisters, children and alone. We hope that we can share some of our experiences with you and that you will have as memorable, as interesting and as happy travelling as we have had. Good Luck!

1
Thinking Ahead

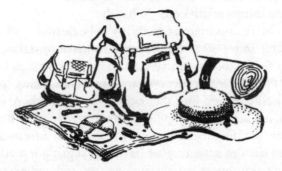

Too often the whole idea of travelling instantly conjures up images of discomfort. The assumption seems to be that whereas the tourist will be sitting in the luxury of an air-conditioned coach or lounging in the lobby of a famous hotel, the traveller will arrive in town, sweat-stained, wild-eyed (male and probably bearded), emerging from the bush after weeks of roughing it to stagger over to the local bar and spill out his tales. The harder the circumstances he has had to endure, the more determined he has needed to be in pursuit of his aims, the better and tougher traveller he seems to be.

Some people, women as well as men, undoubtedly do set out to travel in this way. They bemoan the increasingly civilised nature of countries the world over and long for the days when real excitement and possible danger could easily be found by the intrepid few. Moreover in their eyes, those of us who don't begin in like-minded fashion, prepared to endure everything — bed bugs, filth, real hardship, disgusting food and above all disease — 'everyone picks up hepatitis in Nepal' — hardly deserve to be called travellers at all. Anyone who's going to be cautious and nervous should simply retreat and settle for the package tour, all mod cons. Well, that is one point of view and good luck to them. However, the sharp dividing line such people draw between tourists and real travellers doesn't reflect many women's experience of travelling.

To enjoy independent travel you do not need to be prepared to wrestle with wild beasts, fight off hostile crowds and put up with non-stop diarrhoea. Nor do you have to know how to collect water in the middle of an oasis-less desert, survive on a diet of plant roots and grubs and be fluent in at least a dozen different languages, though of course any of these things might come in handy.

What is more important is an ability to be flexible, to learn as you go along and above all to be prepared to make mistakes. Patience, rather than fearlessness is probably the traveller's greatest virtue. And for those of us who aren't sure how well we'll cope, being comfortable needn't mean escaping into the cocoon-like atmosphere of the first class hotel, nor settling for a holiday somewhere just like home. What being a traveller does mean is using the available information to our own advantage, not assuming we have to just grit our teeth and bear whatever circumstances fate throws our way, and understanding that there are often choices to be made and alternatives to be had. Indeed half the fun of travelling is often making the decisions.

DECIDING WHERE TO GO

Some of us have no problem making up our minds where to go; we are simply obsessed with a particular place and have been for so long we can't even remember why or how it happened.

'I've always wanted to visit Macchu Picchu. I started out travelling through South America just to get there.'

South America

Others are more vague about their final destination:

'Why did I travel? To see the world, escape home for a while, work abroad, find myself — all the usual reasons.'

China

'My reasons for travelling: pleasure, enjoyment, an eye opener, to learn.'

Indonesia, Malaysia, Thailand

There are probably as many reasons for heading to particular places as there are travellers and certainly there is no one way of making up your mind. If you're thinking of starting on a long trip but aren't sure where to aim for try asking yourself the following questions.

Do you have friends or relatives in a particular part of the world who would enjoy showing you something of ordinary life in their country?

In which countries could you expect to share a common language?

Are there any countries whose present-day or historic culture interests you and makes you feel you'd like to find out more?

Do you know any other women who have travelled? Ask them for their impressions or their advice.

Do you have any particular goals in mind? Mountains you want to climb, things you want to learn about yourself? What sort of environment would suit your purpose best?

What is the status of women in the countries you might visit? How might this affect you?

Some countries will be very different from back home, their ways of doing things unfamiliar or unexpected. Do you feel fitting in and learning new ways could be an exciting challenge or is this something you'd rather not have to deal with. (You can always begin somewhere relatively familiar for a first trip.)

How important is your own level of comfort? Will this influence where you travel to? (If you are dreading poor standards check with a reliable guide book to see if you're right.)

Do you want to have a very physically active trip, a leisurely time, or a combination of both?

'I should have seriously considered my personality — not a "viewer" but a "doer". I'm interested in people and their way of life, and needed a specific area of interest which would have connected me with like-minded locals.'

Australia and New Zealand

GATHERING INFORMATION

Since the first edition of this book there has been an explosion of information aimed at the traveller and tourist alike. All the main British newspapers have regular travel columns, as do many magazines. Television programmes offer tantalizing glimpses of far away destinations. And of course so do returning travellers:

I don't think I would ever have gone travelling if it hadn't been for my friends all going off to India.'

Depending on your friends' propensity to exaggerate for the sake of a good travellers' tale, returned women travellers, coupled with a good guide book, are more likely to be reliable than other sources.

Many travel journalists get their information first hand on organised trips laid on by Tourist Boards who are keen to encourage visitors to their respective countries. Trips like these which include 5 star hotel accommodation, guided tours specially laid on for journalists, first-class travel and a whirlwind itinerary taking in all of the sites, but none of the people, are unlikely to provide much in the way of information for independent travellers, especially women (although they may whet your appetite). TV programmes also have their drawbacks; it's easy to forget that the apparently lone woman presenter is in fact accompanied by a (maybe all male) camera crew, and is being filmed at a location already researched by the rest of the team earlier.

Guide books

A good guide book should make you feel reassured that you WILL be able to find somewhere to sleep, that the transport system IS useable, and that you won't starve. You should look for detailed information about accommodation, with names, addresses and phone numbers of local hotels; advice about using public transport; where (and what) to eat, and what to expect to pay.

The best include background information about the historical, geographical and political contexts in which you will find yourself. They will give information about the culture, the environment and, depending on the interests of the writer, information about development issues, conservation — even the impact of tourism! Most have a fairly youth-orientated backpacker approach.

At long last, more guide books are beginning to give a passing nod to the information needs of women travellers. They are starting to provide some information about the status of local women within local cultures, and about cultural and safety issues for Western visitors. Two of the best known series are Lonely Planet Guides and Rough Guides (see page 273 for details of these and others mentioned in this section).

There are also a small number of travel guides written specifically for women, by women. Virago publish a series of six city guides. Rough Guides, in conjunction with Penguin books, publish *More Women Travel*, a compilation of women's experience of travel in over 70 countries.

Guide books for minority groups Mature women, lesbian travellers, disabled travellers and black women, however, are still not as well served as they should be. For mature women the problems are really one of style. The standard guides for independent travellers will provide most of the information they need, particularly the Lonely Planet series, which does provide information about a range of types of accommodation, to suit different budgets. However, it is presented in a relentlessly downbeat manner.

Gay women will find some information in the Rough Guide Series about local scenes, with contact addresses, clubs etc. You may also find

Virago's *Are You Two Together?* useful. Also available is Ferrari's *Places for Women.*

Disabled women have *Nothing Ventured — Disabled People Travel the World* (also Rough Guides) to turn to, and may find a paragraph or so in some other books in the Rough Guides Series. For specific information there is a new series out called Smooth Ride Guides, covering Australia and New Zealand, with the USA, Canada and other destinations to follow.

Black women are the least well served. Those we spoke to before updating this edition were concerned about the lack of information available to them.

'I'm worried about how I will be received, about being turned away from accommodation.'

'There is definitely a need for information about what travelling is like for black women. I mean, before things changed in South Africa, I wouldn't have known whether or not I could travel on a bus.'

There is very little information at all about how you might be received as a *black* woman from the *West*, either in traditionally white societies, or in black ones. Both Rough Guides, and Lonely Planet do attempt to describe the local cultures in some depth, so at least you can find out whether the countries you will be entering are multi-cultural or not.

In view of some of the comments I received about the poor reception of black women in some parts of Eastern Europe, and Japan in particular, more positive information is overdue. Happily, more and more black women *are* now travelling, so we would hope that the information you need will become more easily available. *More Women Travel*, mentioned above does include one or two entries by black women — let us hope this is the start of a new trend!

Disadvantages of guide books   Do you need a guide book at all? Once you have shaken off your fellow travellers and headed for a new destination, there is nothing more annoying than to find them all again, in exactly the same hotel, bar and cafe that you are using,

because you're all clutching the same guide books!

This does happen — in fact it happens all the time — so there are drawbacks to relying solely on guide books from home if you wish to get off the beaten track.

Local tourist offices

Once you have found your feet, you will be able to judge for yourself what offers of accommodation from other sources might turn out to be like and you will pick up ideas on other places to visit. Tourist information offices usually have lists of places to stay, or you may be accosted by local touts, eager that you visit their 'brother's', 'sister's', 'cousin's' guest-house. These may often thrust under your nose written testimonials from other travellers who have stayed there. You will also get recommendations about where to stay and where to go from other travellers direct, or you may be bringing these from home. Background information about the country(s) concerned is also available from local tourist boards, although it is likely to be highly selective and uniformly glowing in its praise.

Some suggestions

To help you make up your mind about where to go, here are some recommendations suggested by our contributors.

Some Easy Countries

Japan — I was told that Japanese surgeons have to practise stitching up stab wounds in the U.S. They don't have enough!
China
Bali
Seychelles
Thailand
Kenya
India — much innocent harassment — very little danger

Nepal — although, alas, not as crime-free as it used to be
Malawi

Some Less Easy Countries

Rural Turkey
Pakistan
Morocco and Algeria — usually o.k. in tourist areas although travelling with male companions does minimise hassles
South America — the problems are of robbery rather than being pestered by men.
Egypt — high incidence of pestering. Recent terrorist attacks on tourist groups in some areas.

TRAVELLING COMPANIONS?

Almost as important as where you go are your decisions about whether to travel with just one other person, in a group, or to travel alone. It's more than just a question of having or not having someone to play cards with at the airport terminal. Who you travel with and in what numbers affects your whole trip — what you see, what you do, who you meet and who meets you.

During my first trip I had experience of all the different permutations, and their advantages and disadvantages. Rather foolishly I set out with a male companion whom I hardly knew, having advertised for someone to go with in a magazine. When the inevitable happened and we parted company (me in tears, he stony faced), much to the entertainment of the local market, I joined up with a group of other Westerners until I felt confident to strike out on my own. At each stage I was developing my travelling ability. Without someone to go with I would never have left Europe; when the advantages of travelling in a pair began to pall, I joined a group for the security it offered, and when finally I had found my 'travelling feet' I set off on my own to sample the delights of travelling solo.

Travelling with a companion

Most people, especially on first trips, do as I did and look for someone else to go with. (Hopefully you and your companion will get along better than we did!) Not only is it much more fun if you are setting off with a friend (all that planning and arguing about what to see first), but it's like an extra insurance policy. Having someone else to help decide which of the hotels on offer is going to be the best bet for an undisturbed night, someone else equally dubious about buying duck's feet, for example, from an incomprehensible Chinese menu (chewy bits of blackened stick, in case you're wondering). It can also be easier getting through the practicalities — between you, you can halve the time spent waiting in queues for tickets. One person can go off to find somewhere to sleep whilst the other keeps an eye on your backpacks.

And it's not just the advantages of sharing practical problems, sharing the emotions of a trip can be good too. When you're tired, or apprehensive it's nice to have someone else there for support, even if they don't do much except listen.

> 'I travelled with one other woman. Visiting another country can come as quite a culture shock if one hasn't experienced it before. We were able to offer each other a great deal of support and comfort.'

Telling the day's events to someone else can help bring things into perspective if you've had an exasperating time, or add to the pleasure if you've experienced the moment of a lifetime, seen your first camel caravan or just exchanged grins with local women on the bus.

> 'One thing I did miss out on by not having a travelling companion was someone to talk to.'

Travelling companions bring different outlooks, interests and skills with them. One of you may be good at languages and at negotiating with local people, the other a genius at currency transactions or skilled at first aid. If one person is mad about plants and the other goes hunting round bazaars for local embroidery it rubs off, so you both actually see *more* than you might have done on your own. One person's interests can take the other into more museums, more markets and around more monuments.

Besides, particularly for women, there is the fact that it may feel safer to be travelling as one of a pair, than to be alone (see page 248).

However, there are of course some drawbacks to sharing your travels. Perhaps really passionate enthusiasts are best avoided. The train spotter who can't be persuaded to leave the engine shed or worse, the medic who insists on a tour of every local clinic, hospital and operating theatre, require considerable tolerance unless you happen to share their fanaticism. Not least because with such companions you can get a very one-sided view of the country which you are visiting. An Australian I once met was watching her companion struggle to fit a surf board into a taxi. They'd travelled right round the Far East, but only to within three miles of the beach in each country they had visited.

Even where your chosen partner has not got an all-absorbing hobby to follow up, the ordinary differences between you can sometimes cause problems.

You wake up feeling dreadful and your companion is dying to get going. You worry about them getting ill, and they get fed up with your penchant for getting both of you lost. A view which has stunned your companion with its colours, shadows and heights leaves you cold, whilst they insist on a detour to a totally unimpressive monument miles from anywhere which means that you miss out on the day's shopping you'd promised yourself.

Travelling, to use a cliché, *does* broaden the mind, but everyone reacts differently, often in an unexpected way, especially on first trips. Away from the familiar routine, quirks that you or your fellow traveller may regard in each other with amused tolerance back home, suddenly take on an undreamt of significance. Attitudes to money, or even differing opinions as to what constitutes an early start (one person's 'dawn' being another's 'lie-in') have caused many travellers to temporarily or even permanently, part company in a rage in the middle of nowhere.

Not only this, but new sides to your character may appear. The enthusiastic partner with whom you set out may become more and more timid, and more and more impossible with every day's travel further from home; or it may happen to you. Until I found my feet, I hid behind my companion on that first trip at every new town we came to. Every contact with local people, every decision, every responsibility I left to him - no wonder he found me a dreary contrast to the apparently self-confident woman he'd met in England.

Several contributors to this book wrote to warn of these sort of strains and the effect that travelling can have on personal relationships:

'I would prefer to travel with other females because there seems to be less chance of arguments and disagreements arising than when I travelled with a boyfriend.'

'If you are going to travel with someone, I feel you must be very close to them. The inevitable hassles of travelling do not need to be added to personal relationship problems.'

Happily, if you feel the advantages of travelling with someone outweigh any disadvantages, there are steps you can take to make shared travelling easier on both of you. Most crucial, *before* you set out is to talk through the sort of trip you both want and are expecting. This is essential if you and your companions don't know each other very well. Even if you are going with a really close friend from work you may only know them at the office or see them 'off duty' during a coffee break. You could be surprised by how much you *don't* know about each other. The time to talk about your possibly conflicting ideas is before you go, not halfway up a mountainside when one person is impatient to make it to the top and the other's inwardly groaning about their feet.

There's little point for example in setting out on a gourmet tour of the world's best restaurants if your companion would rather economise on food so that her budget will go further. And although both of you may be pining to visit the same country, China to one person may mean a boat trip down the Chang Jiang, to the other, the Great Wall. Are you sure you are going to be able to do both?

Be honest about your attitudes to money — are both of you expecting to travel at the same level — (dirt cheap, tourist class or in luxury)? It helps if you have roughly the same amount to spend. When travelling companions are operating on wildly differing budgets, problems are bound to arise, if the less well-off has to act as a brake on the travel plans of the more affluent of you.

Be realistic about your personal differences. On your travels you don't *have* to do everything together *all* the time. After all at home you wouldn't insist on sticking to your best friend all through the day no matter how well you enjoy each other's company. Establish from the outset (and look forward to the fact) that there are going to be times when you'll be on your own. Try arranging breaks away from each other. Do different things and then meet up later at your hotel, or even at the next town. Splitting up occasionally takes the pressure off, and allows you to explore and experience at your own pace.

Some travellers end up in a situation during their travels when one person is always the initiator, the leader, the other constantly the acquiescor, the follower. Although this may seem to emerge naturally, it seldom works well for long periods. The initiator may end up resenting the feeling that they are expected to take all the decisions, all the responsibility, the acquiescor that they haven't had the chance to do the things they wanted to. Unfortunately the usual alternative to this sort of set up is the eternal compromise, where both of you are so concerned to be fair and take each other into account that neither ends up particularly happy with a decision which in any case usually takes far too long to reach. How many of us are only too familiar with the 'I don't mind, what do you want to do?' syndrome? One way out is to agree to take turns to choose what to do, so that each person gets a chance at decision-making and at asserting their own preferences.

Above all during your travels, be aware of each other's need for time. Time to digest, to reflect, to absorb what's happening and time simply to be on your own once in a while, so that this can happen.

Travelling in groups

The sense of security that comes from travelling as one of a group appeals to many women, particularly if it's a first trip, or a trip to a remote and little visited area. Many travellers find themselves in groups for part of their travels as they meet up with other Westerners, other travellers from home. Others join an organised group from the outset.

Group travel has advantages, particularly for those single women who otherwise might not travel at all, but it has some drawbacks as well.

On the plus side, groups allow different permutations among members. You're not always spending time with the same person. You also have a wider pool of experience to draw on. Other members' knowledge can make up for the political or geographical gaps in your own; your own contribution adds to the overall picture the group builds up during the trip.

The security of a group can be reassuring. Although you may feel you are having your fair share of trouble with officious hotel managers, local Romeos and pick-pockets, being in a group means that there are more people around to call on if you feel you can't handle a problem on your own. Groups also have more power than individuals. Threatening to leave if the loos aren't cleaned cuts more ice if there are ten of you, than if it's just you and a friend complaining. Requesting a 'tea-stop' from the long-distance coach driver is more likely to get results if a dozen voices are raised, than one.

Moreover, in some situations, it would be positively foolish to travel alone, or even in pairs — pot-holing, mountaineering, desert or arctic travel are all better undertaken by a small party with few enough members to move around easily, but enough people to be able to cope in case of accident.

However, against these advantages are several drawbacks that put many women off group travel altogether. Firstly, the number of people involved tends to make groups less flexible than individual travellers. What can get lost is the spontaneity and freedom which makes it possible for couples or solo travellers to make the most of an unexpected festival, village wedding or just an unexpected break in the weather. Secondly, there the problems of actually organising the group:

> 'Travel arrangements are so complicated, time consuming and bureaucratised that if travelling in a party of more than two, one would spend all one's time sorting out each other's affairs. It was bad enough with just two of us.'

Part of the fun and excitement of stepping off the package tour circuit is making your own arrangements about where you stay and how you travel. But it's very difficult with more than four to come up with a satisfactory way of organising yourselves.

Inevitably, sooner or later (preferably sooner if your travels are to proceed smoothly) the group has to become 'organised'. It quickly becomes easier to appoint a spokesperson who can take some or most decisions and who can do most of the negotiating with people outside the group. Individual members then become less and less involved with the day-to-day arrangements and plans.

> 'I would go as a member of a smaller group (next time) when I could take more part in planning and decision-making.'

The problem of organising the group can present particular problems for women in mixed parties. These have all the usual traps for women members, particularly if they are in a minority. Far too often women find they have to work twice as hard to be heard, to be involved in decision-making and to have their perspective taken into account by the male members of the party. This isn't always entirely the men's fault. Local people may often reinforce any stereotyping that's going on by automatically expecting the men to act as spokespersons for everyone else, by approaching male members first when decisions have to be taken, by assuming that women in the party will come second.

Dealing with assumptions by local people is difficult if not impossible because the culture clash involved is so great. Dealing with assumptions by male group members will of course depend very much on who you're with.

However, without doubt the biggest drawback to group travel is the way groups isolate their members from local people.

'If I travel with other people I tend to spend all my time in their company, whereas travelling alone, I make more of an effort to meet people.'

Group dramas, personalities and relationships can swamp what is going on outside and you are cushioned from the exciting process of exploring and examining your own cultural ideas in comparison and conflict with those of local people. I certainly felt more relaxed and at case when travelling onwards as one of a party of Westerners on that first trip, but that was a reflection of how little adjustment to non-Western culture I was having to make during this time.

Local people also react very differently towards groups than they would to one or two travellers in their midst. You only have to consider your own reactions to individual tourists having difficulty finding their way round your home town, and then compare this to your feelings towards the large party who are blocking the pavement whilst you're trying to reach the shops before closing time. Or think about the time you met a couple on holiday in the pub, in comparison with the time your favourite drinking place had been completely taken over by a coachload on their way to the nearest monument.

Groups repel the merely courteous and polite — who can afford to offer hospitality to so many? Who can be bothered to help? 'Let them look after themselves, with such a crowd, they can manage.' Groups put off those who are simply friendly — how can anyone approach such a number of people all at once if all they want is a chat and the chance to try out a foreign language?

Groups also act as a magnet to those for whom tourists are the means to a livelihood — 12 people after all, means 12 chances someone will buy something. Finally, especially in non-Western cultures, groups attract the curious in larger numbers than do solo travellers who blend in better and offer less excitement.

I remember a noisy party of Italians who took over the local ferry boat on a trip down the backwaters of Southern India around Allepey and Quillon. They dominated the whole boat, drowning out local people who stopped what they were doing in order to watch this free entertainment. Several running jokes from the group comic took up much of their time, as did pretending to push one of their members overboard. I enjoyed the trip, but my memories are as much to do with what was happening with them as it is to do with what I actually saw on the way. What a contrast to a day spent paddling the lagoons around Ambalangoda in Sri Lanka. We were heavily outnumbered by our boatman, two of his kids (and their friends) as well as three neighbours who came along just for the ride. It culminated in a visit to a tiny temple where the children brought flowers to offer to the enormous statue of the reclining Buddha. On the way back we stopped off at our boatman's home and his wife invited us inside their thatched one-room house. We sat on the bed and drank tea and admired her children's school certificates.

Unfortunately, avoiding some of the problems of group travel is impossible unless you avoid large groups altogether. But it is important to sort out any decision-taking process and organisational problems before you go. And it is important to allow time for members to spend some time on their own.

Organised tour groups

Although organised tours have all the disadvantages of group travel, we certainly don't believe that women travellers couldn't or shouldn't ever consider joining prearranged trips — especially as for many women these prove to be a stepping off point for travelling independently on return trips. Despite the fact that one of the aims of this book is to help and encourage you to become independent to move safely and enjoyably around on your own (or with a friend), in control of your own arrangements, we can't all be like Dervla Murphy or Christina Dodwell! There are several specialist operators that offer adventure trips, some to very remote areas indeed, and there are many good reasons why you might consider joining them. (A low budget is not however one of them, for most are not particularly cheap.)

Firstly, many people are happy to hand over to others some or all of the responsibility for day-to-day arrangements and organisation.

Secondly, as a lone woman, you might have genuine misgivings about your ability to move around easily on your own, in the areas you wish to visit. You might prefer the reassurance of a group. Thirdly, in some countries, independent travellers are strongly discouraged. A group may be allowed where an individual would not. Fourthly, prearranged group travel is ideal for those whose time is limited. Making all your own arrangements is fine, if you have time to do so before you go (and plenty of time during your travels to sort out those arrangements when they go awry). Not everyone is lucky enough to have three months, six months, or even more to spend wandering the world. For them a prearranged month's trek in Peru or Nepal could be the alternative to an otherwise ordinary holiday at home.

There are several things to consider when joining such a group. You do first of all have to weigh up what you lose (flexibility, closeness to local people), against what you'll gain (security, like-minded travelling companions etc.). Once you've made up your mind, there are several things to consider when choosing which company to travel with. What sort of briefing material is provided? How sensitive is it? (Some tour operators blatantly treat other countries and cultures as consumer items which happen to be conveniently around for the pleasure of their members.) What information is given specifically for women group members? What evidence is there that the company has thought about the needs of women travellers? What is the decision-making process — how much say do group members have, and over what sort of choices? Is the group leader male or female?

You should also find out if the group sets aside any time for its members to spend exploring on their own. If it does, take every opportunity to get away with just one person, or by yourself, and *enjoy* feeling more exposed to local traditions, and less sure of yourself. Try to find local women and their families to chat to. A list of some tour operators offering interesting trips to more unusual destinations begins on page 276. Those we have contacted told us that overall they catered for slightly more women travellers than men, but in any particular group it would be impossible to predict whether there would be more male or female members. Most companies however agreed that they aimed to get a 50/50 mix of men and women. Ages range from about 25 to 45 (although there are upper age limits for long overland hauls), with the majority of group members being under 35. Most group leaders are male because group leaders have to be able to carry out major repairs to tour vehicles and it is difficult to find suitably qualified female leaders. Destinations range from trekking in Thailand to caribou stalking in Canada. You could go mountaineering in the Sinai or visit troglodyte caves in Turkey. Further information about group travel can be obtained from good independent travel agents (see page 277).

TRAVELLING ALONE

'If you go alone, although it is terrifying sometimes, you look around much more and have a much more "exciting time".'

Asia

It's difficult to talk generally about what you can expect if you travel by yourself because travelling alone is such an intensely personal experience. It is also one that is easy to become almost addicted to. Many of the world's great travellers — Dervla Murphy, Christina Dodwell — habitually travel on their own, as do several of the women who contributed to this book.

I never set off on my first trip with the intention of striking out by myself (I didn't feel nearly brave enough!). But, like a lot of other women travellers who end up alone, it happened partly through circumstances. It also happened because, to my surprise, I suddenly found I was no longer automatically looking round to see who else was going in my direction. Even more to my surprise, once I'd tried it, I found I really enjoyed the experience of travelling solo.

There was the sense of freedom that came from knowing I could choose where to go, when to go, or whether to move on at all. From now on I could pace my travels to suit myself. If I wanted to slow down, or double back or just lounge around on a beach it was up to me. And I could spend the days as I wanted — eat when I felt like it, explore, shop, visit a temple, go up this street or avoid that one all without consultation or negotiation with anyone else.

There was also the unexpected pleasure of having so much time to myself. I had never before been on my own for such a long period, no friends, no family, no colleagues meant having time, as much time as I wanted to sit and think, to read, to watch. To my amazement I found I actually *liked* my own company, and found I was no longer daunted by the thought of empty hours which I alone was responsible for filling.

For many of us — before we actually try it the thought of this emptiness is as daunting as any fears we might have about our personal safety. Most of us are used to having almost continuous input from others, to being part of something, whether that's a family, a shared house, a partnership or an office. To be alone for long periods, for days at a time, let alone weeks or months, can be a novel experience. To be responsible for your own input, for making sense for yourself of what's happening, with no-one else around to bounce ideas off, try thoughts out on, or talk to as you try to make sense of what you see can be unnerving at first. No wonder many travellers are afraid of being lonely by themselves. And if the idea of their own company doesn't bother them; many are put off by the idea of so much freedom of choice. At home we're so used to highly structured days where other people tell us what we are to do and where we are to go; to suddenly have so much freedom can be daunting in itself.

These fears did worry me to start with, and particularly because this first trip was outside Europe in an unfamiliar culture.

However, I found that travelling alone in a really different society can be unexpectedly easier than travelling alone in the West. There are several reasons — spending time by yourself just observing is never dull in countries where everything is different. You're unlikely to find spending a whole morning watching passers-by over a cup of coffee 'boring' or a 'waste of time' if the scene includes a sugar-cane juice extractor; a seller of folk medicines whose stock includes a dried cat and several live lizards, and half a dozen small boys touting shoe-shine and cigarettes. You are unlikely to be without any direct human input for long in countries where local people take the initiative and come and speak to you. They may have none of our inhibitions about talking to strangers and find a single woman easier to approach than a group, or even a couple.

'I enjoyed being completely independent and feel I met more
local people being alone.'

I also found that in a well-visited developing country being alone
seldom meant being without any contact with other Westerners for
long. As most solo travellers find (sometimes to their cost), other
Western travellers always come up for a chat. I felt a great deal of
protectiveness was extended towards me by people passing on
suggestions of places to stay, places to visit, places to avoid. On the one
occasion I fell ill by myself I was grateful for the support I received
from the other women in the budget hotel I was staving in. Taxi
drivers and others tend to assume you wish to be with other travellers
and will automatically take you to hotels, however downmarket,
where other travellers stay. Once you get addicted to travelling alone
you may indeed find that this wears a bit thin, you may go out of your
way to *avoid* other non-locals, but at least the choice is yours.

Travelling round Europe and the United States on your own is
certainly possible — many women do it — but in some ways it can be
harder work, especially when it comes to meeting both local people
and other travellers. You may no longer stand out, so other travellers
don't recognise you as a fellow visitor and talking to local people may
be left much more up to you. In Britain you're likely to be ignored
unless you make the first move to chat to a family in the park or an
elderly pensioner in a bus queue, although not all European countries
are like this. Italians for example hardly suffer from the famous British
reserve, but Paris could be hard work for solitary travellers who are
shy.

However, wherever you go, as a solo traveller, you will find that
being alone forces you to become more involved in the country you
have come to visit. There's no-one to cushion you from having to
adjust:

'You are exposed to the country and the people, for better and
for worse.'

It is the complete opposite of travelling in a group. Lone travellers are
forced to accept challenges to the 'My Country Right or Wrong' and

'West is Best' attitudes that far too many of us unconsciously believe
in because there's no-one with them to help fend off challenges from
local people. You are much more likely to explore ideas about new
ways of doing things if there's no-one else around to back you up when
you try to insist on 'your way'.

Because I was on my own I was offered accommodation with a
university lecturer (who would certainly not have been prepared to
take in more than one Westerner). Long conversations with him and
his family gave me more food for thought than all the books I'd read,
or all my discussions with other travellers. Hours spent watching
undistracted by any companions gave me a much better idea of life in
his small town than I would have got on any group visit to the area.

Above all, what many many women find they gain as a result of their
travels alone, is a huge increase in their confidence and self reliance.
(I actually changed my posture as a result of my new-found confidence. Instead of walking head bent, eyes down, I came back happy to
look people in the face, to hold my head up, literally to 'walk tall'.) For
many this spin-off is what makes travelling by themselves so exciting
and so worthwhile.

With no-one else to help them or to answer for them, solo women
learn, perhaps for the first time, to ask for and get what they want.
They learn that being conspicuous and making mistakes *doesn't
matter*, so they are no longer held back from trying things out from fear
of looking foolish.

Calmly walking into a bar on your own, a single woman, and
perhaps the only Westerner, is nerve wracking at first. But once you've
had to do it (if you are going to eat at all), you will discover that nine
times out of ten it only *feels* as if all eyes are on you. And if everyone
at the next table does turn round to stare, you learn to ignore them with
equanimity. The first few times it may be with a faked confidence,
your palms sweating with embarrassment and fright, but gradually on
your travels such things cease to bother you. You find you're no longer
daunted and can go anywhere.

'I shared a boat trip with a French woman who said of the
women travelling on their own that she'd met, how they
seemed to have an aura of strength and calm about them. I

explained that I developed this front to keep hassles at bay...
Yet in the process of developing this shield I had indeed
become stronger and more calm as a result and I can feel it
still.'

India

You may start out cowed by waiters, unnerved by hotel staff or border
guards and passport officials but your self confidence will grow as you
discover that they're only human after all. You *can* ask for a better seat,
a smaller room, an extension to your visa, and get them!

You also learn that you can cope with most incidents of sexual
harassment (see Chapter 11 on page 236) and that in fact the world is
generally a safer place than you might have supposed:

'I came back a different person. I learnt how to take responsibility for my own safety. I can't say how I'd cope in any really
serious situation because so far I've not got into any. I've learnt
how to take preventative steps to make my own travelling
relatively trouble free. Without relying on other people.'

'I think it is definitely easier travelling with others ... but I
personally found the experience of travelling alone really
rewarding because I gained in self-reliance and independence.'

Being a lone woman traveller isn't always easy, but it's an exciting
experience that many women value so much that even where they
know there are difficulties, they don't want to give up:

'Being a single woman becomes tiring after a while because of
the inevitable hassles and these begin to outweigh the advantages of being alone. But I wouldn't want to be all the time in
company.'

Don't feel you must try solo travel unless you are ready to. Build up
slowly and wait until you are feeling fairly confident before you go,
you'll have a much pleasanter trip than if you're always nervously
looking over your shoulder.

Boost your confidence by taking at least one of the following steps before setting out: learn enough of the local language to hold a limited conversation. Talk to other women who have travelled alone, especially in the country you wish to visit. Find one or more contacts that you can stay with for part of the time when you've arrived.

2
What To Carry

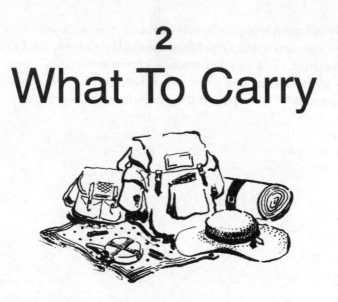

LUGGAGE

There is a Travellers' Law which states that you fill up any bag *whatever the size*. In other words, if you go and kit yourself out with an enormous case instead of something of a more reasonable size, you will find plenty to fill it up with.

Do *not* therefore go straight out and buy one of these gigantic backpacks that makes you look from the back like a rucksack with legs, or a suitcase big enough to pack yourself inside. You'll only find yourself open to abuse from busy commuters trying to get round you as you block passageways and trip up elderly ladies. In addition you'll find you can hardly pick up the thing, and that moving around for any distance at speeds above a crawl is impossible.

Instead think first about where you're going and what you're doing — mountaineering or serious hiking, overlanding, catching a lot of trains, buses and planes or mainly staying put?

Next assemble the minimum amount of luggage you expect to take with you. Spread it out on the floor — are you horrified at the amount? Now aim to HALVE it. Be as ruthless as possible — if you're a first-time traveller you've almost certainly got twice what you need.

Remember, you are aiming, above all else, to be able to travel easily, comfortably and with the ability to *run*, at least to catch a bus.

Ideally at this stage you need to cram the lot into a borrowed container (or plastic bags) to be able to give yourself some idea of the weight — this will help you know whether you should try and whittle down the amount still further (or whether you dare add anything else).

Once you've got a fairly clear idea of the amount of stuff you'll be taking and how much carrying you expect to do, you'll be able, finally, to start deciding what sort of bag to go for.

Rucksacks

Rucksacks are ideal for travellers who have a fair amount to carry (they're designed to distribute weight properly), and who want to keep their hands free. If you're mountaineering or hiking they're essential and the most sensible way to carry heavy loads over any distance. However, despite their popularity they do have some disadvantages — rucksacks are an awkward shape to fit into luggage racks and car boots and they can get tangled up easily, caught on luggage carousels at airports, or under your seat. They are also fairly expensive. If you do decide to buy one take a long-term view and think of your sack as an investment for many trips to come.

The old style external 'A' and 'H' frame rucksacks have largely disappeared. they were heavy, prone to damage (especially from people like us who would sit on them), they were too high and they often positioned the load badly. And the awkward frames got caught up or dug themselves into fellow passengers.

Today's backpacks have neat internal frames instead. Manufacturers love to talk about their 'advanced engineering design' (there can be up to 265 parts to one rucksack), or about 'integral carrying systems' and adventure technology'. As one Y.H.A. shop manager said:

> 'The thing to watch out for is to separate manufacturer's hype from common sense. We get a lot of men in here trying to be technical, or women who just say they don't know what they want. It's common sense really.'

In fact all internal frame sacks work on the same principle. The load
is shared between the wearer's shoulders and pelvis. The bags have
shoulder straps and a padded hip belt which transfer around 60-70 per
cent of the weight from your hips directly to your legs.

Women should not be put off by catalogues that habitually show
burly men posed against rugged cliffs. Tucked away in the text you
will find most manufacturers do in fact make models suitable for
usually smaller female frames. If the circumference of your hips at the
top of the hip bone is less than 75 centimetres you may need to look
at smaller sizes, and you should also take your *back* length into
account.

Some of the more expensive models have fully adjustable backs
where you can alter the length to get an individual fit, however you
may find a small-size, non-adjustable style just as suitable (and less
expensive).

Although most modern bags are made from waterproof material
(smooth or textured nylon) rather than old-fashioned cotton canvas,
you will need to line your rucksack with a waterproof bag (use a black
plastic dustbin liner and carry a spare) because water can get in
through the seams. Even if you're going somewhere where you're
expecting dry conditions it's worth doing this. Inevitably either it's
raining when you set off or you arrive back to a typical British
downpour, or the airport staff (who loathe backpacks) will drop your
sack in a pool of oil or a puddle of rusty water when you're not looking.
Some retailers sell ready-made liners or pack covers.

When packing any rucksack you want to keep your centre of gravity
as near normal as possible i.e. around chest height. Pack heavier items
towards the top and make sure the bag sits close to your back, this way
you won't end up stooping too much. Put things you'll need during
the day, penknife, tampons, etc. where you can get at them, not right
down at the bottom of the main compartment. Try not to have things
hanging off your pack or strapped insecurely on top or underneath —
you're asking to have them stolen or lost, and you add disproportionately
to the overall weight.

Some travellers feel that backpacks have an 'image problem': they
feel they're automatically stereotyped as either young and penniless,
or as hearty outdoor types.

These days you can buy travel bags which have been designed as a compromise between a soft suitcase and a backpack. Usually rectangular in shape, they have a hidden frame and shoulder straps that can be tucked out of sight when not in use. Inevitably these are not as good for serious walking as a properly designed rucksack but a smart hotel won't look askance at them.

Travel packs are often manufactured by the same companies who make rucksacks so look out for them at good outdoor pursuit suppliers.

Do take care of your sack. Don't sit on it. Clean it occasionally with pure soap and a nail brush (no, you cannot put it in the washing machine), and don't store it away damp.

Three well-known British manufacturers are Karrimor, Lowe and Berghaus, all of whom make sacks suitable for women. Any good outdoor supplier will stock these and other makes.

Frameless rucksacks   Small frameless rucksacks are not intended for the serious hiker. They don't distribute the weight very well and any lumps and bumps in your luggage stick straight into your back. However, I have successfully used one for all my belongings when going on short trips round Europe. I was lucky, I persuaded airport staff that my small pack was hand luggage (and with some pushing even managed to squeeze it into a cabin locker). Those with double zips can be closed with a miniature padlock.

Suitcases

Suitcases should be avoided by travellers who will be moving around taking all their things with them. They aren't designed to be used like this. On the other hand if you will have one permanent base which you can reach without a lot of carrying, suitcases are a convenient way of packing a lot of stuff in. Take a small rucksack or shoulder bag with you as well so you can go off on short trips with enough stuff for four or five days at a time.

Day bag/bumbag

As well as your suitcase or backpack, you will need a smaller container for everyday use. It should be strong (slash resistant), waterproof, and with a strap long enough to go crossways over your body The bag should be lightweight and have plenty of secure pockets. The size will depend very much on whether or not you need to conceal a large camera inside.

All the pockets and the top of the bag should either be fastened with a catch, good poppers, or better still, zip fasteners that you can make more secure by closing with an additional safety pin. (This — instead of a tiny padlock — is enough to deter most pickpockets.)

PRACTICALITIES

The list of items you *could* take is almost limitless, particularly if you are one of those people that suffers from the 'better safe than sorry' syndrome.

If you are one of these, a trip to any camping shop will provide you with bags full of cunning little gadgets that promise to maintain body weight, stop bottles leaking, de-odorise loo seats and keep fleas at bay. It is easy to get carried away and before you know where you are, spend a fortune on items that, in a simplified form, you already own anyway or that you will only use once on a trip lasting six months.

The problem is knowing when to stop, because it *is* useful to have some gadgets with you. What you need depends on where you are going and what you are going to do when you get there. For nearly everyone the most useful thing overall is the ability to move around easily unencumbered by a heavy pack, so don't take more than you absolutely have to. *Don't* go and get one of everything on the following pages: do try and assess each item in the light of its usefulness to *you*.

Most people end up taking one or two items not so much for their inherent usefulness but for the comfort and sense of security they bring. This security factor is usually entirely proof against reason and common sense. One of us only feels safe if they've taken a plastic survival bag along (even to the tropics), the other is able to jettison everything else but a scrubbing brush. And each of us is convinced the other is quite mad! Including *one* comfort item in your pack is worth it for your peace of mind. Taking six things chosen on this basis alone is five too many.

Sleeping kit

Sleeping bags and survival bags   Good sleeping bags are not cheap and you get what you pay for, so it's worth doing a bit of research before you go. It's also worth taking a long view and thinking ahead to other trips as well.

The basic points to consider are: weight, bulk, warmth, durability, ability to withstand damp, and price. Not necessarily in that order, as obviously different travellers will have different priorities depending on the sort of travelling they intend to do.

How important is it that your bag weighs as little as possible and takes up little space? What sort of weather conditions are you trying to meet?

A sleeping bag is designed to keep you warm at night by trapping your body heat (but not moisture) and insulating you from the cold. How efficiently it does so depends on two things: the material it is filled with, and the construction of the bag.

Natural fibres combine greatest warmth with least bulk and least weight. Synthetic fillings are less expensive than down, and machine washable, they perform better when damp and are unlikely to affect allergy sufferers.

The amount of filling used will affect the amount of warmth the bag provides. Bags designed for Arctic conditions will hold more (and be heavier) than those designed for use in the British summer. However just as important as the type and weight of filling, is the way your bag is constructed.

The filling has to be kept in place between the inner and outer covers. The simplest way to do this is to quilt the bag by sewing through both covers and filling. This stitch-through method produces a bag suitable for indoor use, or for use if you are camping out in the mild summer conditions. It is not suitable for low temperatures as cold-spots result along the lines of stitching.

A more efficient method for bags for use in colder weather is to have two layers of quilting arranged so that the stitched areas overlap, or better still, the bag is of a walled construction.

Internal 'walls' separate the filled sections and allow the filling to expand. This provides a continuous layer of insulation with none of the cold-spots you get from sewn-through quilting. Depending on the quality of the filling, and the construction, bags made this way can keep you warm in the harshest of conditions. The top quality ones are used on Arctic and Himalayan expeditions.

The shape of a bag also affects its ability to keep you warm. Mummy-shaped or tapering bags are warmer, although more constricting than roomier rectangular ones. Most sleeping bags are made with zips to give you some control over the heat — you may not want to have maximum warmth all the time. In a good bag the zip will be properly backed to ensure that heat doesn't escape when it's fully sealed. Some of the bags made for extreme conditions also incorporate a hood.

For those who are intending to sleep out regularly in fairly rough conditions it could be worth considering a waterproof outer cover. In order to avoid condensation, waterproof outers need to be water-vapour permeable in order to let the moisture your body naturally produces escape, without letting in rain or dew. Gore-Tex or similar modern synthetics are used to achieve this. If you're not planning on sleeping rough, but might run the risk of getting caught out in the open in inclement weather, you can avoid serious problems of hypothermia if you have a plastic survival bag. This is simply a plastic bag large enough to get you and your sleeping bag into. It won't cope with the problem of condensation and isn't suitable for more than emergency use, but taking one could save your life. They come in various weights. Very light bags have a relatively short life — they are designed for occasional emergency use and would not stand up to regular use on rough ground. There are more substantial bags available, including one endorsed by the British Mountaineering Council which is bright orange to make you easier to spot by rescuers. Some bags are made of a heat reflective material and you can also obtain silver 'space blankets' that work on the same principle.

Sleeping bag liners Some travellers take their own sleeping bags not for warmth but simply because they prefer to use their own bedding when they're staying in budget hotels. At least they knew who slept in it last!

However, if you are unfortunate enough to sleep in a verminous bed, using your own sleeping bag won't keep out the wild life. You are more likely to end up with any nasties climbing in and taking up lodgings for the rest of your travels. Simply removing already flea-ridden bedding and substituting your own doesn't avoid the problem because fleas and bedbugs also inhabit carpets, rugs, mattresses and bedsteads. Once they've moved into your bedding they are almost impossible to remove without thoroughly soaking your sleeping bag. Sprinkling insect powder into a sleeping bag is unpleasant and not particularly effective. It can also be dangerous.

A sheet sleeping bag, or sleeping bag liner is a better alternative, used in lieu of sheets with the hotel bedding (verminous or otherwise) used for warmth. Liners are made of lightweight cotton or calico and are easy to wash and dry if you are unlucky enough to pick up unwanted insects. A liner is worth having even if you are taking your own bag, in order to keep it clean, and if you are off to the tropics (and don't expect to be at high altitudes) a liner is all you will need. They are obtainable from any good camping shop, or alternatively you can make one yourself. Most designs include a pouch at the head where you can tuck a towel, or your clothes, as a pillow. You can also sew in a pocket to hold valuables at night.

Finally, in addition to their sleeping bag and liner, many travellers also buy a sleeping mat. Sleeping mats insulate you from cold, damp ground; or pad out a hard bed. they can also serve as beach mats, or cushioning. Mats are usually made from foam, plastic or rubber, with or without air cells. As they come in two sizes, full length and three quarter length, travellers who want to travel light can choose a hip length mat and save a little on space as well. Mats should be carried *rolled*.

Mosquito nets
If you are travelling to areas where Malaria is prevalent, or if you are the sort of person that mosquitoes seem to seek out, you might consider obtaining a mosquito net.

Good, up-market hotels in malarial areas should provide their own, but at cheaper budget hotels you may find the nets ripped and tattered, if indeed they exist at all.

Nets can either be woven of cotton or nylon; or made of plastic mesh. The basic shapes are a pleated conical affair that is suspended

from the ceiling over your bed and pulls out to tuck under the mattress;
a cage shape with a suspension point at the head end, or a fitted cage-
shaped net that is draped over poles at each end of the bedstead like
curtains on a four-poster.

Although the fitted square is neater, it is only effective if you've
actually got a bed with a frame to take it. As I know, to my cost, if you're
sleeping on a bed without the necessary poles, the only way to tie up
this type of net is with yards of string, turning the whole thing into a
booby trap, liable to collapse at any moment. If possible therefore, get
a net which only needs one suspension point.

Mosquito nets can be bought locally, although you may not get a
choice of designs. In the UK, they are available from Safariquip (see
page 278). Choose one that is light and not too bulky and include a
needle and thread in your kit for instant repairs. The tiniest hole is
quite large enough for mosquitoes to squeeze through, and it's easy to
snag the fine mesh on something.

It is obviously worth seriously considering a mosquito net if the
area you're travelling in is malarial, but what if you're visiting places
like Scotland or northern Scandinavia? A mosquito net is probably the
last thing on your mind in areas like this where these insects are a real
nuisance, but don't present a health risk. If you are the sort of person
that mosquitoes seem to love, the type that attracts them when they
ignore everyone else, you might consider taking a net and putting up
with the funny looks you'll get. This is particularly true if you are also
one of those people that reacts badly to bites. For non-malarial areas,
especially where you will be sleeping indoors, insect sprays and
repellents may be sufficient to keep most of the pests at bay.

Insect repellant   Take some. You'll certainly need it. The best
ingredients for keeping insects at bay are diethyltoluamide and
dimethyl phthalate. Check the label to see how high a percentage of
active ingredients any one brand contains. The higher the amount
present the more effective a repellant will be. Specialist shops such as
those which sell camping or fishing gear are most likely to stock the
more powerful sorts. Some brands contain as much as 95%
diethyltoluamide!

Repellant can be bought as aerosols, liquids or in solid sticks. An
aerosol will take up most room in your luggage though it does have the

advantage of being easy to spray on clothes. Don't spray directly into your face — spray a little on your hands and then apply from there. The liquids tend to be stronger than the sticks.

You can buy aerosol sprays and mosquito coils for use in a closed space. These contain the natural insecticide pyrethrum.

Torches   In countries where the electricity supply is at best limited to a couple of hours each evening, and at worst limited *and* erratic, a torch can be a useful piece of equipment.

Choose a lightweight model and the more expensive longer lasting batteries. Don't take those torches which automatically come on when you flip up the top. Unfortunately the tops too easily get caught up in your luggage, you find that the torch has been on for hours in your pack, and the batteries are worn out. If you think this is likely to happen, pack the batteries separately and fill the case with spare pairs of knickers instead.

Alarm clocks and watches   You may be the sort of person who loathes watches and never wears one, and who prefers to use the clock on the cooker rather than hang a time piece on your wall. If you are, it's tempting on your travels to make the romantic gesture to dispense with time and to leave a watch or clock at home. This is all very well if you are also the sort of person who can wake themselves up at different times according to need, or who has an infallible internal clock that can cope with international time zones. If you are not, it would be a mistake always to rely on other people.

> 'I asked a taxi-driver to wake me at 4.30 a.m. to get to the station on time. He spent the night sleeping outside the hotel to be sure of waking up. It never occurred to me that he might have no way of knowing the exact time either.'
>
> *South India*

Most travellers, if only at the beginning and end of their travels have buses or planes they *have* to catch, quite apart from numerous occasions during their travels when it would be more convenient to get a particular train at a particular time. As cheap digital watches incorporating an alarm can be bought in any high street, it makes sense to take one. You don't have to wear it all the time.

The days when travellers could take the cheapest pocket calculators and watches with them to sell at a huge profit abroad have gone. There has been a flood of cheap electronic goods round the world and most local people who can afford to own a watch will have one at least as good as those your local garage sells back home.

Earplugs   Uncomfortable at first to get used to, wearing ear-plugs is not nearly as bad as being unable to sleep on a coach, or being woken up at some ungodly hour in the middle of the night.

> 'Chinese people seem to thrive on noise. It towns and cities it can be unbearable until you get used to it.'
>
> *China*

Earplugs are cheap and obtainable at any chemist. They are more efficient than cotton wool. Eye masks and a blow-up pillow make long journeys comfortable — and you may even get some sleep!

Washing, drying and mending

Shampoo and toiletries   Unless you are going for weeks into uninhabited or deeply rural country, take a normal supply of soap, shampoo and toothpaste and enjoy trying out local alternatives when these run out. (If you can get them that is, Colgate, Palmolive and Johnson's products seem to have a world-wide distribution and Sainsbury's own brand soap has even turned up in Sri Lanka.) Shampoo is easier to take in sachets. Although this is more expensive than by bottle, bottles leak or crack or break.

Soap is obtainable just about everywhere. However camping shops sell concentrate in tubes (bio-degradable and useful if camping) which saves taking a heavy bar that gets sticky when wet. Unfortunately some soaps sold in developing countries promise to 'whiten' the user's skin. Such soaps should be avoided as they may contain mercury which is dangerous, particularly for pregnant women.

Toothpaste is perhaps not quite as widely available outside Western countries as soap. Local people may use soot or salt which you can safely try, or more dubious local preparations. 'Monkey powder' made from dried camels' dung actually turned up in London from North Africa some time ago. A brave colleague of our dentist tried it out ... it is *not* recommended! Although toothpaste contains a mild abrasive, it is the brushing action that counts, not the paste which mainly makes cleaning your teeth pleasant.

Although it is better to take a proper toothbrush, in some Third World countries local people use twigs instead. *Not* any old twig, but sticks from particular types of tree which you first chew to produce a frayed 'brush'. Each twig is used only once — the original disposable!

If you really care about your teeth, dental floss is a useful inclusion in your pack especially because it can double as string, or in emergency thread. Floss is lighter to carry than toothpaste, and, used as well as a brush, makes paste redundant.

You may feel particularly attached to your usual skin care products but in Europe there is very little to distinguish between different makes apart from packaging and cost. If you have sensitive skin and are at all worried look for cleansers, moisturisers and lotions on the babycare shelves.

If your supplies run out or you're travelling in a country where cosmetics are either not available or are imported at extortionate prices you might prefer your own home-made remedies. Rolled oats or oatmeal can be mixed with cold cream to make an exfoliate, or you could use ground aduki beans or almonds. An oat and water paste or plain yoghurt will make a face mask — just rinse off with plain water. Slices of raw potato or cucumber can be used as skin cleansers. Mix honey with water or glycerine to make a moisturiser. Cold porridge has a similar effect.

Suncare preparations   If you are going to hot countries, visiting any part of Europe in summer, or will be outdoors for much of your trip, you must include some form of protection against sunburn. This is also true if you will be in snowy conditions or at high altitudes.

Sunburn is not just unpleasantly painful but, as we are all more aware these days, serious burns can be dangerous, and so can prolonged exposure to the sun. Westerners who have fair skins do not have as much protection against sunburn as those with dark or black skins. (Although these can, and do, burn.) Suntanning is entirely a Western idea. Elsewhere local people cover up and protect their skin from exposure to sunlight by wearing all-enveloping clothes and by using sunshades. You should include clothes in your pack with long sleeves, collars etc. to protect you but you should also take *ample* supplies of suntan lotion for your face and for those parts of your body that are exposed. (This includes your feet.) You need a sun protection factor of 12 and above to protect you adequately. You should also take a lip salve with a *total* sunblock.

Suntan lotions are readily available throughout Europe and the West, but may cost more in holiday resorts. Look for the same brands at cheaper prices in cut-price chemists and supermarkets or chain stores.

If you are going outside the West you should *not* rely on being able to buy supplies locally. In countries where local people don't use tanning products only up-market hotels catering for overseas visitors are likely to stock sunscreens, and if you are lucky enough to find some, be prepared to pay double what you would at home.

So, stock up before you set off, choose a sunscreen with a higher protection factor than you usually would and take an amount of *total* sunblock. Even if you tan easily at home, it is likely that on your travels you will be spending far longer out of doors than normal. Not only this but the sun may be far stronger than you are used to. This is particularly true if you are travelling at high altitudes where thin air allows ultra violet rays to burn more fiercely.

Sunglasses   Sunglasses are useful if the light is strong. If you wear glasses to correct your sight consider getting photochromatic lenses that go dark in sunlight. I have twice bought glasses like these in India at half the price they would be back home. The choice of frames is more limited but local opticians can be relied on to make up a prescription brought from home accurately.

Loo paper Loo paper is a Western invention and as such is available throughout Europe and the West. Unless you are camping you won't need to carry your own, however some public toilets are better supplied than others, and it is useful stuff for blowing your nose and mopping up spilt drinks.

Outside the west loo paper is unknown and unused by millions of people around the world. Travellers can learn to do without by adopting the perfectly hygienic local method of washing instead. If you can't face the idea, you will have to carry your own supplies. No easy thing to find space for if you plan to be away for months. Flat packs are easier to fit in, and at least the stuff is relatively light. Look at it as ballast, to be used up as you go and the resulting space filled with bargains, presents and souvenirs to take home. If you run out in areas used to tourists and you can't find any in local shops, desperate travellers will find supplies in the cloakrooms of large hotels catering for tourists.

Tampons and sanitary towels For the reasons given on page 179 it is easier to carry the supplies you think you'll need with you. You should do without panty-liners if travelling beyond the reach of Western-style sewage systems.

Detergents and scrubbing brush The penalty you pay for packing as few clothes as possible is the daily wash — enjoyable when you are splashing about in cold water on a warm evening in hot countries, less so in freezing cold conditions, and impossible where water is scarce.

There are special travellers' detergents available either in a tube, as a concentrated cream, or in packets of soluble tablets. Of the two I've tried, the cream works well in cold water, but the tablets are only suitable for use in countries where you can rely on hot water being available. Both are more convenient to carry than loose powder.

If you decide to get supplies locally in developing countries, the cheapest type of soap for clothes washing is the old-fashioned yellow block. This is not particularly efficient and you may prefer to go for whatever is the local brand of detergent. Often this turns out to be a familiar make, but why is it so much better than our own brands back home? All this advertising hype about new formulas for low temperature washes is revealed as the slogan it is. The detergents you will find on your travels may have to work efficiently in cold water, and people don't expect to use great cups at a time either. A small box (decanted into a plastic bag) will wash everything beautifully and last for ages.

A small plastic laundry brush (larger than a nail brush, softer than a scrubbing brush), also makes it easy to clean travel-stained clothes.

For drying, many women recommend the peg-less clothes lines available from camping shops, but if you always carry string, use this instead, or find something to drape the washing over.

Washing should not be hung outdoors in Africa, particularly near fruit trees or on the ground, unless you can iron it afterwards. A particularly nasty bluebottle-like fly — the tumbu fly, lays its eggs on damp washing. These then hatch into tiny maggots that burrow into the wearer's skin.

Washing should also not be hung where you can't keep an eye on it:

'We left our washing outside on some railings. When we came back someone had stolen all our spare clothes.'

Morocco

In Northern Europe where drying weather is unpredictable you may have to try and dry clothes in your hotel room. Drip-dry things can be hung over the bath or in the shower cubicle, other stuff should be rolled in a towel first to get rid of excess moisture, then draped near or over the radiators.

On some trips you won't in fact need to take anything for washing clothes. It's not always necessary to do your laundry yourself. Most up-market hotels offer a laundry service, but so do many smaller ones. The latter don't always advertise the fact because whether or not they're happy to accept someone's dirty clothes will depend on someone having time to fit in an extra chore on top of running a hotel and coping with their own household. Often however they will agree to take small amounts, even if they wait for you to ask. (Where there is no printed rate to refer to, check what you will be charged first.)

In Europe, other Western countries and increasingly in large cities round the world, travellers can use launderettes (laundromats). If you don't have enough washing to make it worthwhile to use the machines, it is usually possible to bring damp (not wringing wet) clothes that you have washed out yourself to put in the driers.

In rural areas in Southern European countries you may find old fashioned village wash-houses. These are provided with running cold water (occasionally with a hand pump), stone troughs and plenty of space for scrubbing clothes. These days you are likely to have the place to yourself as more and more villagers can afford automatic machines at home. The most famous laundry service in a developing country is that of the Dhobi Wallahs in India.

Mending   A sewing kit costs very little and is easy to pack. However, unless they happen to match your clothes, don't end up with just fragile cottons in pinks and blues. Make sure you've also got sufficient supplies of *strong* thread to repair a torn shoe buckle, sew together a broken rucksack strap or mend a camera case. Strong needles are essential for these sort of repairs, and in some of the remoter parts of the world, make good presents.

The other invaluable mending material is the elastoplast from your first aid kit — the sort in a roll without a lint dressing. You will however need to include either a pair of folding scissors, or a sharp knife to cut it with. Elastoplast can repair torn canvas, a ripped cagoul, or a cracked cup.

Towels

'Take an old middle-sized towel, for lying on, washing with, wearing if you are desperate, making shade, being sick into, carrying melons, sieving petrol through etc.'

Jordan

Quite! Towels are certainly adaptable, but unfortunately they are also bulky. As an alternative you might consider taking a piece of thinner material, or using a sarong. Apparently the S.A.S. recommend a baby's nappy, which after all is really only a small absorbent towelling square. There are also travellers' towels on the market made of a very thin synthetic material. Although not very pleasant in feel they do actually get you dry and certainly take up very little space, they are not as versatile as towelling however and can't cope with large amounts of water.

Pastimes

Games   Travelling sets of chess, Scrabble, Mastermind and cards can be more than just diversions to pass the time when you're bored. Games like these, especially where you don't need to share a common language, can be real ice-breakers with people you meet.

Mastermind is small and light and can be played without words; many people know the basics of chess, electronic games are popular everywhere, and card games are also universal.

However, for the most basic of skilled pastimes all you need is a piece of string or paper. Cats-cradle is a very old tradition and one shared by many cultures. Local children will be delighted to teach you the games and patterns they know, and in some cultures you will find adults do not dismiss cats-cradle as a diversion for children only. Cats-cradle may be part of an oral tradition where string figures and configurations are incorporated in story-telling and used as illustration.

Origami is well known to be part of Japanese traditional craft, but again you will find people in other cultures interested and amused.

If these are new to you, the children's department in any good bookshop will have books on string and paper games and can even supply you with special paper.

Books   All my own packing is done with one aim in mind — to reduce everything else to as little as possible in order to get in more books. However exciting your travels you are probably going to have more time to read than you ever have at home, so make the most of it. Now is your chance to actually get through *War and Peace* or Gibbon's *Decline & Fall of the Roman Empire*. It is worth being selective about what you take. Books in English, although usually fairly easy to obtain in capital cities, are often expensive in non-English-speaking countries.

Even if you have already done some reading up on the area, try to include at least one book that will help answer some of the puzzling questions you will find yourself asking: choose something that provides a historical, cultural and geographical background in a little more depth than a standard guide book. Although such volumes may seem rather 'dry' on the shelves back home, they often make more sense and come alive when you are actually in the country in question.

Look out for novels by writers from the countries you are visiting. There has been an increase in the publication of overseas literature, particularly from the developing world. It is no longer hard to find Asian, African and South American novelists in paperback.

If you are taking a novel, remember that a book of reasonable quality is not only going to last you longer than a piece of popular fiction you can zip through in two days, it's going to command a better deal on the 'swap' market.

English speakers will find they have ready takers for books they have finished with amongst other travellers and sometimes amongst local people as well. In countries where budget travellers are particularly numerous, you may even find secondhand book-swap shops on tourist beaches or in popular towns. Beware, however, when choosing or swapping books of the most curious attacks of culture shock. For example, Dickens, the perfect complement to a modern Indian city, could be positively mind-boggling in rural Africa. And be warned that far too many travellers seem to end up trying to rid themselves of copies of *The Ape Man on Mars*. If nothing else is available at least console yourself that you are getting a varied literary diet.

Diaries Avoid purpose-made diaries with hard covers and a set amount of space per day. They are heavy and unnecessarily limiting. Take a standard notebook instead, and if you are any good at sketching, buy one which includes some blank pages. Even if you have never kept a diary before, you may be amazed by how strong is your need to record things on your travels. Don't worry about future publication, but do consciously try to make your entries as full as possible. You will find you appreciate all the detail when you read it back to yourself a year or two later. Not only that, but recording the detail actually encourages you to notice more. (Unfortunately both of us have admitted that our longest entries seem to be devoted almost entirely to food, and its results on our digestive systems — this makes a disappointing, if gory, re-read at home.)

A notebook is a good place to explore your reactions and responses to a strange culture, and to life on the move, as well as the place to record highlights and low spots, addresses, travellers' tips, information about train times and recommendations of places to stay.

It's also a place to store travel ephemera — pressed flowers, old laundry bills and spent railway tickets — all souvenirs and memory joggers to have back home.

Binoculars Binoculars are more or less a necessity if the main part of your trip is birdwatching, going on safari, or will be spent out in wild countryside. For other travellers binoculars are useful, even fun to have, but more of a luxury item than a necessity. Unfortunately good pairs are either heavy or expensive. For the real enthusiast it is probably worth paying the extra and investing in a decent set of lightweight miniatures. If you are going to Hong Kong or Singapore you might find it cheaper to buy there; if you will be passing through a *good* duty-free airport shop such as the one at Schipol Amsterdam you might do better than at home. In Europe, Andorra, sandwiched between France and Spain, is a duty-free shopper's paradise. If you are heading that way, bear this in mind.

As an alternative you might consider a monocular. This is a single eye piece which is almost as easy to use as binoculars (and for people with eyes with very differing vision, actually easier). A monocular is about half the weight and half the price of the more conventional binos, and although it would not suit a really keen ornithologist, if all you want is something to inspect the carvings on a temple more closely, or pick out a footpath you might find one worth taking. In those parts of the world where binoculars are a rare Western commodity, local adults as well as children enjoy having a look through them. However be warned that this is a good way of spreading eye disease. Wipe the eye piece with a piece of lint soaked in disinfectant if you are worried about conjunctivitis.

Security

Padlock   In Europe and the West, the mortice lock has superseded the old fashioned padlock, at least for doors in houses and hotels. If your travelling is confined to the West you won't therefore need to take a padlock with you. However, in many other countries room security, especially in budget hotels, depends on the padlock with which you will be issued by the hotel staff. As these are often flimsy, and you may not be convinced that you are the only one with a key, you may prefer to use your own, good quality, combination lock instead.

One place where you will need a padlock is in India, if you want to leave your bags with the Left Luggage Departments on Indian Railway Stations. Indian bureaucracy has made this a staff-rule, and without a padlock hanging off the side, your baggage will not be accepted.

A combination lock is better than one with keys (less to lose) but keep a note of the number somewhere separately.

Personal alarms   They are reassuring to have and may very well get you out of a tight spot but there are other strategies you can use with the same effect — like screaming for instance.

An aerosol alarm looks rather like a perfume dispenser:

'The one and only room maid ... spotted my personal alarm and the poor woman almost blasted out her ear drums when she attempted to "spray" it behind her ears.'

Morocco

These alarms emit a loud shriek that can be deafening at close range. NEVER let one off next to your ear or near small children unless you are desperate. They have the drawback of a limited life. Once the gas inside the aerosol has been used up (25-40 presses) they no longer work.

Sprays that contain a small amount of tear-gas obtainable in the U.S. are *not* legal in Britain. You would have problems with airport security, border guards and customs here and abroad if discovered with one. If you do carry such a spray keep it inconspicuous and expect difficulties if it is found by officials.

Where aerosol alarms undoubtedly do work is on animals. Dogs and other creatures hate them, and stray pariah dogs, rabid or otherwise can be a real problem to travellers even in European towns and cities.

For travellers more concerned with attracting help than frightening off an attacker there are flares available for use in wild country or at sea. In sunshine a mirror can be used to alert would-be rescuers.

Personal alarms are available from many security companies, or in the U.K. from the Automobile Association. Flares and rockets can be bought from shops that supply yachtsmen or those involved in outdoor pursuits.

Meeting people

Photos   Taking along photos of your family as a talking point is an old travellers' idea, and along with postcards of the Royal Family, a bit of a cliché. However, you will find they are looked at with interest by local people who, if they have photos, will also enjoy showing you theirs.

Some women say a photograph of a 'husband' is a useful standby in countries where the local Romeos have a lot of difficulty understanding a woman traveller's solo status. If you think you would whip it out and show it to a would-be leerer, swallow your pride and get the most macho looking of your acquaintances to pose.

Contacts   Compile a list of contacts before you go — mine proved invaluable on my travels. Besides providing somewhere to stay, they also allowed me to see a very different side of things and to get off the narrow tourist track.

If you end up with a list of people you've never met — all friends of friends — then ask your mutual acquaintances to write explaining who you are and roughly when you'll be arriving. It makes things easier than just turning up out of the blue and expecting to be welcomed. Offer to take news, letters or presents from those back home or if you're visiting ex-patriates, some of those small items which are unobtainable abroad. A friend I stayed with in the States had a craving for old-fashioned liquorice sticks which I was happy to supply. All of this smooths the introductions. If you can, write yourself, a week or so before you're planning to arrive, asking if it would still be all right to call.

Other useful addresses to carry with you are:

- The British Embassy/Consulate (although I'm afraid few of us can expect to be a welcome visitor to British Consuls around the world). There is a useful leaflet called *Consular Assistance Abroad*, available from travel agents and Citizen's Advice Bureaux.
- American Express and Thomas Cook local office addresses. English is usually spoken here.
- Local addresses to contact for traveller's cheque refund services.
- Address of local office of the airline with which you are booked to go home.
- Address of an overseas branch of your home bank, or the address of a bank with whom your own bank does business.
- Student travel office if you hold a student card.
- Address of your insurance company and its emergency number.

Presents   Accepting hospitality and present giving is discussed elsewhere in this book, and you will find that present giving is not always an appropriate response to the friendliness you will meet from local people. However, there will almost certainly be one or two occasions when you feel that giving a gift would be appropriate and it is nice to be able to find something suitable in your pack. You will be severely limited by space and weight so anything you decide to take must be small, light, and preferably of little monetary value so that it doesn't matter if stolen. Some of the souvenirs from tourist shops in this country are suitable (forget about Union Jack knickers), or you might find something in one of the National Trust shops. I usually try and take something small and pretty for the women in any family I meet, who often get forgotten by travellers, especially if unseen. After all, who does all the work!

I would prefer to take useful presents, but this is difficult without knowing in advance anything about your possible host and their circumstances. If you do know you will be staying for sometime with a particular family, you could write and ask if there is anything special you can bring out with you (but don't get yourself entangled with customs regulations).

Present giving to children should definitely be limited to one-off occasions only. Coins from home, or postcards showing scenes of your home country are light and easy to pack.

Eating & drinking

Travellers who are not self-catering should limit what they take to the bare essentials. You do not for example need to include a fork. A spoon will hold all that a fork can carry, and will manage yoghurt as well. In China consider taking your own chopsticks instead:

> 'It's advisable to take your own chopsticks around with you. Local restaurants and food stalls supply them but it's one of the best ways of getting ill — they really are disgusting.'
>
> *China*

For picnic foods such as paté, ham and cheese, you will need a knife that will spread as well as cut, but you don't need an extra one in addition to a good penknife. The Swiss Army Range of knives can provide you with a knife with suitable blades for dealing with food as well as for cutting other objects. Useful gadgets incorporated in a penknife are a pair of scissors (or you can get folding traveller's ones), and a corkscrew, a bottle-opener and a tin-opener. Forget gadgets for taking stones out of horses hooves unless you are absolutely sure you will need them.

At times of tension, airport security staff can be over-zealous about traveller's pocket knives. I once saw a German tourist relieved of her fruit knife at Colombo Airport (at the time Tamil terrorists were causing a lot of problems). She was furious when half an hour later, and at several thousand feet in the air, we were all supplied with much more substantial steak knives with which to tackle our meal. If you are carrying a fairly large penknife it is better concealed in your backpack and consigned to the luggage hold rather than smuggled on board in your hand luggage.

As well as cutlery to eat al fresco, you will need a water bottle. Something to carry hot or cold drinks in might be more essential than you think. I have twice been caught out. Once on a long and freezing rail journey here in England when the heating had failed and the buffet car never materialised, and secondly (and potentially more hazardous), on a particularly long train journey in rural India. On this latter occasion it wasn't that water was not available, it was, in fact the carriage full of people begged me to drink some as the day wore on and it got hotter and hotter. But we were deep in the countryside on a slow stopping train and all there was to drink was village well water. Without a bottle to hold it and some sterilisers in, I continued to refuse whilst feeling more and more uncomfortable in the heat. (Eventually, to my immense relief we arrived at a station large enough to have a tea seller.)

Avoid cheap plastic containers — they make all the liquids they contain taste the same — nasty. Look instead for a lightweight metal container with a fabric exterior. The cloth isn't really very effective at keeping drinks warm, but wetted, will keep cold drinks cool by the process of evaporation. A thermos flask is ideal for both hot and cold liquids but is not so easy to carry.

Some travellers are prepared to carry around bottles of drink bought locally and to dispense with a container of their own. There is, however, a problem with relying on local containers and that is the occasional difficulty of persuading vendors to part with them. In developing countries recycling is a way of life, there is none of the litter

of our throw-away society and a drink bottle will continue in circula-
tion until it eventually breaks. Drink sellers often insist that you drink
what you have bought at the stall. If you want to take the bottle away
you can expect to pay a 'deposit' — in effect to buy it as well as its
contents.

As this then means you have ended up with a water container after
all (but a heavy, breakable and possibly unsealable one) you might
wonder if you shouldn't have bought a purpose made one in the first
place, at very little extra cost.

Where you want to sterilise your own water for drinking and
cleaning teeth etc., a container is essential.

Water sterilisers   To sterilise water you either have to bring it
to a rolling boil for five minutes or use chemicals. Sterilising tablets
can be bought at any chemists. Puritabs and sterotabs are chlorine
based, potable-aqua contain iodine. You can also buy tincture of
iodine. Iodine is more effective because it kills a wider range of
contaminants than chlorine, including the cysts that cause amoebic
dysentery. If the water in the area you're travelling in is likely to be
impure you must take a means of sterilising the water with you.

Finally it is worth repeating here that the most useful thing for any
traveller is the ability to move around easily. The worst thing you can
do is weigh yourself down so that travelling around becomes a chore,
not the pleasure it should be. It takes courage, at first, to do without
the safety and security of all the things you may be tempted to pack just
in case. Pack *light*; you will have a better trip for it.

3
What To Wear

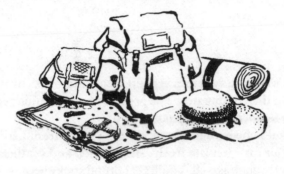

It takes considerable effort for first-time travellers to actually believe, let alone follow, the Golden Rule: *You need as many clothes for three months (or three weeks) as you do for three days.* One set of garments to wear, one set of things that needs washing, and a few spares for emergencies (including one smart dress) is the *maximum* to aim to take.

This does presuppose that you're happy to wash out your clothes frequently, or to exist in garments that are dirtier than you might accept at home. Once you've tried it you'll know that either is infinitely preferable to an enormous backpack that makes moving base a struggle, and running for a bus an impossibility.

The actual items you choose depend on where you're going, the climate you expect and the sort of trip you're planning (e.g. trekking versus business or staying with a maiden aunt in the diplomatic quarter in Cairo). But for women travellers in particular there are certain important considerations about clothing and sexuality, and about fitting in with local people.

CLIMATE

Do check on the climate before you travel. It is easy to forget that even
in the desert nights can be cool or that in Russia summers can be hot,
whilst the nearer you are to the equator the more temperatures will
vary according to the altitude you're travelling at rather than season
of the year.

Heat

Your body's cooling system is very efficient, and works by producing
sweat which then evaporates. The process of evaporation reduces the
immediate temperature and cools you down.

You should choose light, loose clothing made from natural fibres
so that the air can circulate freely. *Avoid* nylon and synthetics which
don't let air through as well. You'll get hot and sticky because the sweat
is not evaporating properly and you'll be liable to uncomfortable sweat
rashes like prickly heat (see page 152).

You also need to choose clothes that provide some protection
against a sun that may be far stronger than you're used to. Anyone who
has seen over-enthusiastic tourists who have turned lobster red knows
the danger areas: shoulders, upper arms, the back of your neck and
knees are all liable to sunburn unless you keep them covered. This
applies to your face as well, so you should include a hat or shawl to
shade your head.

As a general rule light colours are best as they reflect back the sun's
rays, but white is hardly a practical colour for most travellers.

Where it's hot and wet, the most practical item of 'clothing' might
be a small umbrella! Getting wet whilst it's hot doesn't have the same
dangers attached to it as getting wet and *cold*, whilst there is nothing
more unpleasant in a tropical downpour than wearing a rubberised or
plastic cagoul next to bare sweaty skin. If an umbrella's not feasible
then keep one set of clothes aside to get wet in, and pack a separate dry
set in a plastic bag to change into once you're under shelter.

Cold

Instead of helping the air to circulate as in hot climates, dressing for cold conditions is about trapping your body heat in a layer of air around you. The best way to do this is to choose several *layers* of clothes to wear over each other with air between them, rather than single, bulky garments. These clothes should be made of fibrous fabrics that themselves trap air, such as wool, brushed cotton, down padding etc.

As well as trapping your body heat you need to keep it there by keeping out of the wind, otherwise your nicely heated layer of warm air is constantly being blown away, and constantly having to be replaced. You also need to keep out water. Water, as it dries, conducts heat away from you, and in cold conditions, your body temperature can quickly reach a point where it's dangerously low and you start to suffer from 'exposure' or hypothermia. The outer layer of clothing should therefore be made of a fabric that is wind and waterproof. There is however a problem in finding clothes that keep your body heat *in*, and the wet out but which still let the moisture you produce evaporate, otherwise you can produce enough moisture yourself to make clothes damp.

There are a number of specialist clothing manufacturers catering for the outdoor-pursuits market that have attempted to come up with solutions to this problem, using new man-made fabrics. The best known of these is Gore-Tex which is used to make cagouls, anoraks, sleeping bag covers etc.

Gore-Tex is expensive but if you are expecting severe weather conditions you should visit a specialist supplier and discuss your trip with them and consider whether or not it would be worth paying the extra money involved. Several of the specialist magazines such as *Climber and Rambler, The Great Outdoors* etc. run occasional articles on new developments in outdoor cold-weather clothing and equipment. You can also get advice from the Royal Geographical Society's Expedition Advisory Service. (See page 278).

Finally, when choosing clothes for cold conditions you must include a hat, for a considerable percentage of body heat is lost from the top of the head which should preferably be protected by two layers — a warm woollen hat next to the skin, and an outer waterproof hood which can be put up when necessary.

Temperate and mixed climates

Most of us are fairly adept at dressing for our own climate, and own clothes that can adapt to a range of warm-cool, wet-dry conditions. You may still need to pack layers of clothes not so much to beat the cold, but for maximum flexibility in countries with unpredictable, changeable conditions — conditions in England for instance where May can bring a heat wave or snow flurries, as well as the expected showers and mild spring days. A vest, T-shirt, light jumper and cardigan/jacket are more adaptable than a choice that limits you to either a shirt or a thick, knitted sweater. Avoid single bulky items such as heavy jackets, overcoats and thick pullovers which take up far too much space and take ages to dry when they get wet. Go for cotton and polyester mixed fabrics which drip dry easily, and wool synthetic mixes that wear better than pure wool. As temperate climates are damp, with showers all the year round, choose a lightweight waterproof, and pack watertight shoes.

Comfort

Not many travellers are likely to set off in high heels and a hobble skirt, but although choosing comfortable clothes might seem obvious, it is easy to make mistakes. The commonest is to pack just a couple of pairs of jeans. Comfortable? Practical? Well, ... trousers turn out to be less than ideal when you need to go for a pee miles from the nearest bush, can be far too hot if you're jammed on a bus with scores of other people, and are most uncomfortable if you are sitting for ages cross-legged. All-in-one jumpsuits are even worse, being impossible to take off without removing virtually everything else as well.

Comfortable clothes are loosely cut, easy to get in and out of, and cover you sufficiently so you don't have to hold anything down if you're climbing into trucks or trains.

CULTURALLY APPROPRIATE

It's best to stick to straightforward conventional Western styles when it comes to deciding what to take. At home we expect people to be tolerant about the garments we wear. We also expect a fair amount of tolerance about how much or how little of our bodies we choose to cover or uncover. In many cultures outside the West, things are different. The idea of dressing to express individuality so crucial to us, may be discouraged and local attitudes be much more conservative than we're used to at home.

Even where Western-style clothing is worn, local people do not expect a wide choice of styles. Where money is short clothes have to be practical and are chosen to suit the lifestyle and the climate rather than the whims of fashion. They're discarded only when worn out, not simply because they're 'old-fashioned'. Local people are also likely to be far more constrained by taboos and traditions about covering the female body than we are, especially where these are supported by religious beliefs.

Local people not only have fairly fixed ideas about what is and isn't suitable for themselves. They often have preconceived ideas about what is suitable for *us*. Even city dwellers may be more used to foreigners who visit on business, or may increasingly get their ideas from imported American TV programmes.

'In the Pacific Islands they expect all Westerners to go round dressed like the characters they see on American satellite programmes.'

It was a clash with these sorts of expectations that gave 'hippies' and independent travellers such a bad name in the 60s and 70s. Some local people, when faced with Western fashion as it actually was, simply refused to believe that these travellers were wearing exactly what they'd be wearing at home. The same would apply to some of the street fashions and clothes of today.

However, as long haul travel becomes more and more possible, local people in popular tourist areas are surprised by very little, and in all but the Islamic Countries have politely resigned themselves to the Western Culture imposed on them by holiday makers. Attempts to resist more unacceptable practices such as the wearing of shorts and topless sunbathing are still made, but in the face of the indifference of many tourists, these become more and more half hearted. (Anyone who's visited Greece and seen faded local graffiti begging sun-bathers to wear bikinis totally ignored by nude foreign sun-worshippers will know what we mean.) But just because local people may have given up expecting visitors in holiday areas to be sensitive to their ideas, doesn't mean that they don't appreciate those who use their imagination and are prepared to go some way to fit in with local expectations. Away from tourist areas visitors who venture off the beaten track can be surprised by reactions to clothes that hitherto people have appeared to ignore.

> 'Away from the beach everyone stared at our cycle shorts.'
>
> *Gambia*

Do therefore choose ordinary, simple skirts, dresses, tops to take on your travels. Leave at home the more exotic and especially the more revealing articles in your wardrobe.

> 'The more modestly you dress, the more culturally comfortable and assimilated you will feel.'
>
> *Indonesia*

> 'In cities wear normal town clothing. Try to be clean and as smart as you can manage.'
>
> *Colombia*

It isn't just polite to be sensitive to local ideas and expectations, it makes practical sense as well. Unless you positively revel in attracting attention you'll find you have a more enjoyable trip if you blend in with the local scene and leave more extreme styles at home.

Wearing local dress

Fitting in to the extent of wearing local dress is something some travellers have strong feelings about. Those in favour feel that by wearing local costume travellers are showing respect for local traditions and that anything less is an attempt consciously or unconsciously to impose 'superior' Western standards on local people. They go on to argue that if travellers insist on parading Western clothes in front of local people they gradually come to see these as more 'modern' and more desirable than their own traditional costumes which are abandoned in favour of ubiquitous T-shirts or cheap nylon dresses.

Those in favour of wearing local dress also point out that in most cases local clothes have developed in response to the climate and the conditions in which the wearers live and are therefore far more comfortable and practical than Western clothes.

'Wear Indian clothes — saris, salwar-kamiz and a bindi (red-spot painted on forehead) — I got a lot of respect for doing this.'

India

Not all women however agree:

'Wear your own cultural clothes, Europeans in saris attract attention.'

India

'I saw some Westerners trying to wear local dress (sarong and jacket). They looked rather ridiculous and some local people were offended that they weren't "properly" dressed, i.e. in Western clothes.'

Indonesia

Those against the idea of travellers adopting local dress wholesale say that they feel that this is being condescending and is seen by local people as 'dressing down'. They agree that local dress is in no way inferior to Western dress but go on to say that local costume is part of the wearers' *own* heritage and tradition, and should be respected as such. That travellers only adopt such costumes temporarily when convenient to themselves, and wouldn't wear them at home.

Personally I feel that most Westerners in local costumes do tend to look rather self conscious, as if they are in fancy dress; or downright awkward and insecure, unaccustomed to moving in the long folds of a sari or sarong. However to be *invited* to try on, and wear local clothes is a real pleasure and to refuse this would certainly cause offence.

The compromise that is the most acceptable is to choose Western-style clothes that serve the same covering-up purpose as local ones. So where local women wear loose baggy ankle length trousers and tops choose trousers and a loose shirt; or at least a skirt that is mid-calf in length. Where local people prefer shoulders and armpits to be covered, choose T-shirts and blouses with sleeves.

Don't wear shorts away from the tourist beaches in areas where local costume is obviously designed to cover up the wearer's legs, and if this is the case, especially don't wear shorts if you intend to visit religious sites.

In the Islamic countries local people will make it much more obvious what is considered acceptable, and in recent years traditional Moslem dress has been re-introduced and re-adopted by fundamentalists even in previously relaxed Islamic countries such as Malaysia.

Loose clothes with long sleeves, full fairly long skirts and a headscarf are generally acceptable throughout Islamic countries.

SUGGESTED CLOTHING

The following have all been recommended by the women who contributed to this book. It's not a list to rigidly adhere to, but a set of basics to pick and choose from to suit your travel plans. We do recommend that you don't limit yourself to just trousers — take a skirt or dress as an alternative.

Underwear, including bra and socks,
Skirt — mid calf, full or gathered, and/or
Dress — mid calf, full or gathered,
Long-sleeved shirt,
Short-sleeved shirt (including T-shirts),
Trousers, *not* jeans,
Pair of sturdy walking shoes,
Pair of lightweight shoes or sandals,
Pair of flip-flops,
One large and one small cotton or wool scarf,
Jumper and/or cardigan,
Cagoul,
One-piece swimsuit; or bikini for tourist areas only,
Hat.

Underwear

Always choose cotton underclothes whether you're packing for hot or cold climates. Synthetics don't allow sweat to evaporate properly (you can sweat on Mount Everest), and this encourages prickly heat and thrush to develop. For cold, temperate and mixed climates invest in good quality thermal underwear to wear over the cotton knickers you've taken — light, easy to wash and dry and incredibly warm and comfortable, they take up little space.

Thermals can be used to sleep in, which saves on packing night clothes; and they are an ideal layer to keep the heat in. This means that worn under other garments, they can take the place of far more bulky sweaters. Britain's best known manufacturers, Damart, supply numerous expeditions to cold climates, but also have a wide range of less specialised underwear that I've taken even to Mediterranean countries in summer. One vest worn under daytime clothes is warm enough for cooler evenings in the tropics.

Not everyone wears a bra, but if you prefer to go without, remember that bare breasts under a thin T-shirt do cause unfavourable comment in countries where women dress to minimise bosoms. Choose cotton rather than nylon.

Socks are useful even in hot countries as a (slight) protection against insect-bites. You can usually keep them on if you are visiting mosques and temples, where shoes are removed. (I planned a dignified approach to Gandhi's monument near Delhi, but ended up frantically hopping round the black marble slabs because I couldn't bear the heat on my bare feet.)

In cold countries you will need two or three pairs, and wool reinforced with nylon at the toe and heel wears better than pure wool.

Skirts and dresses

The most useful skirts and dresses are cut fairly fully. It is much easier to hide a money belt under pleats and gathers than under a straight or A-line skirt, and they make it much easier to go to the loo in the open without embarrassment (see page 126).

Elasticated waists or wrap-around skirts are more comfortable than fitted waistbands. You will be amazed what different diets and climates can do to your weight (and you don't always get thinner).

Always choose skirts with pockets, but where possible stick to pockets let into the side seams which are less obvious to thieves than open patch pockets. You can also slit a side pocket to allow yourself easy access to the money belt beneath (see page 255).

Acceptable everywhere, mid-calf skirts are easy to move around in, comfortable when sitting cross-legged, and long enough to be decent at all times.

Shirts and tops

Long-sleeved shirts are useful even if you're packing for the heat, for protection against sunburn, and against insects.

T-shirts are actually hotter than loose cotton or seer-sucker blouses, but are useful if you want to take clothes you can build up in layers.

Shirts with short sleeves are more widely acceptable than sun tops away from tourist beaches, and anyway offer better protection from sunburn.

Cotton sweaters and jumpers are as heavy or heavier than a thin wool pullover or cardigan and are less practical. They don't keep their shape as well as wool, attract dirt more easily, don't dry as quickly and crease badly. They also soak up water like a sponge, where wool is *relatively* water repellant.

Loosely cut tops which are long enough to go over or under your waistband are preferable to ones that will ride up to reveal your midriff everytime you want to raise your arms. (In Islamic countries choose loose tops that are also long enough to cover your hips.) This isn't just because you might not want to display bare skin; in cold climates you want tops that are long enough to tuck in and *stay* tucked in to lower layers so that you keep warm.

Choose garments with button down pockets if possible — the more the better.

As indicated above, layers are more practical than single garments, so for mixed or cold climates choose vest-T-shirt-shirt-jumper-cardigan-cagoul, rather than just a shirt and a couple of sweaters.

Waterproofs

Cagouls in man-made fibres have widely replaced the old cotton anoraks, and are available in different fabric weights, as well as in different lengths and finishes. For extreme weather conditions take specialist advice and be prepared to spend upwards of £60 for a knee-length garment that has seams which are wind and waterproof, seals at neck and wrists and is also made from material such as Gore-Tex which allows moisture to pass from the inside, out.

At the opposite end of the market are plastic cagouls which will tear along poorly finished sewn seams and which if done up, produce so much condensation that you drown in your own sweat.

If a cheaper version to cope with the odd shower or cool day is all you need, go for a middle range, lightweight garment from a good outdoor clothing shop.

Trousers

Choose loosely-cut comfortable trousers — in cotton for hot climates to let air circulate; and in corduroy, wool mixes or brushed cotton for the cold. If choosing for cold climates they should be roomy enough for you to wear long-johns and tights underneath and still be able to bend your knees comfortably.

Avoid denim jeans unless you're travelling in temperate areas. Although denim is tough and hard wearing, it is difficult to keep clean without scrubbing in plenty of hot water, and it takes a long time to dry. Denim is also too heavy for hot climates, and not good at providing insulation in cold weather. In cold, wet conditions it can even be fatal, holding moisture next to your skin and conducting heat away from you. Even in the comparatively mild climate of the U.K. denim is not recommended wear if you're out mountain walking.

On the market there are both specialised lightweight travellers' trousers and a new insulated winter range, in safari-look designs. We haven't tried these ourselves, however I have spoken to travellers who have been very happy with the lightweight (wind and shower proof) pairs they have bought and feel them to be well worth the extra money.

Trousers with cuffed bottoms are warm and easy to pull socks over. As with skirts, the more button down or zipped pockets the better.

Shorts

Like bikinis, shorts are widely worn 'leisure wear' for Westerners in tourist areas. Shorts aren't just limited to the beach, but are worn along popular trekking routes, on safari trips, or for general sightseeing.

However away from holiday areas, shorts are *not* recommended for women travellers. Unless it's clear that shorts are acceptable wear for local women, you will find that they attract unfavourable comment and attention. Unfortunately tour operators who arrange overland expeditions to even quite remote areas seem to recommend members to bring shorts. Our experience is that away from the 'security' of the group, women in shorts in these areas often cause offence and attract unwanted harassment. Mid-calf skirts are a much better alternative, allowing the same freedom of movement, as well as being cool. They are much more acceptable to local people.

> 'Everything is acceptable except short shorts ... I was always embarrassed when I saw tourists dressed in these, they looked out of place or ridiculous.'
>
> *Tanzania*

Footwear

Hookworms, chiggers and verrucas are just three of the parasites and infections you can pick up through bare feet. Snakes, scorpions and leeches are other hazards you will be anxious to avoid and even ordinary cuts, grazes and blisters can easily turn septic and ruin your trip.

All travellers should therefore wear comfortable shoes even down to the beach where sand can hot up enough to burn the soles of your feet.

Buy footwear at home and *wear it in before you go*. Don't rely on being able to find what you want abroad. My beautiful all leather Turkish slippers with curled-up pointed toes are unfortunately enlivened by a sharp tack protruding through each sole.

Of course you can get excellent shoes on your travels and cheaply as well but don't rely on it! Look for footwear that is made from leather; or canvas (if you're going where it's hot), both materials let feet breath so you are less likely to develop athlete's foot. Check the stitching along seams and where possible buy shoes where the soles are stitched on rather than stuck. It's easier to get these repaired locally.

Don't take tight-fitting shoes — your feet swell in hot weather, and in cold climates you'll want to fit in extra socks.

Flip-flops — either made from rubber or plastic can usually be bought locally. They're worth getting not only because they're comfortable to wear in hot dry conditions, but also because they're useful to wear in the shower, in less than clean public loos, and on the beach.

Scarves

My cotton shawl which is two by five feet has been used as a towel, a pillow, a headscarf when entering temples, it has carried hard-boiled eggs through mountains, covered me up during naps, hung as a curtain across windows etc., and it *still* looks nice on the wall at home. Slightly larger sarongs or kangas can be worn as skirts, tops, beach wraps and houserobes; and smaller squares as evening wraps, head coverings or used as bandages, or bags.

Women all round the world use simple unstitched pieces of material as the basis of colourful costumes; to carry babies in, or pleated and knotted as all kinds of distinctive headwear.

If you're going anywhere in Asia, the Far East, Africa, the Middle East, or South America it is hardly worth buying one before you go — you'll have great difficulty in restraining yourself from filling the remaining corners of your backpack with all the local examples of colour and pattern you'll find on offer in any bazaar and market. Luckily they're cheap and light, they make wonderful presents to take home and you can buy as many as you can carry, or afford to send back.

Hats

Unlike a headscarf, the brim of a hat will keep the sun off your face and out of your eyes. Even though straw hats are difficult to pack it may be worth taking one, although some kind of local headgear is almost always available. Winter hats are much easier to pack. You don't need anything with a brim, just a woollen pull-on which comes over the ears and can be squashed into a pocket easily.

Swimwear

What to take depends very much on where you're going obviously.

> 'We were told off for sunbathing in bikinis on the university campus.'
>
> *China*

In countries where there are tourist beach developments bikinis are now accepted and even topless bathing is now becoming more usual as visitors import Western ideas of what's acceptable with them. However, away from tourist areas, observe local women, who in many countries, if they bathe at all do so fully clothed and then decide the likely reaction to even a modest swimsuit.

If you don't know the area, take a one-piece costume, not a bikini. If topless bathing turns out to be O.K. you can always get away with just a pair of knickers.

Clothing tips

Don't take garments you're particularly attached to. Apart from anything else that might happen to them, it's too handy to be able to ditch your own clothes and replace them with local alternatives if you see something you like.

Don't take military-style clothes anywhere. Khaki or mock camouflage flak jackets and trousers come regularly into fashion in our shops. In other countries where the army is much more in evidence than at home, where things may be more unstable, and where women regularly do military service, wearing anything that looks even remotely to do with the armed forces is asking for trouble.

Don't let all your clothes become equally travel worn. Try and keep at least one top that is clean and unmarked (preferably with a skirt as well) for occasions when you may want to dress up. I was once a positive embarrassment to my hosts who asked if I would like to give away prizes in a local school. Presumably the principal assumed I owned something other than the jeans I stood up in. Alas, no. The recipients were all immaculate in spotless pressed uniforms. I was still in jeans and stuck out like a sore thumb, the only person who had apparently made no effort for the occasion.

You will definitely want a set of smarter clothes if you intend job hunting on your travels. If you have an interview it might be worth paying out for a laundry to get your clothes into shape, or investing in some new ones, if your own have gone past the point of no return.

Finally, in developing countries, don't underestimate the fashion consciousness of contacts you may have in government circles, amongst professional people, or with those who are wealthy enough to have travelled widely themselves. Often these people will be among the privileged upper classes and may have adopted Western dress themselves. If this is the case their clothes will almost certainly be 20 times more expensive than anything you've got with you.

'The volunteers were all much scruffier and less fashionable than the people who invited us to parties.'

VSO Volunteer Zambia

'Evening dress tends to be very formal but nobody seemed to notice my cheesecloth skirt at a "posh" party.'

Pakistan

COUNTRY-BY-COUNTRY GUIDE

The following are tips for particular countries passed on by other women travellers. Always check up on the weather conditions you can expect at your time of travel, and don't forget to allow for the influence of altitude on temperature.

Islam — The Gulf States, Middle East, Libya and Iran

The Islamic religion has very strong expectations about what is suitable dress for women and there may be considerable opposition towards Westerners who are not prepared to fit in. In recent years there has been a rise in Islamic fundamentalism which is often associated with patriotism and anti-Western feelings. In some countries local women have readopted Islamic dress as a statement of their beliefs and patriotism. The Gulf States, Middle East, Libya and Iran are generally the most 'strict' Islamic societies. Travel and tourism is not encouraged in these countries, however if you are granted a visa, or are in one of the Arab States working, take *modest, conventional* Western clothes.

Tops with long or three-quarter length sleeves and fairly high necklines are advised.

Take mid-calf loose-fitting skirts and dresses, and loose-fitting light trousers. A headscarf is essential for Iran and Libya, and appreciated elsewhere.

Shorts, short skirts, suntops and bikinis are *OUT* except in expatriate compounds where you can wear what you would at home.

Take a light cardigan or sweater to counteract ferocious air conditioning in public buildings, offices and homes. Warm clothes may also be necessary where desert temperatures drop at night or during winter months (particularly Iran, which gets very cold).

Islam — Around the Mediterranean

The Islamic countries of Egypt, Morocco, Jordan, Tunisia, Turkey and Algeria are more relaxed about what is considered suitable for local women. In urban areas modest Western dress is fairly common (but still covers the wearer), particularly on younger women. In rural areas Islamic traditions are strong although veils are less common than in the Gulf (and forbidden in Turkey). Many of these countries welcome visitors, so for travellers, Western dress is tolerated and acceptable in tourist areas. However, avoid shorts or tight or revealing clothes away from sightseeing areas and tourist beaches.

Loose trousers are acceptable everywhere.

Take a light cardigan or jumper in spring and autumn and warmer clothes during the winter months. Temperatures can get quite low around the Mediterranean in winter (you can ski in Algeria); inland Turkey can be as cold as minus 20° centigrade during the winter, and snow falls are common.

Pakistan

Islamic traditions are strong in urban and rural areas. Only a few 'modern' upper-middle-class urban women wear Western dress, even at home. Most women wear the traditional *salwar-kamiz* (loose top and tight trousers). Veiling is common as most keep purdah.

Take loose trousers and hip-length tops; or a mid-calf full skirt. Cover shoulders and upper arms. A shawl or headscarf is useful especially for visiting mosques. If visiting the northern, mountainous region in winter take plenty of warm clothes, it gets very cold, with plenty of snow.

Do not take shorts, sun tops or bikinis. A one-piece swimming costume is for hotel pools only.

Islam — Asia and the Far East

India, Indonesia, Maldives, Malaysia. In these countries Islam exists alongside other religions, and although there has been some rise in fundamentalism recently, attitudes are generally more relaxed. Local women still wear modest clothes but veils are rare.

In Malaysia in the last two or three years many young women, particularly students, have adopted Islamic dress and now wear long dresses, head coverings and in extreme cases, gloves and socks.

Travellers should dress for tropical conditions and avoid shorts and bikinis away from tourist beaches.

Islam — North Africa

Islam has had a major influence on Black Africa. The nearer north to the centre of Islamic influence, the stronger Islamic traditions of dress become. As elsewhere take modest skirts and dresses and loose trousers. Cover shoulders and upper arms. *AVOID* shorts, sun tops and bikinis.

West Africa

Nigeria   In the cities Western dress is widely worn and Nigerians are generally very tolerant about Western clothing, although about 40 per cent of the population are Moslem. Shorts are not really acceptable outside Lagos.

You can buy lengths of cloth locally to wear as wraparound skirts — very colourful, cheap and practical.

Gambia and Senegal   Local women wear traditional wraparound long skirts or T-shirts and skirts. Buying well-made Western clothes locally is expensive, so bring what you need with you. Western holiday styles are acceptable in Dakkar and on tourist beaches, but in non tourist areas shorts are frowned on.

Topless sunbathing is O.K. in *some* tourist areas.

Ghana, Togo, Mali   In non-Moslem areas trousers, shorts and skirts are acceptable although shorts are more for 'work-wear' if you are out in the bush. In Moslem areas keep legs covered. For large towns take a smart summer dress; in more provincial areas clothes are more casual.

North East Africa

Ethiopia The highlands get cold at night so include a warm jacket, vest and pullover as well as lighter daytime wear. You should bring a scarf for visiting churches, and avoid skimpy, figure-revealing clothes.

East Africa

Kenya   Along the tourist routes shorts and holiday wear are fine, but away from tourist areas trousers are stared at. T-shirts are widely worn and can be bought locally.

Tanzania   In the Moslem coastal areas local women wear black *bui-bui* (a long robe which falls to the ankles) but Western dress is widely seen in towns. Trousers are stared at in rural areas, as are shorts. Shirts with sleeves are better than those without; skirts and T-shirts are acceptable elsewhere.

You will need warmer clothes if visiting the uplands, e.g. Mount Kilimanjaro, Arusha or Ngarongoro.

Zambia   Shorts are suitable for tourist areas only, pack a pullover and/or cardigan for cooler months of the year.

Malawi   You will not be allowed into Malawi if you are wearing trousers, and skirts and dresses must cover the knee. You should keep to this standard of dress during your stay.

Asia and the Far East

India, Sri Lanka and Nepal   Local women wear *salwar-kamiz* (trousers and tops) in North-West India and saris elsewhere. Tribal costumes are seen in the hills and in Nepal. Western dress is seldom worn, even in urban areas.

Northern India and Nepal are cold during the winter months and at high altitudes; hill stations everywhere are cool. Trousers are acceptable everywhere, although skirts are cooler and more practical in the heat. Dress to cover legs, shoulders, upper arms and bosoms.

Modest one-piece swimsuits are much more acceptable than bikinis, local women only bathe fully clothed. Topless bathing is OUT (except on some beaches at Goa), and is forbidden in Sri Lanka.

A headscarf is essential if you want to visit Sikh temples, and a sun hat is advised.

Cheap, light, Western-style clothing is available in large cities or at beaches frequented by travellers. Local tailors can copy most garments and make things up for you. A good selection of thong-type sandals (*chappals*) is available at most towns — small sizes only. Woollen clothes are available in Nepal and North Indian hill stations.

Thailand, Malaysia, Indonesia, Myanmur (Burma)
Western dress is widely worn by local women, especially in urban areas, but traditional sarongs with blouses and tribal costumes are also seen.

The climate is hot so light skirts or dresses will generally be more comfortable than trousers, blouses cooler than T-shirts.

It is preferable to cover shoulders and upper arms, shorts attract unwanted comments and are not advised away from tourist areas. Local women bathe fully clothed so wear bikinis on tourist beaches only.

Temple scarves are essential if visiting temples on Bali. They are cheap and easy to obtain locally. They are worn around the waist and hips.

Light clothing is for sale throughout the area, particularly in cities and in tourist areas, however, quite a lot on offer is synthetic.

Philippines, Hong Kong, Japan, China
Conventional Western dress is worn by local women in most areas. Styles are generally fairly simple, nothing too way out or extreme, though young urban women in Japan and Hong Kong will be wearing much what you might at home. Many Chinese women still wear traditional trousers and jackets, but Western styles are now more common in urban areas.

Choose light clothing but take sweaters or a jacket to cope with air-conditioning in public buildings.

Winters in part of China and Japan are *cold*. Take plenty of thermal underwear.

Bikinis are acceptable on most beaches, but one-piece costumes are preferred in China.

Central and South America

Urban women dress smartly in fashionable Western clothes, whereas in rural areas many peasant women wear their own traditional woven and embroidered costumes.

Pack for a mixed climate. Conditions vary from tropical on the coast to cold in the high mountainous interior. A waterproof is essential. Woollen jumpers, hats, ponchos and jackets are available locally.

Short-sleeved T-shirts and jeans are acceptable everywhere, but shorts are NOT recommended, and upper arms, shoulders and knees should be covered when visiting churches.

Bikinis are worn by urban women on popular beaches.

Job hunters need a smart outfit and should not attend interviews in trousers.

Russia and Eastern Bloc countries

Styles are similar to those for Britain although outside major cities, styles in Russia and Eastern Bloc countries may look dated. Warm clothes, good quality thermal underwear, warm footwear, gloves and a hat are essential in Northern Europe and Russia in winter, but clothes should be worn in layers, as houses and public buildings are well heated. Waterproofs should also be packed, although the winter cold is dry. However, it can be hot in summer so pack accordingly. Bikinis are worn by local women, but topless bathing is not usual in Russia or other Eastern Bloc countries.

Clothes are often difficult to find in the right sizes so take what you need with you, although traditional felt boots are a good local buy.

4
Getting Ready
To Go

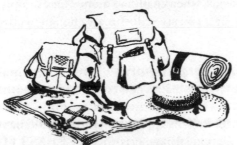

PASSPORTS AND VISAS

A quick scan through the pages of any directory listing the entry requirements of different countries in the world gives a graphic (if depressing), picture of the squabbles between nations.

Israelis, or indeed any other nationals who have visited Israel are unwelcome in any of the Arab League countries; Iran, at the time of writing, was making it virtually impossible for Americans to enter their country. Bulgaria is not keen on nationals of the Korean Republic or holders of Taiwan passports (amongst others). This may be the age of mass tourism, and international air transport, but it is by no means an open world where any traveller can turn up at the borders of any country they choose and expect to be politely let through.

All travellers therefore find themselves in need of various documents. Exactly what you will require depends on your nationality and status, and the relations between your home country and the country you wish to visit. It may also depend on the purpose of your visit —are you entering as a visitor, student, business woman, or diplomat? Finally what you require in the way of documents can change according to political circumstance, sometimes, dramatically, overnight.

Passports

Your passport is your most important travel document because it verifies your national status and your identity. You will be asked to produce it at the borders of every country you visit (although neighbouring countries often have reciprocal arrangements where an identity card or similar may be used in lieu of a full passport). Your passport may also be requested for scrutiny by officials on many occasions during your travels, when changing money for example, when checking into hotels, or if you are unfortunate enough to cross swords with the local police.

United Kingdom passports   If you wish to apply for a United Kingdom passport, or obtain a new one to replace one that has expired, you should ask at your local Post Office for Form A and a copy of the notes that go with it. This application form should be completed and returned to your regional passport office AT LEAST FOUR WEEKS in advance of your departure, LONGER IN THE SUMMER. If you are going to a country which will require a visa you should make sure of getting your passport even earlier by several weeks (see page 77).

Although your passport will be posted to you by first class post, you can ask for it to be sent by registered post if you enclose an extra amount to cover the costs.

In emergencies you might be able to obtain a passport more quickly by travelling in person to your regional office. There is also a duty officer available outside office hours in the London office to deal only with serious emergencies (death or serious illness). Evidence of the emergency has to be produced. The duty officer is available from 4.30 p.m.–6.00 p.m. Mondays to Fridays, and Saturdays 10.00 a.m.–12.00 noon. Normal passport office hours are 9.00–4-30 Monday to Friday. Your area office will be entered in the local yellow pages.

When you send off your application form, keep a note of the exact date of posting, in case of a query later with the office.

Enclosures — birth certificate   You will need to enclose your birth certificate with your application form, *not* a photocopy. This is all well and good if you can find it, if not you can obtain a birth certificate from the local Register Office of the district in which you were born. Alternatively you can apply to the General Register Office in London (see page 278). Your birth certificate will be returned along with your passport.

Photographs   Two identical passport photographs must be enclosed with your application. These can be in black and white or in colour. They must be taken full face, without a hat, and must be not larger than 2½ inches by 2 inches. Most people use the photographic booths found at central Post Offices, on station platforms, and in large stores. Despite the fact that they give everyone the expression of a startled convict, they are cheap and the right size. If you prefer a more artistic effort, go to any professional photographer.

Don't have your photo taken with an outrageous hair style you intend to change for ever next day, and if you habitually wear spectacles keep them on. Dark glasses, unless worn continuously for medical reasons, are not allowed. If you are applying for visas at the same time or travelling outside Europe, you should have at *least* six copies of the photo made, preferably a dozen.

Countersignatories   Every applicant needs a 'referee' who will sign the application form and endorse the back of one of your photographs to confirm that it looks like you. Your countersignatory should have known you for at least two years and should be 'a Member of Parliament, Justice of the Peace, Minister of Religion, Lawyer, Bank Officer, Established Civil Servant, School Teacher, Police Officer, Doctor or person of similar standing' (sic). The notes accompanying your application form add darkly 'Passport Office procedures include a check on the authenticity of countersignatories'.

Marital status   If you are getting married you have several options open to you about the name you wish to have on your passport, as well as a decision to make about whether or not to opt for a joint passport with your partner.

Joint passports are cheaper and can be in either partner's name (not just in that of the husband). However the drawback is that although the name-holder can travel alone, whichever of you is down as the dependent can not. That person can only travel accompanied by the person in whose name the passport has been issued.

If you decide to remain a passport holder in your own right, you don't have to use your married name if you don't want to. If you have already got a current passport in your own name you can go on using that (but take along your marriage certificate as some countries won't consider an unamended passport valid). Because your passport is an identity document it should be in the name you will be using for all purposes at home. So if you want a passport issued in your maiden name you can do so, provided you make a statement declaring that this is the name you use for every occasion.

Alternatively you can apply for a passport in a double-barrelled name, amalgamating your own name and your husband's name (again declaring that this is how you are known for all purposes).

Finally you could have the best of both worlds by keeping your own name but have a statement entered reading that The holder is the wife of ...

If you do decide to have your existing passport amended in your married name, allow several weeks. If you wish to apply for a passport in your married name *ahead* of the actual wedding (for use on a honeymoon immediately afterwards), not only is the Passport Office accommodating, but just to prove that romance beats even in the dry heart of the Civil Service you can pick up a special gold coloured form, embellished with honeysuckle, from your Post Office, that will tell you how to go about it. Ask for Forms PD1 and PD2.

Divorce   If you were previously on a joint passport in your ex-husband's name but are now divorced, you can apply for a passport of your own or jointly with a new partner. You don't have to produce the old passport, even if this is still current, but should fill in the appropriate boxes on your application form and enclose either a marriage certificate or divorce documents.

Children   Up to the age of 16, it is usual for children to be included on their parent's, or guardian's passports. A child can be entered with both parents, so they are not always limited to travelling with the same one.

A child can also be included on the passport of a close relative, provided the parents give their consent. If a child is illegitimate, consent must be given by the mother.

Children between 5 years and 16 years may hold passports of their own, if they will be travelling without a member of their family (expatriate children returning home to school for example).

Exceptionally, children under five years may be issued with their own passports.

British visitor's passport   Under E.C. regulations, your travel agent must advise you about your passport requirements. British visitor's passports are valid for one year only and can be used for holidays or unpaid business trips of up to three months in the following countries:

Andorra, Austria, France (incl. Corsica), Germany, Gibraltar, Greece, Italy (incl. Sicily, Sardinia & Elba), Liechtenstein, Malta, Monaco, Portugal (incl. Madeira & the Azores), San Marino, Switzerland, Tunisia, Turkey,

Belgium ⎤ Children under 16 years cannot go on their brother's
Luxembourg ⎬ or sister's passport
Netherlands ⎦

Denmark ⎤
Finland ⎥ Trips to these as a group must add up to less than 3
Iceland ⎬ months in a 9-month period.
Norway ⎥
Sweden ⎦

Spain   Spain may decide not to recognise British Visitors passports from 1995.

The main advantage of these short-term passports is that they're obtainable over the counter of main Post Offices in England, Wales and Scotland. They *are* cheaper but as they are valid for such a short time, they work out more expensive in the long run.

To apply you complete Form VP, available at the Post Office, supply two photographs (see above), and *one* of the following: A birth or adoption certificate (NOT a photocopy); National Health Medical Card; D.H.S.S. Retirement Pension Book or Card; or an uncancelled Standard British Passport (which will be surrendered for the duration that you hold a Visitor's Passport).

British Excursion Document for travel to France This has been introduced in response to the growing number of Britains who wish to go on weekend or day trips to France (usually either for sports events or on shopping expeditions). The Excursion Document is valid only for France, and only for a stay of no longer than 60 hours. You must travel on an excursion ticket and normally go out and return by the same seaport or airport. Again, apply at a Post Office. You need one of the following documents:
A birth certificate or adoption certificate.
A D.H.S.S. Retirement Pension Book or card.
An uncancelled British Visitor's Passport or Standard British Passport. Also one passport photograph which must be endorsed by a countersignatory who must be a 'responsible British Citizen' (sic) — see above. The countersignatory must also sign the application form for you.

Children can be included on both a Visitor's Passport, or an Excursion Document.

Changes Since 1987 new-format passports have been issued which recognise Britain's membership of the E.C. The new passports are machine readable — computerisation is being introduced both at the Passport Offices and at immigration points. New format passports are gradually being phased in by replacing existing ones, as and when these expire. The procedure for applying for a passport remains the same as before.

Visas/entry permits

A passport is issued by your home country and endorses your right to travel outside that country. A visa is issued by the country you wish to visit and gives you permission to enter (although the final say rests with the immigration officers who will inspect your documents at the point of entry).

You won't need a visa (which is stamped on the pages of your passport) for every trip. It depends on your nationality and where you wish to go. At the time of writing for example a U.K. passport holder did not require visas for travel within Western Europe, nor for many of the Commonwealth countries. Provided that you travel with a recognised carrier, you can visit the U.S. for up to 90 days without a visa, if you have a British passport. Visas are required for British women visiting Eastern Bloc countries, Australia and many of the smaller, more remote (and more interesting) countries of the world.

However visa requirements can change rapidly as the political situation within a country changes, or increasingly, as a response to international terrorism.

Many years ago India did not require U.K. passport holders to apply for visas. However, all that changed, virtually overnight, with the assassination of Mrs. Gandhi. The Indian government believed that Sikh extremists, living in Britain, with British passports, were finding it too easy to travel between the two countries, so visa regulations were introduced for all. (I suspect they're likely to remain; they must generate a handy amount of foreign currency ....)

Travellers therefore need to check out well in advance of their trip whether or not they need to apply for a visa. Under E.C. requirements your travel agent must advise you.

Applying   You apply for a visa at the consulate or embassy of the country you wish to visit which is based in your home country.

Usually you can apply in writing by obtaining the necessary forms either from a good travel agent or from the consulate. You return these along with the required number of photos, the fee and your passport. Enclose a stamped-addressed envelope (recorded delivery) to make sure your passport gets back safely. Always allow several *weeks* especially if the country you are visiting is out of the ordinary. Applying in person by visiting the consulate can speed up the process (it can also involve waiting in queues for hours). Applying for a visa to India, for example, can take up to 6 weeks by post, but 2 days in person.

If the country you wish to visit doesn't have official representation in your home country you will have to apply to one of its other overseas offices. Travel agents, and in particular, Thomas Cook can advise you.

A few countries prefer you to apply to their own government departments direct, but avoid this if at all possible. Your documents sink without trace in an office miles away. No one who answers (eventually) your desperate phone calls knows anything about them and the only person prepared to take responsibility for your visa will be out and 'back tomorrow'.

Applying during your travels   You don't have to obtain visas at home; you can apply at consulates based in other countries during your travels. Sometimes this is necessary. On a year's trip you may not intend to arrive at a particular place for ten months. If the country concerned will only issue a visa six weeks ahead of entry, you will have to *plan ahead* to make sure you can obtain one en route. You should check that visa regulations haven't changed whilst travelling by checking 1-2 weeks before arrival in the next country as to what the then current regulations are. Things change overnight sometimes.

Contact the consulate for their advice at home before you leave but check this against what other travellers tell you.

Sometimes it's an advantage to apply for a visa elsewhere. Local peculiarities may mean that a procedure which in London takes weeks and is fraught with obstructions, takes only hours with smiles and a cup of tea, in smaller offices elsewhere. The opposite can also be true. Again check with returned travellers or contact the smaller tour operators who specialise in overland long haul trips and ask what their experience is (see page 276).

Entry restrictions and conditions   If all the above sounds confusing, don't worry, in well visited countries your application for entry is going to be treated as a rubber stamping exercise (really concerned with generating a little useful foreign currency, not with keeping you out); your passport and visa will be issued in a day or two and without fuss.

However, in many of the more remote and interesting countries of the world you may find your application hedged with provisos, forms in triplicate, photos by the dozen and all sorts of documentation. If this is the case, don't panic, allow *plenty* of time, and console yourself that if it's difficult to get in, at least it should be unspoilt when you've got there!

Below are some of the more common restrictions and conditions that might be imposed.

Length of stay   Visas are almost always issued for a defined length of time. Usually for visits between 30-90 days, but sometimes for as little as seven days, or as long as two years.

You must find out in advance whether or not it will be possible to renew your visa whilst in the country and what the procedure is. Getting caught with a visa that has expired can lead to tedious explanations to the local police, possibly large amounts of baksheesh, deportation, or at worst, accusations of espionage and imprisonment.

Purpose of visit   Different types of visa may be required depending on the purpose of your visit:

(a) Tourism and Travelling
Some governments, keen to attract visitors, issue 'tourist visas' to any *bona fide* applicant, with a minimum of red tape. Others, whilst keen to develop a tourist industry, are not keen to encourage independent travellers. They only want to see visitors as part of a group, booked

onto a proper tour. Alternatively they may expect you to produce
evidence of pre-booked accommodation and an itinerary outline. In
the past this has applied particularly to Communist countries, however Russia and its former republics and China have become much
more relaxed about independent travellers in recent years.

A very few countries discourage tourists and casual travellers
altogether — Saudi Arabia and Albania are examples where you may
be refused entry other than for business reasons.

(b) Business Travellers
Women visiting for business reasons may be welcome, where 'tourists' are not. Expect to be asked to produce a company letter stating the
nature of your business, and the address of your contacts within the
country. As Britain is keen to develop exports and business contacts
abroad, you can get considerable help and advice from your British
Overseas Trade Board regional office.

(c) Scientific Expeditions
You may require a special entry permit as a member of a scientific
expedition. This can be more difficult to acquire than a straightforward tourist visa but if you decide to try and do without, you could find
yourself with a lot of explaining to do to interested customs officers
who want to know why you've included five ice-axes, eight hundred
metres of rope and twelve jerry cans in your luggage.

Contact the Royal Geographical Society Expedition Advisory
Service in London (see page 278) for help.

Evidence of sufficient funds/repatriation   Obtaining a
visa may be dependent on your producing evidence that you have
sufficient funds to support yourself on your travels. You may be asked
to change a set sum into local currency, or show a return ticket home.

Health certificates   You may be asked to show certificates of
vaccination when applying for visas (see page 139).

Visa applications and women travellers   In almost all
countries no distinction is made between male and female travellers as

far as right of entry and visas are concerned. However some of the fundamental Islamic countries have strict regulations and expectations about women and may make it difficult for you to obtain the necessary permits.

Iran Photographs to accompany your application must show you with your head covered with a head scarf. Your hair must be drawn back so that it is not visible.

Women who intend to apply in person at the Iranian Embassy (not recommended) must enter with their heads covered and preferably wearing a modest dress with long sleeves.

Libya It is possible to apply for a visa through the Saudi Medical Office. Check with your travel agent.

Saudi Arabia Although Saudi Arabia attracts large numbers of foreigners who enter to take up employment, there has been some difficulty in the past for young (under 33 years) single women wanting visas for jobs in the country.

Appearance Women (and men) may be refused a visa because of their appearance (although it's more likely that it will be at point of entry that your looks may cause problems).

> **'Any person who does not conform to accepted standards regarding dress and appearance will be refused entry.'**
> *Malaysia*

These rules date from the '60s when mini-skirts and flower children shocked more formal societies, and today are much less strictly applied, but travellers should produce photos of themselves looking neat and tidy when they apply for visas, and generally try to look as conventional as possible when visiting consulates or when entering a country. If there is any problem with your visa application you don't want to give officials any extra excuses for turning you down.

Transit, exit, multiple entry & re-entry permits

Transit   It is almost unheard of for any air traveller who touches down to change planes, and who will not be leaving the airport to be asked to produce a visa. But travellers passing through who expect to stay overnight or for several days may need a transit visa. Having over-zealous officials barge onto your train and into your sleeping compart-ment, and then start angrily shouting something incomprehensible because you didn't find this out is alarming (and possibly expensive). I know because it has happened to me.

Exit visas   Most visas automatically allow for your exit from the country concerned, but you may need a separate piece of paper or stamp for when you want to go home.

Multiple entry and re-entry   If you're intending to do a lot of coming and going, check whether you can apply from the *outset* for a multiple entry visa which will save separate application every time you want to re-enter the country, or whether you need to apply for a re-entry permit once you've arrived

For information on all of the above see a travel agent or tour operator; use a good *up to date* guide book; talk to returning travellers and take advice from the relevant consulate. Never accept the first piece of information you're given, even from the consulate itself (and in some cases, especially if it's from the consulate!). *Always* check your advice against other people's experience.

Travellers to Israel   Travellers to Israel are reminded that if they wish to go on to visit any of the Arab League countries they must not have their passports marked to show that they have been in Israel. If this is explained to Israeli officials they will arrange for you to have any entry stamps, visas etc. stamped on a separate piece of paper, not on the pages of your passport.

MONEY

Currency regulations — what to look out for

While you're waiting for your new passport or twiddling your thumbs between pleading phone calls about a visa you need to be getting on with sorting out the finances of your travels. I'm afraid that like many other travellers, I find information about people and places infinitely more interesting than dry nuts and bolts about currency regulations. Well, you can learn the hard way. Like the time I spent my last handful of coins on a farewell round of drinks, only to discover that I needed to find around ten pounds in airport taxes. Like the time a friend had to change a fairly large denomination travellers' cheque in order to pay for a taxi to the airport and then discovered she wasn't allowed to change the money back into currency she could use at home, nor could she take the now worthless coins out with her.

As with visa regulations, a little research into the small print before you go can save an awful lot of trouble later on. Governments, particularly those with weak currencies, are naturally keen to protect themselves and to encourage you to bring in and spend as much 'hard' currency as possible. (Most of the strong Western currencies come into this category.) Many governments in developing countries organise their currency restrictions to maximise the amount of overseas currency they can earn from a developing tourist industry which may be a source of much needed foreign income. This doesn't necessarily mean making things harder for travellers. Where tourism is a major generator of revenue there may in fact be regulations in force which give preferential treatment to tourists to encourage them to spend more. But the reverse can also be true and travellers can in some countries find themselves hedged about by all sorts of restrictions and forms to be filled in in triplicate. Below are some of the commonest ways which governments have devised for getting their hands on your money.

1. By limiting the amount of local currency travellers are able to obtain *outside* the country before they arrive. This means you have to change the bulk of your money within the country at rates favourable to the government. If you are ordering foreign currency at home, your bank will advise you about the maximum amounts you're allowed to have, before you set off.

2. By making sure you change money at the 'approved' (i.e. government set) rate through authorised exchange counters. In order to keep you away from black marketeers offering a more competitive rate, a government may ask you to declare on your arrival the amount of money you are bringing in. (Forms to fill in will be issued on the plane, or at the airport, or at customs.) You are then expected to get proper receipts that account for all your money-changing transactions. You will be asked to produce these and account for any discrepancies when you try to leave the country. Woe betide you if you failed to find this out and have thrown all your receipts away, or if you were persuaded to change money illegally and therefore haven't got the right number of receipts in any case.

3. By persuading you to spend more than you are hoping to. Obviously governments can't force you to buy things you don't want to, but they can try and encourage you to by only letting you through customs if you have a (large) set sum of money with you. Or by requiring you to change a certain amount of money immediately on entry (at sometimes higher rates preferential to the government). You might even be required to buy vouchers for sums you had no intention of spending.

4. By not allowing you to export currency. You may have budgeted carefully and be left at the end of your trip with some unspent local currency, only to find that you are not allowed to change it back into pounds or dollars, nor are you allowed to take it with you to change at home — so your only recourse is to spend it after all.

5. By imposing airport taxes or by charging for transit visas etc. or by charging exorbitant commission on transactions. By setting up government-controlled shops where goods can only be purchased at government set prices, in hard currency only.

6. By having a special 'tourist rate' of exchange. This may even work in your favour where the 'tourist' rate is better than the 'official' rate.

Some, all, or, if you are lucky, none of these regulations may affect you during your travels. To avoid unpleasant surprises, look up the rules before you go. There are several sources of advice. Travel agents are issued with *A.B.C. Guides* and other trade journals that are regularly updated and provide just this sort of information. However these guides will only give you the official regulations. What happens in practice may be slightly different, particularly when it comes to exemptions; ways round the system which whilst not illegal, aren't necessarily as widely publicised. For this sort of information you can ask returning travellers (often the most *up-to-date* source of advice), or you can use an up-to-date guide book, or better still try one of the tour operators that run regular small group holidays to the area you are going to.

Don't, during your travels, change larger amounts of money than you need to, especially just before you leave. Even if you can take excess out with you, you won't get a particularly good rate when you come to change it back into your own currency.

Do find out about exemptions. (Travellers to Egypt for example, who could prove three nights pre-booked accommodation were at one-time exempt from immediately having to change 150 U.S. dollars into Egyptian pounds at the high rates set at Immigration.)

Don't be tempted to try and break regulations or cheat your way round them.

Carrying money with you

There are a number of different ways of carrying money in your travels. You want a system that is safe, convenient and inexpensive, as well as appropriate to the different levels of sophistication in banking services you will find on your travels.

Below are the main options, together with a reminder about what to do if you run out of funds altogether.

Cash Most travellers prefer to bring some local currency in cash with them. You need enough for immediate use e.g. bus and taxi fares from the airport or station, and if you can get hold of it, enough to cover the first two days' expenses. This is in case your arrival coincides with a bank holiday, festival, strike, or simply closing time at the nearest exchange counter. By bringing enough with you for your immediate needs you also miss out on the queue at the airport bank (which seldom offers as favourable rates as do places in town), and are therefore first in the queue for bus, taxi etc.

Foreign currency is much easier to obtain in the U.K. than it used to be. Most high street banks carry (or can obtain very quickly) all the European currencies as a matter of course, Middle and Far Eastern currencies (stocked for business travellers), and monies for North America and Australasia. In the U.K. foreign currency is also available from bureaux de change, the Post Office, foreign banks, Thomas Cook and American Express offices. It pays to shop around as they do charge different rates.

It is worth noting that in some countries it is not possible to obtain money in advance; in fact, it is sometimes illegal to import local currency. Always check with your travel agent if in doubt.

Do allow several days' notice to be sure of getting what you want. It really isn't the bank's fault if they can't supply you with enough Australian dollars the day before Christmas Eve when your flight leaves on Boxing Day. For currency for more unusual destinations, especially where supply is notoriously erratic (Thai Bahts, Venezuelan Bolivars etc.) allow several weeks to be on the safe side. When ordering try to obtain as many small denomination notes as possible — change is often a real problem and confronting a local bus driver with the equivalent of a £20 note for a 50 pence fare is unlikely to go down well.

In addition to some local currency for immediate use you may also want to take an emergency supply of cash in one of the world's strong currencies. It's usual to recommend U.S. dollars, but depending on the exchange rate and your destination you might consider pounds sterling, Deutsch marks, or even Japanese yen. In many countries you will find people keen to obtain these 'hard' currencies and you may be offered a good rate for them (but see below about the black market). You may also find that officialdom has dreamt up good excuses for relieving you of such money. In Costa Rica for example, only U.S. dollars can be exchanged into local currency, whilst in Russia travellers shopping at the special tourist shops must pay in acceptable foreign currency. If you do take U.S. dollars, take 50 dollar notes rather than 100 dollar bills. There have been problems of forgery in the past and the latter are not now universally popular.

Travellers' cheques   Travellers' cheques are a long preferred method of carrying money abroad. Invented in 1891 by the American Express Company, the largest and most well known suppliers today are American Express, Thomas Cook, Visa and National Westminster Bank. Of these, travellers to countries outside the West should choose either American Express or Thomas Cook's which are the most widely acceptable.

Travellers' cheques are now available in a range of foreign currencies. American Express offer seven including four European currencies, Japanese yen and Canadian dollars. Thomas Cook offer eleven, including Australian and Hong Kong dollars. This means you may have the choice of buying cheques in your home currency and changing them into local currency as you need; or carrying cheques in local currency and being able to use them as you would bank notes to settle bills without having to convert them first.

If you are travelling outside Europe, or where local currency cheques are not available, choose cheques in pounds sterling, or preferably, in U.S. dollars. Travellers to the Americas, north and south, *must* take dollars.

As with cash, it is useful to take a mixture of large and small denominations.

The great advantage of travellers' cheques over bank notes is that they are replaceable if you're unlucky enough to have them stolen or lost. Suppliers have a network of overseas offices, agents and sub agents who will replace cheques for you. In Western countries travellers will find they can get new cheques within forty-eight hours or even sooner. But be warned. Although all suppliers make a great selling point of their 'instant' or 'twenty-four hour' service, things don't always work out like this in developing countries. Firstly, because in countries where communication systems are less well developed, agents may be extremely slow in arranging replacements — days even weeks may elapse, and secondly because the network of agents and offices may be less widespread than you think. On my last trip I took cheques issued by my high street bank. There was no problem cashing them, but the day I discovered I'd lost the lot was the first day I looked to see where was the nearest replacement agent. Needless to say there were only two, the nearest 600 miles away, the other nearer a thousand. On my return to England I found that both Thomas Cook and American Express had had agents approximately 300 miles nearer. This information would have been easy to obtain before I set out, if I'd taken the trouble to ask. Suppliers have lists of their offices and agents abroad and will either look up the information for you or give you a booklet with all the addresses in. Do compare the different replacement services for the country you intend to visit *before* you buy your cheques. Shop around, explain exactly what your travel plans are, and ask for full details of agents, offices and services to take with you.

Once you have bought your cheques, sign each one immediately as no refund can be given for unsigned cheques. Only countersign when you want to cash a cheque, and do so in front of the person accepting it. Keep a list of your cheque numbers separately and mark them off as you spend them so you have a record of what's gone missing if you're unlucky enough to have them stolen.

When cashing travellers' cheques SHOP AROUND. It is normal for exchangers to offer slightly differing rates, and to take differing amounts of commission. As a general rule, you will almost always be offered a poorer rate at the first counter you come across at airport or immigration.

Credit cards   Plastic money can be a useful back up to your other resources, enabling you to settle some bills without cash and obtain some items on credit. Generally speaking the more developed a country's tourist facilities, the more outlets there will be that are happy to accept your card. (Don't assume that because you're outside the West you'll necessarily get longer to pay. We used ours in Sri Lanka and the bill, disappointingly, turned up at the usual time.) You can also use your card to obtain local currency at banks participating in Visa and Mastercard schemes.

There are two pluses that card-holding travellers are automatically entitled to. The first is that a certain amount of accident insurance is automatically included by many credit card companies if you book travel tickets this way. What you get varies from company to company and is unlikely (and not intended) to provide full travel cover. However as it's a free bonus, it's worth reading the small print to find what you're getting. You usually need to make a claim fairly rapidly — within a matter of days — and you will need proof that you used your card to buy your tickets, so keep the relevant pieces of paper.

The second plus is that in Britain you also get cover under the Consumer Credit Act. This means that if you pay for your travel arrangements by credit card and the company or airline goes bust, or similar disaster strikes, you may be able to get your money back by taking up the matter with your credit card company. This applies for sums over £100 and less than £15,000. The Consumer Credit Act also limits you to £50 maximum liability if your card is stolen. Report the loss promptly to cover yourself.

For information and advice on all aspects of the Consumer Credit Act, contact your local Trading Standards Department.

One final advantage is you can arrange for your home bank to pay up for you if you're on the move and will not have a permanent address where monthly statements can be sent.

Service cards   Service cards (cheque cards) with the Switch logo are widely used in the UK. With Maestro and Cirrus logos, you can use your service card in the same way abroad, either to pay, or to obtain cash from a cash machine.

Charge cards   American Express and Diners Club are not credit cards but charge cards where you have to settle up the full amount each month. Aimed particularly at business travellers they offer a range of 'extra' services including immediate spending money if your luggage is lost or delayed, guaranteed hotel reservations and special airport departure lounges. Promoted as 'prestige' cards they're popular throughout the Middle and Far East. Charge cards are expensive to obtain, you have to pay a membership fee and an annual charge as well. But the prestige is good for business women.

Unlike credit cards there is no preset spending limit so you could charge an expensive emergency flight home to your card (but remember you have to settle up in full within a month). You can't obtain emergency cash with American Express and the Consumer Credit Act doesn't apply so you don't get the same cover if your card is stolen or if the person you've bought your ticket from goes bust.

Eurocheques   As the name implies this scheme applies mainly to Europe although some Mediterranean countries and a few banks in capital cities elsewhere do participate (Australia is fairly well served).

You draw money as you use it directly from your home account using a special Eurocard and Eurocheque in exactly the same way that you would at home. You can either draw cash from a bank or use a cheque to settle bills. You can also take out money from cash dispensers in countries which are participating.

You must apply in advance for your card and set of cheques through your own bank at home (allow several weeks). Ask for a list of cash dispenser locations and if your travels will also take you outside Europe, a list of other participants.

Expect to pay a charge for the use of the card. Don't be surprised when these charges show up eventually on your bank statements back home. Carry your PIN number separately.

Money from home   READ THIS BEFORE YOU GO.
Running unexpectedly out of cash is never less than inconvenient. Usually, it happens miles from anywhere, or on a Sunday, or at the start of a three-day festival when everything is closed. Friends went recently on a short trip to Europe. On the last day, the car already

packed for their return drive home, they went for a final dip in the sea. Their car was stolen and they were left, crossing Europe in shorts, swimwear and flip-flops. No money, no passports and getting pretty funny looks at midnight on the Paris Metro, carrying their rolled-up beach towels. It can happen to anyone, but you will feel a lot better, if it happens to you, if you know what to do.

- Don't set off without leaving some money at home stashed away for just such emergencies. If you haven't got any money, at least try and find a relative who will be prepared to bail you out if disaster strikes.

- Don't run out of money! Take precautions by, for example, splitting up the money between the members of the party. *Never* leave cash, travellers' cheques, or other valuables in the car.

- Don't phone your family and ask for 200 dollars in notes to be posted immediately, temptingly easy as this may seem. You are almost certain to attract the attention of dishonest Post Office staff, in which case you won't receive it, or of honest Post Office staff, in which case you may have to explain yourself to local police (and may also not receive it).

- Discuss running out of cash with someone at home, AND your bank manager, BEFORE you go.

- Make sure you, and the person at home who is responsible, knows what procedures to follow, and what the options are.

- If you need to send a particular form of cable with specific wording, or contact a special address make sure you know in advance what this is, and carry details separately from all your other documents.

- Arrange that you will have confirmation of the exact amount of money *and the date it was sent* posted to you separately, on paper that is properly signed with a legible signature. Unfortunately officials do not always let you know that they have received your money, or may deny its arrival. The more impressive looking your 'proof' the better.

The options

1. Money can be sent to you through the Urgent Transfer System via your high street bank to a bank near where you are staying. You will need identification. Allow at least 24-48 hours for the money to arrive. Unless you are fluent in a local language, you may have extreme difficulty in obtaining money through the banking system quickly; it may take days — even weeks.

2. Payment can be made through the Post Office. In some countries you can pick up your money in cash over the counter, in others money paid in at home can only be presented through a bank account. The Post Office has a useful leaflet on Sending Money Abroad which warns that as theirs is a 'mail service it should NOT be used for emergency as no guarantee of delivery time can be given'.

3. Money can be paid through Thomas Cook or American Express Offices. Where Thomas Cook do not have a local office, they may use local banks instead.

4. Replacing travellers' cheques — see page 87.

Dealing on the black market

A Black Market exists where individual dealers operating independently, and *illegally*, offer to change your money and travellers' cheques for a better rate than the one officially offered by government regularised banks and bureaux de change. Amongst some travellers there seems to be a lot of pressure to run all the risks associated with illegally changing money. Not only are you promised a better deal, you're somehow made to feel that 'real' travellers would never be seen standing meekly in the queue at the bank; that 'real' travellers should outwit officialdom and somehow be one up on everyone else by achieving extraordinary deals at street level. The fact is that the only extraordinary deals are the ones where travellers are cheated, sometimes spectacularly. The dealers who offer such enticing rates are only too often prepared to operate outside the law in more ways than one. Knowing that you are hardly in a position to complain to the police, black marketeers are notorious for cheating if they think they can get away with it. Of course some travellers do get slightly better rates changing money this way. But very few travellers make a fortune from dealing illegally at street level with people who are making a living from currency transactions.

Needless to say the best way of avoiding all the problems is to avoid dealing this way in the first place. Unless you have been long enough in a country to really know your way around, our advice is DON'T.

Independent dealers

In some countries, independent dealing is not illegal. This is confusing, especially for first time travellers who, anxious to heed warnings about the Black Market, are suspicious of individuals offering to change money who are not attached to respectable banks or similar institutions. You may be offered a better rate by legitimate dealers that you can safely accept, but how can you tell a straight dealer from a petty criminal? First, by instinct — if it appears shady, it almost certainly is. If the deal you're being offered sounds too good to be true, it is! Second, by circumstances — someone who approaches you in the street or is hanging around at borders is not *necessarily* crooked, but you will be a lot safer changing money with an independent dealer you can return to. A hotelier can't afford to lose good hotel business by having it known in travelling circles that he or she cheats on money exchange. The proprietor of an exchange 'shop' which is permanent, is likely to offer a safe deal, however scruffy looking the premises. The money dealer who *regularly* frequents the café you go to, and has changed money for other travellers you can check with, is worth doing business with, if the rate offered is better than elsewhere.

INSURANCE

Adequate insurance cover is an absolute must for all travellers. We've tried to avoid horror stories in this book, but the following should (we hope) act as an awful warning — a true tale that happened some years ago to friends of ours.

They went on a straightforward holiday to Europe. Nowhere very exotic, and because of this, and because it was a last minute, spur-of-the moment decision, they didn't bother with insurance cover. All went well until a car they hitched a lift in collided with a lorry. The driver died and both friends were seriously injured — they needed immediate emergency treatment in hospital and long-term convalescence before anyone could even think of getting them home. Acting on bad advice they were moved from the inadequate public hospital to an even more inadequate private one. (The standard of nursing was such that one friend still has the scars from the bed-sores she developed from not being properly nursed.) Time passed with the hospital bills mounting, until eventually both were able to travel back to England. As both friends were in plaster from the hips downwards and were still immobile they took up *three* seats each on the plane home, at full schedule fare!

The resulting bills ran into thousands. Their experience put them off travelling outside the U.K. for years. Neither has ever hitchhiked since.

Insurance cover could have paid for proper medical care, their flights home, for a family member to have flown out and for all the other expenses involved. Convinced?

Most people make sure they do take out insurance cover but there are literally hundreds of schemes to choose from, so how can you sort out what's best for you? First of all *don't* take the first scheme you're offered without reading the small print. Even if it does look all right, don't accept it without shopping around to see if you can get an equivalent deal cheaper elsewhere.

The key things to look for are adequate medical cover (especially for visiting the U.S. where costs are astronomical); personal liability (in case you cause damage or injury to anyone else); cover in case of cancellation or delay, and baggage cover.

In addition, independent travellers may have special needs that are not covered by the sort of standard policies that are aimed at package tour members.

Questions to ask include:

● What happens if your companion has an accident? Carrying on alone on a package holiday is one thing, you might feel differently about continuing your travels by yourself.

● Is the cost of any medical treatment paid up by your insurer directly to the hospital or medical centre, or do you have to pay the bill and wait to be reimbursed later? If you are confining your travels to Europe and the West, where there are fast and efficient banking systems, you may be able to rustle up the necessary money for yourself fairly quickly. If you are in more out of the way places, waiting for a reimbursement of funds after you've parted with your last penny could take a long time.

● Does the policy include a 24-hour emergency service providing immediate assistance, in English, wherever you are?

● Are you covered for dangerous sports if your trip includes mountaineering or scuba-diving? What about trekking? Be warned that many standard holiday policies do not cover you for riding on motor-scooters — a popular and cheap way of getting around for visitors to countries like Greece.

- What is the baggage cover like? For low budget travellers the baggage cover on more expensive policies is often too much. If you have taken our advice and are travelling with the minimum of stuff, don't over-insure yourself where you don't need to.

- What arrangements are there for you to make claims during your travels?

- Can you extend your cover if you are away longer than planned?

- Are there exclusions for pregnant women?

Make sure that the travel agent or broker you are buying from understands exactly what your travel plans are and what sort of cover you need. Too often travellers end up fitting their trip round their insurance policy exclusions, not the other way round.

Women joining pre-arranged tours with companies that specialise in overlanding will find that adequate insurance cover is compulsory. Some tour-operators prefer you to use their own schemes (and you are advised to do this even if it's not compulsory); others will want to see a copy of any policy you take out independently to check you have proper cover.

British travellers to European countries which are members of the E.C. should obtain the D.H.S.S. brochure SA30 and an E III certificate to take advantage of reciprocal medical arrangements between the U.K. and other E.C. countries. However you may need additional cover as well, particularly if you are visiting Greece.

Finally, as you will be aware, travel today is not particularly cheap. You will need cancellation cover if you are booking through any of the reputable travel agents.

5
On The Move

MAKING PLANS

There's no easier way of turning a holiday into an ordeal than by badly organising your travel plans. This is particularly likely to happen when the pressure is on to complete the trip of a lifetime. If you've given up your job, or saved up enough money to make ambitious plans you'll want to do and see everything you can manage. Scanning the guide books seems to confirm that wherever you're setting off to there's an endless succession of sights and tourist musts waiting to be visited whilst you know that friends back home will eagerly be awaiting photos and souvenirs from all the major tourist attractions. 'That's me in front of the Eiffel Tower; me again outside the Louvre.' Even if you're not the sort of person to set out on a whistle-stop cultural tour of Europe friends will probably have plenty of alternative expectations about what you'll do, and will gaze at you in disbelief if you confess to having missed out: 'You mean you didn't visit the tribal peoples of ..., take magic mushrooms in ..., sit up all night to watch the dawn rise over ... ?' With all these expectations to fulfil it's not surprising that many of us end up creating an exhausting schedule for ourselves and a few opt out altogether by determinedly doing nothing except lying on the beach. These are not the only options.

Taking the pressure off

Be realistic about what you can do. This means thinking about the
time you have and how to fill it. So that you don't end up travelling
under pressure or regret missing out on things, try thinking about
your itinerary before you go. This doesn't mean drawing up a rigid
plan of exactly where you intend to be on which day. If you were going
to do that it would be far easier to have professionals do it for you
and book yourself in with a group package. Anticipating in advance
exactly what you will want to do is not only impractical for the
independent traveller, it will leave you no room for flexibility. Always
give yourself enough time to enjoy unexpected diversions — that's
half the fun of travelling.

What's more important in terms of thinking ahead is to know what
you really want to see or do whilst you're away. What are the few things
you will regret not having done once you're back from that trip of a
lifetime? This should not be a long list, maybe two or three things, or
even only one, certainly no more than five no matter how long you're
going for. By keeping these to a bare minimum you will then leave
yourself free to make the most of the opportunities you hadn't
foreseen.

Timing

Again be realistic. You're not going to be able to do everything all at
once all of the time. Whether you're driving yourself, bumping
around on the back seat of a bus or even strolling comfortably up and
down the corridors of a train, long journeys are always tiring. You
won't be full of energy and raring to go at the end of them, so besides
beginning to work out what you want to do and where you want to go
on your travels, add in some rest times when you can just hang round
and do nothing. If you don't give yourself a break and stay put for a
while your whole trip could just become one long attempt to find
another hotel or somewhere to eat, the most restful times being when
you're tied to one spot in that car, or on that train. Perhaps the most
punishing method of travelling is to stick to a consistent pattern of say

always two nights in any one place, then moving on. You don't always have to move at the same speed. You can travel long distances fast then slow down, spending a week or two in one place, perhaps taking day trips out or just breathing in the atmosphere. Varying the rhythm can be one way of avoiding travellers' burn out — the glazed look in the eve, the incessant need to keep on moving, rush round every available museum, craft centre or street market; these are all signs you've been doing too much and need to slow down to appreciate what you're seeing.

If your aim is to travel through a series of countries or states allow for the fact that at the beginning you'll probably find yourself moving quite slowly. This is inevitable. You'll be more baffled by complex border procedures, disoriented by not speaking the language, intimidated by the thought of finding somewhere to stay. You're also more likely to be suffering from jet lag, worn out by adjusting to a humid climate or simply bemused by culture shock. Don't get panicked about the time you could be wasting. After a while you'll unwind and find your feet. As you become more used to your surroundings you'll be able to travel faster.

'At the beginning of my travels we only ever left anywhere at a civilised hour like six or seven o'clock in the morning; by the end, making a 3 a.m. bus for a journey which would last two days seemed unexceptional, whilst the down-market hotels we'd felt nervous of staying in began to look like palaces in retrospect.'

South America

By starting off without an overcrowded agenda or unreasonable assumptions about what you'll manage to do you'll find yourself far better able to cope when your plans go astray. For instance in developing countries travel by road is notoriously unpredictable:

'Travelling by road is generally difficult for most visitors — you must be prepared to wait, and expect delays. If you can afford to fly from one main town to another, do so as it's the easiest and by far the quickest option.'

Zambia

Landslides or floods in the rainy season can snarl up a particular route for days especially if the roads are unpaved, whilst dilapidated vehicles are always breaking down — anything from a slow puncture to a broken axle. Even without mishaps services may be wildly off schedule and the Western obsession with knowing exactly what's meant to be happening when, entirely inappropriate to the situation.

'Remember you are in a land where everything happens "with God's will" so don't expect buses etc. to run on time. It's pointless to plan a timetable for your trip, just get there when you can.'

Pakistan

'When travelling by bus expect the combination of dramatic scenery, interesting people and complete mishap. We rarely arrived anywhere at the appointed hour, whilst those who sold us the tickets remained engagingly optimistic about the time it would take.'

South America

As you have no control over what goes on, short of choosing an entirely different means of getting to your destination — like flying or taking the train — the best strategy is to relax and accept that most such road journeys will take much longer than you think. Instead of fretting when you've broken down, get out and have a look around. Talk to your fellow passengers, enjoy the view. When travelling under these sorts of circumstances, setting yourself a tight schedule with deadlines to meet and connecting services to make is a sure way of ending up angry and frustrated.

Finally, do look at the local calendar before you decide when to travel. The day before a public holiday everything is likely to be packed with locals, whilst on the holiday itself there may be few or no services running.

Hearing from home

Most of us write letters home or send postcards whilst we're away. Letters home can act as an extension to your diary. Collect them up later, if friends or relatives will part with them and they'll make nostalgic and interesting reading one day. If you're sending postcards, persuade the recipients to keep them for you — unless they want them themselves — and you can build up a picture collection without the aid of a camera. Unless you're a skilful and committed photographer, postcards often give better pictures of national monuments, taken at the best angle in the best light — moreover postcards often offer the sort of images of local street life you'd love to take yourself but may not dare to.

If you're writing home you'll want to hear back. The easiest way is to provide your friends with a list of addresses along your itinerary and then keep them informed as to which places you're still going to visit, and when, as you go along. The sorts of places which will keep mail for you include embassies (check first), American Express and Thomas Cook Offices (they each provide their own list) and main Post Offices.

If mail is being forwarded to Post Offices, letters should be addressed with your name, the name of the town and country where you wish to receive the letter and the words Poste Restante clearly marked in the right hand corner. When you get to the particular town head to the main Post Office and ask for the Poste Restante section. If you have an actual address for a particular Post Office then mail sent to it will be held there rather than at the main Post Office.

Anyone writing to you should print your surname in large capitals. This should make your letter easier to file correctly and therefore easier to retrieve. You will probably have to show some form of identification, such as your passport, in order to claim your mail. At an American Express office you may have to show you are carrying their cheques.

TRANSPORT

Using public transport

To use the transport facilities successfully you have to be something
of your own detective. Besides finding out what's available you also
have to work out the conventions by which the system operates:

> 'This involves watching and learning: how bus ticket-clipping
> machines work, queuing conventions, the metro colour coding
> ...'
>
> *Spain*

Most countries offer a range of transport facilities to travellers,
whether for long distances or around town. Coaches, planes or trains
can be found just about everywhere, though the exact combination
varies from place to place depending on history and geography. If the
British had a hand in a country's colonial past you're particularly
likely to find extensive railway networks, whilst where the terrain is
difficult or distances to be crossed are vast planes may be the best
means of getting around. As the degree of comfort you can expect and
the relative price of a particular means of transport varies from place
to place, one of your first tasks should be to sort out the differences.

> 'There are special arrangements for women travellers only on
> trains where first class compartments are for two people only;

second class are separated into men or women only (the latter all bring lots of kids so it's crowded but fun and very comfortable and cheap); third class is extremely cheap and mixed but not comfortable.'

Tanzania

You may not always want to use the cheapest form of transport, nor always want to travel in luxury, but it's worth having the relevant information so that you can choose.

Don't assume you will be familiar with the full range of services on offer. Some countries may offer a form of transport you've not encountered before — auto rickshaws, for instance (a sort of motorised tricycle), or a cheap way of getting around, such as long-distance taxis or trains, which in your home country you would never consider using on grounds of expense. As far as price goes a lot depends on the degree to which public transport is government subsidised. Where publicly-owned transport is thin on the ground or non-existent, private operators — whether large companies or individuals — may fill the gap with a variety of means for getting from place to place. In the developing countries this can be anything from a space in an open truck carrying goods as well as people, to mini-buses or shared taxis. Rather than travelling to a set timetable these may simply wait until they're full before setting off. Some work to fixed routes with pre-ordained stops — like the route taxis in Trinidad; others head for a particular destination, picking passengers up and setting them down as required; whilst still others may decide on their route depending on where passengers want to go to.

Methods of payment Methods of payment can be baffling. Do you have to buy tickets beforehand, or pay a conductor, or grapple with a ticket machine which only takes the exact fare? Make things easier for yourself by always having plenty of small change available, especially when you're going to be using public transport for short distances around town. To find out what to do ask fellow passengers, or simply watch other people. Of course, some systems may prove incomprehensible:

'We never did discover the method of payment for buses, and travelled free with everyone's persuasion.'

Jordan

Don't bank on a free trip though! If all else fails try consulting the tourist office and getting them to explain how it all works.

The method of payment which causes travellers most anxiety is undoubtedly when rates don't seem to be fixed and the amount you hand over depends on negotiation.

'There's the constant hustle of having to bargain for every single trip however short.'

Indonesia

Without any knowledge of what the going rates are you can end up paying well over the odds if the driver is unscrupulous. Some guide books do tell you what you need to know on this score though of course things may have changed since they were published. Otherwise your best course of action is to accept that you will probably be overcharged on the first day, especially on the taxi in from the airport if you can't find a bus. Cut down on some of that cost by sharing the ride with any other tourists who are making the same trip. Thereafter if you find you're going to be using a particular form of transport which doesn't have fixed prices, ask around before you travel till you discover what other locals consider a fair amount to pay.

'On bemos and colts you usually have to bargain for the fare. It's useful to find out before making journeys how much locals pay and just have the right change ready.'

Indonesia

Alternatively, if you're sharing the transport let the locals pay first and watch how much they hand over. It's best to settle the price before you travel. That way if you consider you're being asked for too much you can always go elsewhere in the hope that you'll get a better rate. You're in a much weaker position arguing over the amount once you've completed the journey.

Comfort

There are various ways of making yourself more comfortable during
a journey. Of course people don't always agree about what they're
prepared to tolerate and some may revel in situations which others
would describe as a nightmare. Nowhere is this more true than when
considering the cheapest forms of travel in developing countries.

> 'Any form of transport is uncomfortable unless you get a lift in
> an air-conditioned Mercedes! Be prepared for overcrowding,
> heat, dirty toilets, no buffet car and an endless barrage of
> questions from inquisitive fellow travellers, though I doubt if
> you will get all these things on one journey.'
>
> *Pakistan*

Yet for some women, journeys in these, the most unpromising of
circumstances, become the highlight of their trip, the moments they
return to again and again when they recount their adventures back home:

> 'But things got crazier still. More and more people kept cram-
> ming in till the whole centre aisle was packed full of people, one
> man sitting on the arm of my seat, a woman sitting on her bag,
> leaning up against my knee, squashing my leg against the side
> of my rucksack just where the frame stuck out! Meanwhile
> every time someone walked past it would be a bagful of
> vegetables in the face, or at least a poke in the eye with a
> poncho.'
>
> *Ecuador*

Often it's hard for the outsider to see quite what they're getting out of
it as disaster after disaster is retold with relish, but those who've been
through it themselves smile knowingly and sigh with nostalgia.
Perhaps it's because such occasions do throw people together (sometimes literally) and provide a chance to talk freely without contrivance:

> 'I always travelled by public transport — much more fun
> and ten times cheaper. Everyone is heaped on top of goats,

chickens, bags of flour and once a whole house — but the
Thais are cheerful, interested and polite and if you can cope
with the heat and squash it's fine.'

Thailand

There's also so much to see and share in:

'I was travelling the cheapest way possible — second class on
the train and that was a free for all. Travelling on the train is
very entertaining in Mexico — at stations people jump on to
sell food and drink. Strolling musicians get on and play until
the next stop.'

Mexico

How you cope depends partly on your own attitude:

'In general if you are prepared to squash in, just take it how it
comes, be friendly and reply to all the questions of "why aren't
you married" etc, it all works out O.K. If you prefer privacy and
insularity then the travel can be frustrating.'

India

But there are also times when even the most seasoned traveller has had
enough:

'The worst journey I had was in a packed bus, people, sacks, no
air to breathe, jolted up and down on hard seats as we careered
across the desert — and then someone turned the radio on —
very loudly.'

North Africa

If you're tired and desperate for sleep then finding yourself in a packed
or noisy compartment or coach may just be the limit, whilst a
succession of lengthy journeys spent in cramped and overcrowded
conditions can quickly make you wish you'd never left home.

Wherever you are travelling, if you have any choice in the matter
try to avoid the most congested services. For instance, if you're staying
in a large city, time your journeys around town outside the main rush

hours. If you don't have a compelling reason for joining in the rush leave that appalling experience to those who have to put up with it. A capital city anywhere is pure hell at this time, morning or evening. Remember too that transport leaving major cities in the early evening, especially at the start of the weekend, will be crowded with homeward bound commuters and anybody trying to escape from the metropolis for a few days. Leave earlier or later. In rural areas of developing countries transport heading into towns on market days is going to be just as congested and uncomfortable. Find out the relevant days before you travel.

These steps may go some way towards solving your problems but, especially in developing countries where transport systems are often overstretched, it can seem impossible to avoid the crowds. If things get really rough then consider whether you wouldn't be better off paying a little more. Save up and give yourself a treat by travelling first class occasionally. In some countries travelling by plane may work out as cheap as making the same journey by bus when you've added in the additional cost of accommodation and food along the way. O.K., so you won't see as much of the countryside but you'll arrive at your destination in a better frame of mind. Find out whether there are any differences in services. Many of our contributors who'd travelled round India recommended always travelling by train. They knew the buses were cheaper but felt they could do without the additional hassle:

'It's always best to travel with reserved seats in ladies compartments on trains if journeying coast to coast or long distances. They're safe and comfortable. I have travelled by bus only twice. To be avoided at all cost — dirty, hot, noisy, cramped, crowded — miserable!'

India

Above all remember to space your journeys (See Making plans, page 97).

When you are faced with the prospect of a crowded journey then, where you can, book yourself a seat in advance. Whatever the circumstances, always arrive early to stake out your space. You should do this even when you know you're unlikely to leave on time. Be prepared to push your way through a crowd, if necessary, just to get on the bus or train:

> 'On city buses it's usually the youngest and toughest who get seats. You have to learn quickly to elbow, shove and push to get on the bus. It's annoying when you see mainly men sitting down and women and old people standing.'
>
> *China*

This sort of behaviour doesn't inevitably lead to frayed tempers:

> 'Women must be prepared to fight to get on buses and boxes (trucks). This is expected. Other women will help you. There is no bad feeling. If you can't get on you can wait for hours in broiling sun. "Fighting" means vigorous pushing, struggling, scrambling, elbowing etc.'
>
> *North Africa*

But you'll have to be determined to succeed. The locals will almost certainly be more skilful at the exercise than you.

Travel tips

Book yourself a seat and turn up early to claim it if the journey is a long one and the facilities are likely to be crowded.

If your luggage is not going to be easily accessible during the trip remember to retrieve what you need before the journey begins and to carry it with you: something to eat and drink (you can never be sure of buying something along the route); something to lean against; something to keep you warm.

If nights are cold and you're not in a sleeper, keep your sleeping bag with you to get into or under.

If you are planning on getting some sleep a window seat gives you something to lean against, the aisle seat allows you to stretch out your legs. Have something handy you can use as a pillow — a spare jumper, a sarong, a towel.

For daytime travel, when choosing where to sit see if you can discover which side of the bus or train offers the best views. Some guide books give you this information. But if the sun's going to be blazing down think about the direction you're travelling in and try and get a seat on the side that is in shade.

Avoid video buses unless you want to see a film. You won't see anything else as the blinds will be drawn and the sound track probably inescapable.

On planes use the toilet facilities early when they're cleaner or at least outside meal times when queues will form. Booking a flight to coincide with meal times can ensure you get a free meal.

Arriving at the bus station or airport in the small hours of the morning is one thing if you already know where they are and have worked out your route. Coming in to a strange town late at night without a clue as to where to start looking for a hotel is quite another. Time your journeys so that you arrive at your destination before nightfall if possible, or at least at a time when other women will still be on the streets.

Special provisions for women travellers

Up until the first half of this century there were still women-only carriages on ordinary British trains. Nowadays you'll only find them on sleepers whilst it is becoming increasingly rare to find a women-only waiting room on station platforms.

Elsewhere you can still find seats and compartments reserved for women on both buses and trains. Oddly enough, judging by the experience of our contributors, this seems as likely to be the case in countries with a British colonial past as in those which are Islamic. India is the best place to find such arrangements. There are women's seats on buses, women-only compartments on trains, and at stations besides women-only waiting rooms you'll also find women-only ticket queues. The latter can be really useful as the queues are shorter.

Travelling in women-only compartments has advantages:

'On most trains there are women-only compartments which I
travelled in as much as possible. Not only are you free from
male hassle and your gear is safer but it's the best chance you
have of coming into contact with the women there who loosen
up a lot when there are no men around. Just write "Ladies
Cabin" under the special requirements section on the reserva-
tion form.'

India

Depending on how you feel about children you may not always want
to travel in the women-only sections.

'"Ladies only" tended to be full of babies. I found it nicer in
open carriages or mixed. No one really takes serious notice of
you, although the men will talk to you. Indian children are
horrible to travel with.'

India

Husbands can also prove a nuisance!

'I remember ladies-only compartments. Great if you want a
break but husbands may well come in to minister to wives
though they usually get pushed out by other women.'

India

Nevertheless, even when not strictly observed it's good to have the
choice:

'Ladies-only compartments on trains are often usurped by
men and used by families. Safer, but it's not much fun being
separated from male companions for a long (30-hour) journey.
I'd go for a normal compartment and a book so as to avoid the
stares.'

India

Where there are no other arrangements for women travellers you're likely to find, as in Britain, that train sleeping compartments are segregated, though again, this isn't always rigidly adhered to:

> 'Some trains seem to have compartments for women, but we travelled in mixed compartments. On long distance journeys, men sometimes found it strange to be sleeping with women but we didn't get the impression it was too terrible.'
>
> *Egypt*

In some countries all the facilities, including sleepers, are mixed. Where this is the case women often seem to look out for and after each other.

> '"Hard" sleepers are arranged in groups of six on trains. There'll usually be men in your section as well as women, but they'll be more upset than you if they see an inch of flesh! People sleep fully dressed on them anyway and you wouldn't be molested. Chinese women on the train will be very protective anyway, especially if you're on your own.'
>
> *China*

Sometimes taxi or truck drivers offer women, particularly foreigners, the 'best' seats: in the front or in the cab:

> 'You pay more to ride in the cab of lorries (rather than in the back with whatever goods the lorry is carrying — onions, sugar, cotton bales, tables etc. and other travellers) and women are often given these coveted, because more comfortable, seats.'
>
> *North Africa*

Whether you want to take advantage of this sort of offer or not depends: sitting in the cab you may not get as good views of the countryside as you would from the back of the lorry or you could miss out on the fun; if it's raining, though, you'll stay warm and dry. As for taxis, sitting in the front can be a dubious privilege:

'In local taxis, white people are often given the front seat. It is often the most dangerous, driving standards being as they are.'

Kenya

It can certainly be unnerving if you're sensitive to the ways others drive.

Hitching

Women are only too aware of the dangers associated with hitching. Warnings are continually being drummed in our ears:

'Although it's a fairly common and incredibly easy mode of travel in Algeria, its drawbacks are obvious.'

Algeria

'I would say not a good idea to hitch by yourself, but that's the same anywhere.'

India

It's difficult to advise on whether you should or shouldn't do it, so much depends on yourself and your judgement of the set-up in any particular country. However the following points are worth making:

1. If you're not sure what the local reaction will be, start out with a companion. Team up with a bloke if that feels safer.

2. Remember, just because you've accepted a lift does not mean that you're obliged to put up with anything. If you don't like the way the driver is acting, even if he's just making you feel uncomfortable rather than threatening you, do something about it. If there's no other way of handling the situation then get out.

3. If hitching is consistently making you feel uneasy or leaving you exhausted at the end of the day, even if absolutely nothing's happened, it's not worth doing.

FINDING YOUR WAY

Working out which train goes where, finding your way round someone else's underground system, sorting out the bus you want, can all
be nervewracking if you don't speak the language, more so if you can't
read the script. The following advice may help to make it easier.

Addresses

Europeans are used to poring over maps looking for a particular street.
We know that each street has its own name but equally we don't expect
the name on its own to tell us anything about where it is. Americans
on the other hand are more familiar with the grid system. The grid
system certainly makes finding your way around a lot easier. When
streets are arranged regularly in blocks all the roads running horizon-
tally across the city will be given the same title (street, *carrera*) and then
numbered from top to bottom, whilst all the roads running vertically
across the city will be given another title (avenue, *calle*) and then
numbered from right to left. The combination of the two numbers
takes you to within a block of where you want to be and you always
know where you are in relation to anywhere else. Simple! In Bogota,
Colombia, they've got the whole thing down to a fine art as buildings
are numbered according to their distance in metres from the nearest
junction.

The most complex system to follow is the Japanese. In Japan they
rarely give streets names, moreover numbers on the buildings indicate
how recently the house was put up, they tell you nothing about the
physical relationship between one house and its neighbours. Instead
the Japanese divide up their towns into named areas, then sub-divide
each area into neighbourhoods and so on. The address will give you
the name of the smallest unit you want and its surrounding neighbour-
hood (this could be as small an area as a couple of blocks). To cope with
all this most people hand out small maps with their address showing
the best route from the nearest public transport stops. Wherever you
are, pick up a map as soon as you can from the Tourist Information
Office.

Different scripts

When you arrive in a country which uses a completely different script you'll suddenly find yourself deprived of all sorts of information you'd normally take for granted. Things aren't so bad in Russia or Greece where the alphabet, although different, is sufficiently close to our own to be relatively easy to decipher. But from the Middle East to the Far East you may find disentangling each script's components much more baffling. Suddenly you're profoundly illiterate. To get by you'll have to rely much more on others. Getting somebody to write down the name of your destination in the local script can be useful, otherwise you'll have to be prepared to ask for help. In both China and Japan you'll often find our own numerals in use. This means you can look for the number of a bus even if you can't read the destination. In the Middle East and parts of Asia it might be worth learning the Arabic numerals. They're quite easy to grasp.

Asking questions

Asking for clear information when you need it has its pitfalls. This is not just because the people you're dealing with may not make allowances for your limited understanding of the language and answer at a speed you can't follow. More important misunderstandings arise when their notion of how your question is best answered is completely at odds with your own. Beware. You may each have very different priorities in the exchange. For instance, those you are asking may feel it's more polite to give you an answer, any answer, than to say they don't know, even when that's the case. Or they may feel obliged to tell you what you obviously *want* to hear rather than disappoint you by telling you what is actually the case, especially if the latter is going to inconvenience you. This is not a question of being devious, it's simply a difference in approach.

If you need to get a clear idea of what's going on, don't suggest the answer you want to the person you're asking. Try and avoid questions which require 'yes' or 'no' as an answer. Instead of saying 'Does this coach go to ...?,' ask 'where does this coach go?'

ACCOMMODATION

Deciding on where you're going to stay is not just a matter of working out what you can afford. Most countries, particularly in Europe and Asia, have more than one type of accommodation available. Besides hotels there may be Youth Hostels (some don't have age limits), guest houses, government-run hostels, traditional inns, and campsites. The YWCA and the YMCA have hostels in over 80 and 90 countries respectively (some YMCAs will admit women), which are often open to travellers whilst some religious communities offer accommodation too.

If you're not happy where you're staying don't just look for another establishment; try a different type of accommodation. You may find that certain kinds of accommodation are more welcoming to women than others. Take guest houses, for instance. I'm using the term to group together any sort of accommodation where a room or rooms are let in somebody's family home. They're called different names in different countries and don't always provide the same service.

In Great Britain 'bed and breakfasts' come into this category and the first meal of the day is always included in the price; Sri Lankan guest houses provide half board, whilst elsewhere you may pay just for the room. In Spain they are known as *casa de huespedes*, in Indonesia *losmans* (though the latter are gradually becoming more like ordinary hotels), in Japan *minshuku*. Perhaps the most familiar name for them is *pensions*, though some countries such as Spain and most of South America, use this term to describe small hotels.

Staying in a guest house rather than a hotel can have distinct advantages for women:

'Sri Lanka has excellent accommodation mainly run on the basis of guest houses where the family will cook all your meals. The guest houses are often run by women, which is nice. All guests are served food together, which is positive in terms of meeting other people. In fact on the whole the Sri Lankan type of accommodation is good for women, you are made to feel at home.'

Sri Lanka

Because they're smaller and more personal they can have a more relaxed and safer feel to them. Staff are likely to be members of the family so you're less likely to get hassled if you're travelling on your own and they'll probably be more concerned for your welfare. Indeed their one drawback is that staff may be over-protective, and very curious about your affairs!

> 'When travelling with my boyfriend I never felt quite comfortable about staying in *casa de huespedes*. The owners would nudge and wink when they saw from our passports that we were unmarried, or look embarrassed when we asked for a double room.'
>
> *Spain*

Judging by the experience of contributors to this book actual harassment of women in the place where they are staying is rare. Being made to feel uneasy and uncomfortable by a predominantly male clientele is not.

> 'In Amman we stayed in the cheap "budget" type hotels — these are generally used by locals and I never saw a local female staying in them. They were manned by males occupied by males and honestly I would have felt very uncomfortable staying there by myself. Eyes watched you all the time and they were certainly interested in me not my husband.'
>
> *Jordan*

Of course it is possible to put up with this sort of attention — by just ignoring it for a start. But that can be wearing. Otherwise sensible male travellers to China can get almost hysterical about the ways in which any foreigner there always becomes the centre of attention for a curious crowd. It's probably the only place they have to endure the same sort of experience! You end up feeling as if you're permanently on show. And at the end of the day when you want to unwind, let alone the morning when you're not yet fully awake, it can be very trying.

> **'Many cheap hotels are run more or less specifically to house young men from the countryside who work in the towns; if you book into one of these expect to have to put up with a good deal of curiosity and downright constant staring. A hassle first thing in the morning if the bathroom isn't "ensuite". Make sure you are modestly attired at these times — just a shirt is asking for trouble.'**
>
> *India*

This phenomenon — being made to feel out of place in an all-male environment — is not restricted to the developing countries. Any women staying in hotels catering for business trade in the West are likely to meet with the same experience. But in Islamic countries especially, it's particularly likely to happen. Where women are excluded from business, hotels will be run by men, and where women have fewer reasons or opportunities to stay away from home overnight, most guests will be male too. In the absence of a local holiday trade, cheap hotels in developing countries exist to serve business men. No wonder women feel out of place. In the U.S.A. some hotel chains which wish to woo the business woman customer are beginning to recognise that there is a problem when women are in the minority. Part of their response has been to reserve whole floors for women guests only.

In developing countries you may be better off trying to find where local women stay when they do travel, though actually working this one out isn't easy. Tourist offices with firmly fixed ideas about where you should be staying — the more upmarket hotels — are unlikely to give you an answer.

These are the sort of circumstances where guest houses, if you can find them, come into their own.

> 'An advantage when I was alone and staying in pensions: the owners, who were always families, were very attentive, ensuring I was in a "safe" room and respected my privacy, inviting me to eat and drink with them. In hotels I found communal rooms full of men who stared constantly when I was the only woman. Pensions were more private and accommodating.'
>
> *Turkey*

Some countries really don't seem to offer anything much in the way of accommodation apart from hotels ranging from the ridiculously cheap to the five star. However, that still doesn't mean that the only choice is over how much you're prepared to pay. By using a popular guide book and sticking to a route frequented by other tourists you can make sure you'll end up in hotels aimed at other travellers like yourself. At least other women will have been here before you and you're unlikely to be treated as a total novelty. Of course staying in these sorts of hotels will mean mixing mainly with other Westerners, and if you've all got the same guide books you may keep on bumping into the same people. This might not be the experience you set off to savour! There are compensations though.

> 'In South America there are a number of "gringo" *pensiones* (very cheap but basic) where a woman travelling alone has not much difficulty in meeting fellow travellers and other women. Very often rooms are shared amongst two to six people. These places are probably the safest (unless you are prepared to spend a lot of money on good hotels) since they are also meeting places for travellers to exchange experiences and go out together.'
>
> *South America*

If you're travelling alone, being able to find people to share a room with has advantages. Some of the cheaper hotels may not have single rooms anyway, or if they do they'll charge more for them. If the management run the sort of system whereby they fill up rooms as guests arrive, ask to share with other women. Besides being cheaper, sharing rooms can also feel safer.

> 'I never experienced any problems myself apart from one uncomfortable night worrying about the lecherous intentions of one particular hotel manager, which happily amounted to nothing. Another woman friend had had more of a problem here and always tried to find another traveller to share a room with, after twice having to fend off hotel managers with set ideas about Western women.'
>
> *India*

One way of dealing with bothersome blokes who are unfortunately resident at the same hotel is to establish quite clearly from the beginning that your room is your own and that if you are in your room you are not available for conversation.

> 'With no other Europeans about and travelling alone I was careful to return to the hotel early with a good book or a load of postcards and keep a low profile.'
>
> *Thailand*

Many cheap hotel rooms particularly in Asia can be locked with padlocks. Take your own. A locked room will secure your possessions while you are out and yourself while you're sleeping overnight, particularly important if you've ended up somewhere unsalubrious.

> 'Small hotels can be difficult because they are often little more than drinking places. Insist on a room with a lock to keep out inebriated men who fancy their chances.'
>
> *Ethiopia*

It may just be chance but the only parts of the world where we've had a few reports of women being disturbed at night in their rooms are Thailand and Indonesia.

'We had a few local guys knocking at our door at night wanting
to "talk a few minutes to practise my English". We never
unlocked the door to any such request.'

Indonesia

If there isn't a lock and you're worried about the possibilities of
intruders during the night you could always barricade the door. Most
hotels are safe. They need to be if they're in the business of catering
for the steady flow of tourists. How do you get to know that the one
you've walked into is not safe?

'I think it's a matter of "gut reaction"; you get to feel that a
particular place looks a bit odd.'

Pakistan

In those circumstances always follow your hunches and go somewhere
else if you can.

'I just knew that the owners of that particular hotel weren't to
be trusted. They looked shifty. Although the two blokes I had
been travelling with were happy to stay there, I definitely
wasn't, so I went and found somewhere else to stay. When I met
up with them again several days later I found they'd both been
robbed during the night.'

Pakistan

Don't worry about appearing foolish or over-concerned — better
safe than sorry.

It is true that in some parts of the world cheap hotels double as
brothels. However, women travellers are extremely unlikely to end up
in them, particularly if travelling on their own. Who would direct you
towards them after all? Or take you in. Male travellers are more likely
to find themselves in this environment and consequently embar-
rassed. There are other possible mistakes: in the United States the
cheapest hotels are actually boarding houses for long-term residents
whilst in Britain some establishments describing themselves as guest
houses or bed and breakfasts turn out to be housing the homeless,

unemployed or down and outs. Most of these operate outside the expected tourist areas. If you turn up on the doorstep the owners will almost certainly put you right, though they may not tell you openly why you should go.

> 'Once we got into the wrong part of town, probably the red-light district, and certainly downmarket. The first hotel we tried there was nobody about except an elderly drunk who took us to look for the owner in a sleazy bar. The price of the room he quoted was about three times the going rate. That was when we realised not only that we'd got well-founded suspicions about the place, but that they were telling us to go away too.'
>
> *Spain*

Of course, misunderstandings can work the other way round too. In remoter areas where the only places with rooms aren't geared to women guests as they simply don't expect them, the management may find your motive for wanting to stay there incomprehensible.

> 'I was once or twice told there were no rooms available and I wasn't always sure this was true. I felt they didn't want a single woman. Smaller hotels in small towns usually. One refused outright — obvious implication that I must be a prostitute if travelling alone.'
>
> *India*

Finding accommodation

You don't have to visit a tourist office or be clutching a guide book to be sure of finding somewhere to stay. All sorts of people who frequently come into contact with tourists will probably be able to help: taxi drivers, bus drivers even shopkeepers or stall holders who work near the major points of arrival in town. Ask them. They'll probably size you up, decide whether you're Hilton or doss house material and direct you accordingly. Whilst they may not lead you to the cheapest or the nicest place, you're unlikely to end up somewhere totally unsuitable. Coming over the border from Venezuela to Colombia in a state of pronounced culture shock, the bus driver took me and my companion to a quietly civilised hotel, not too downmarket. Bumping into him a few days later he said he'd chosen it specially as we seemed rather nervous; a week or so earlier he'd taken another couple of girls somewhere else cheaper, but he didn't think we'd have liked it ... and at the time he was probably right!

What about hotel touts? These can be common and persistent in some countries and some people never use them on the grounds that you end up paying for their services in a higher hotel bill. Personally I've always found the prices they quoted the same as elsewhere and as they take you straight to the hotel they save you a lot of hassle. I'd probably feel less confident about using them if I didn't already know what the going rates were.

If you're looking for accommodation by yourself then start near the bus or train station. The chances are there will be hotels in the area too, to cope with the influx of tourists. Market places are another good location to try. Otherwise try and find out where the best street or area is, rather than asking passers-by for the name of a single hotel. It's usual for tourist accommodation to be clustered together in a particular part of town. If you find the area then you can compare prices and choose for yourself rather than feeling you have to stop at the only place in sight.

Always ask to be shown the room before you book yourself into a hotel. This is standard practice just about everywhere. Scrutinise the toilets, have a good look at the sheets, think about noise. A bedroom facing out onto a busy road or a hotel next to a cinema can mean you lose a lot of sleep. If you are not happy, ask to see another room or politely decline the offer and try somewhere else. Remember, though, it's easy to start a trip with unrealistic expectations about dirt and cleanliness. This can work both ways: you can easily be put off by minor details that actually don't matter much (see page 199) or be over-prepared to put up with squalor to the extent that you don't complain when you could. The dirtiest hotel I stayed in in the whole of South America was the place I spent my first night.

Less easy to anticipate at a glance is the quantity of insect life which may be sharing your room. Mosquitoes are a real nuisance, whether they're capable of transmitting malaria or not. In non-malarial areas clear the room before you sleep by swatting or spraying all the mosquitoes you can find. Sleep with the windows shut, even if it's hot, to ensure no more of the blighters creep back into the room. In malarial regions of the world you may be lucky and find the bedroom already equipped with a mosquito-net. Otherwise, now is the moment when you proudly unpack your own.

Cockroaches are another potential pest. They're not dangerous (unless they're trampling over your food), just unpleasant. They're most likely to be around if your bathroom opens off your bedroom. One way of stopping them trundling through your room whilst you're asleep is to leave the bathroom light on. As they don't like light this stops them from crawling up the drains and so out towards you in the first place.

Loos

Very few guide books mention loos at all, let alone tell you where they can be found. This could just be prudishness about the most basic of bodily functions or perhaps authors find the subject hard to treat seriously — judging by the patter of our stand-up comics many people never really grow out of a childish appetite for lavatorial humour —all the British xenophobia comes to the fore with tales of 'dirty' foreigners, bidets (huge joke) and trench urinals. Yet nothing is more agonising than being caught short and it is a particularly female problem — men in similar circumstances can relieve themselves with relative decency. Perhaps that accounts for the omission.

When thinking about toilets you have to consider sewage disposal as well as the actual toilet facilities themselves. Countries vary in terms of what they offer. In Britain we go for the toilet seat and U-bend with water flush and, unless you are unlucky, loo paper will be provided in public conveniences. The same is true in some, but not all, parts of Europe and in North and South America, though the provision of loo paper varies, and in South America it almost certainly won't be available. Elsewhere, hotels geared to Western tourists will probably try to accommodate our preferences and will provide sit-down facilities. Because we're familiar with these facilities we'll be confident about using them no matter what the local variations.

However, we may be less prepared for areas where the facilities are familiar but the sewage system is poor. In South America and a few European countries such as Greece, each lavatory has a bin for used toilet paper. This indicates that the sewage system can't cope with paper, tampons or sanitary towels. Place them in the container provided. If you insist on flushing them away you may well clog up the whole works, creating real problems for a later user. This will be even less hygienic than doing as indicated.

The squat-and-aim-for-the-hole toilet was probably first encountered by U.K. residents on holiday in France and is most common in the Middle East, Asia and Africa. In Europe these have no U-bend so they tend to smell even when clean. They certainly have a powerful flush, one which will drench your feet if you don't move pretty fast after pulling the chain (or pushing the plunger). In Japan I'm told the system looks something like a man's urinal embedded in the floor — the mind boggles — and only some have a water flush, others lead straight into a septic tank.

In many parts of the world the system will be built on the assumption that the user will clean themselves with their own left hand rather than with paper. Under these circumstances there will be no paper. Instead water will be provided in the toilet, either in a jug or from a tap placed at a convenient distance. This is the case in most of Asia and Africa. If you can it's sensible to acquire the local habits.

'Pakistanis use a water jug to get clean after using the loo. They think it's unhygienic to use paper or to sit on a seat. After a while I got used to crouching and washing myself afterwards. You do feel clean, and begin to appreciate their point when you see piles of dirty paper left around by visiting Europeans.'

Pakistan

It is precisely because of this system that it is considered rude in the East to offer someone your left hand to shake, or to eat with it — sensible precautions to adopt on grounds of hygiene. Carry soap with you rather than loo paper. If you don't feel you can face this then you may have a problem disposing of the paper.

Some countries provide a mixture of squat and sit down toilets. When they do the squat ones will almost certainly be cleaner if only because they're simpler to maintain.

> 'Usually the Western-style toilets are less hygienic (because poorly maintained) than the long drop.'
>
> *Ethiopia*

> 'Toilets for public use available only in cafés, unisex and deplorable. Toilets on boats and ferries and the better type of train are segregated: a fact cheerfully ignored by many Moroccans! It's not unusual for the men-folk to come and chat to the women as they bathe their babies and toddlers in the sinks on the ferries, also wash nappies.'
>
> *Morocco*

Finding good toilets   It's common to moan about the quality of lavatories abroad, and sometimes there can be good reason.

> 'Sometimes there is no toilet and sometimes where there is, it would have been better if there wasn't.'
>
> *Nepal*

As a very general rule toilets with restricted access — in hotels, on stations etc. are going to be cleaner than ordinary public conveniences. If standards are low and you want to find a loo you could bear to spend some time in try pricier hotels. Just walk in with a confident manner and you're unlikely to be challenged.

Museums have reasonable facilities, though you'll probably have to pay to get to them, whilst one of our contributors spoke highly of British Council Library loos.

Finding any toilet   More often the problem is simply to find any toilet at all. In some places public conveniences just don't seem to exist. Depending on how desperate you are try big hotels or restaurants; department stores or petrol stations sometimes have facilities; public buildings such as town halls, colleges, universities or libraries

are possibilities. In New York office buildings are apparently a good bet if you look in the corners on the lower level!

> 'Use the toilet in your hotel before you go out, whether you need to or not. If caught short try hotels/restaurants though these are not always helpful. Use any public convenience you see even if you don't really need to — they're never around when you need them.'
>
> *India*

Finding somewhere to pee is probably most difficult on long coach journeys when there's no toilet on board. Hours pass between proper stops whilst unscheduled stops are most likely to be organised for the convenience of the driver or any male passengers. In other words the chances are that the bus will pull up miles from the nearest hedge, boulder or any other form of cover, or won't stop long enough for you to dash back round the corner or run for the nearest bush.

> 'Every time it came to a stop on a 6-hour journey through the desert, the bus we were travelling on would pull up on a stretch of open road with no bush or boulder anywhere in sight to hide behind. The men would leap out to relieve themselves but the local women and myself sat, legs crossed in our seats for fear of outraging local sensibilities.'
>
> *North East Asia*

What can you do under these circumstances? The most sensible way round the problem is to follow what in many cases will be local example: wear a long, full skirt when you're travelling, or even a long top over your trousers if you prefer, one which will allow you to squat down and pee whilst staying decent.

> 'Peruvians are used to seeing women squatting so if you go about it naturally rather than furtively no one will think anything of it. It's not necessary to go out of sight, merely at a short distance.'
>
> *Peru*

If all this seems too impractical or inappropriate, about the only other alternative is to drink less. In a hot climate taking this single step seems an easy way of controlling your need to go to the loo.

'One sweats so freely that we found only one visit a day was necessary.'

Egypt

But it's *not* a good idea if you can avoid it. If you're sweating you need to replace the fluids and mineral salts you are losing. Otherwise you risk suffering from heat exhaustion and dehydration whilst the more concentrated urine you eventually pass will make an ideal breeding ground for the germs which cause cystitis. (See Chapter 7 page 171) If you must take this course, rather than economising on all fluids try avoiding the ones, like tea, that act as diuretics. If you have skimped on drink, make sure that you compensate by having plenty to drink once you've got to your journey's end.

'I tried not to drink at all while travelling so I would not have to pee. Then drank gallons of water on arrival at my destination to prevent dehydration.'

Peru

If for whatever reason you do end up using the great outdoors as a toilet you do have some responsibilities: unless you're just having a pee lift a small piece of turf or dig a small hole using a knife or even sharp stones if there are any about. Then you can cover over everything including paper and leave the place tidy. Using a stone to cover up after yourself is better than nothing. If the ground's too hard to bury anything then at least burn the paper rather than leaving it as a sorry reminder of your visit.

Public lavatories often don't have functioning locks. Learning to balance on the seat if there is one and wedge the door shut with an outstretched leg is one way of coping; knowing the word for occupied in the local language is another, though being prepared to shout anything might help! On the other hand it wouldn't help you cope with this contingency:

'Toilets are open — no doors. So you can expect to find other
women standing before you while they wait their turn.'

China

Perhaps the answer is given by another contributor.

'Women's toilets are available, but it depends what you mean
by useable! They're often dirty, smelly and crude, but I'm still
alive.'

China

Whatever the system, you must be scrupulous about washing your
hands after going to the loo. If water rarely seems available to do this
then get into the habit of carrying your own. At the very least wash
your hands before eating.

Washing facilities

The British are particularly fond of soaping and soaking in lots of hot
water. Not everybody shares our preference for this method of
keeping clean.

Indeed some regard it as a positively filthy habit; after all you end
up sitting in your own dirty water. Nowhere does this meet with more
disapproval than in the Far East where most bathing facilities work on
the principle that you soap yourself down first with a small amount of
water and then rinse yourself off. In Indonesian bathrooms, for
instance, the large tank of water is not for climbing into. You help
yourself to a bowl full of water and use that to get up a good lather then
scoop some more out and pour it over yourself to get clean. Japanese
bathing facilities, traditionally communal, work in the same sort of
way. You wash and then rinse yourself down at the edge of the main
bath, then *when* you're clean, get into the communal bath water to soak
for as long as you like. To avoid making mistakes when you're in a
communal washing area always carefully observe what other people
are doing before you leap into action, then follow suit. Otherwise you
can give offence.

Communal bathing might sound off-putting at first. One friend who spent some time in Japan said her most embarrassing moments were meeting women she'd been teaching English to in the morning later on at the baths and having to bow a greeting standing stark naked. She never felt quite comfortable about it! But these circumstances aside, they can be good places to meet, talk and relax with other women:

> **'The women found my body surprisingly the same as theirs and were quite happy to look and discuss this with interest.'**
>
> *Japan*

FOOD AND DRINK

Safety first

Getting a gippy tum on holiday is something of a standing joke, one currently being used in an advertising campaign to promote a particular preventative medicine. Yet stomach upsets or diarrhoea don't have to be a feature of a trip abroad. If you eat sensibly and follow certain basic rules you should stay safe.

The trouble is the rules guide books give often sound hopelessly complex and quite impossible to follow. If you obeyed all the don'ts they list you would be left with nothing to eat and no restaurant you would dare to eat in. Consequently most people give up trying, throw caution to the winds and simply assume that they'll get through somehow. Your preparedness to go the whole hog and eat and drink anything has even become a sort of test of how serious a traveller you are. Only wimps are fussy about their food! Further confusion is caused by the fact that some books urge you to eat at roadside stalls whilst others tell you to stick to proper restaurants — in neither case do they really tell you why — and there's now another school of thought circulating which says that all travellers will inevitably get diarrhoea at some stage. The chances are that it won't be serious and is just part of the process of adapting to your environment. As it will clear itself up of its own accord you just shouldn't worry.

What is the truth of all this?

The first point to grasp is that IT IS NOT NORMAL TO HAVE DIARRHOEA WHEN YOU'RE TRAVELLING NOR SHOULD YOU JUST PUT UP WITH IT. If you set out with that attitude it will simply become a self-fulfilling prophecy — and sure enough you'll go down. Moreover staying diarrhoea-free is not an amazingly complex business involving all sorts of bizarre and impractical rituals. It's largely a matter of using commonsense once you understand how food and water get contaminated.

Food

There are a whole range of micro-organisms capable of causing food-poisoning and diarrhoea. New ones are being identified all the time. Many of them, such as salmonella, are routinely present in raw meat: 80% of frozen chickens sold in the U.K. contain salmonella. An astonishing fact. So why aren't we all permanently stricken? Well fortunately these organisms are destroyed if the food is cooked thoroughly, being properly heated all the way through. However, that fact alone is not enough to ensure that the food we eat isn't contaminated. All cooked foods can be recontaminated if they come into contact with these micro-organisms once the cooking process is over. It's for this reason that the catering industry in this country has to keep to strict hygiene practices enforceable by law. For instance it is illegal for raw and cooked meats to be served from the same counter. This is to prevent cross-contamination. If cooked foods are not going to be served straight away the temperatures at which they are stored are strictly controlled. They must not be kept lukewarm. This is to prevent any germs which may have survived cooking from re-multiplying before the food is eaten. They thrive at warm, rather than hot or cold, temperatures and if sufficient numbers are present they will make you ill. Anyone preparing raw foods must wash their hands before touching cooked foods for the same reason. It can give the micro-organisms a chance to spread.

The other main source of infection is faecal contamination. Human faeces can harbour all sorts of unpleasant germs including cholera, typhoid and polio. Contamination is most likely to take place: if the person handling food isn't stringent about personal hygiene, washing their hands carefully before preparing or serving food; if you're not, or if flies, cockroaches or other disease-carrying insects have access to the food after it's been cooked. Animal shit is as dangerous as the human variety.

So how can you stay safe? Follow these rules:

1 *Only eat freshly cooked food.* It doesn't actually matter whether it comes from a market stall or a restaurant with first class facilities. Indeed, the former may be a safer bet if the food is cooked in front of your eyes and then handed to you straight away. Any well cooked hot food you eat directly from the pan will be fine. Conversely, avoid any tepid food especially if it's uncovered (a target for flies) and being kept warm (an ideal breeding ground for germs), over a bowl of hot water, say. Also avoid food which looks as if it's been well-handled since it was cooked.

2. *Be scrupulous about washing your own hands particularly after you've been to the lavatory.* Do it thoroughly. If you haven't managed to do this then at least try to wipe them before eating, or touch the food you are eating as little as possible.

3. *Peel all raw food.* Any uncooked, unpeeled fruit or vegetables are a possible source of contamination particularly if they've been grown in animal or human manure. As they are raw there's no chance that

any micro-organisms clinging to the outside will have been destroyed by heat. This is why salad vegetables such as lettuce should
be avoided.

These are the basic rules. Obviously keeping to them is most important when you're travelling in a country which does not legislate its
food industry, but rules one and two are sound principles to follow
anywhere. Food-poisoning and dysentery are endemic worldwide.
Some travellers opt to stop eating meat while they're abroad because
it can act as a source of infection. That's fine if it's what you want to
do and it's a practical option (in some countries vegetarian foods are
hard to come by). However, you must observe the same rules in
relation to vegetables as you would do to meat. They can be contaminated in exactly the same way that meat can be recontaminated once
it has been cooked. Warm vegetables provide just as good a medium
for micro-organisms to grow in. If you absolutely can't avoid salads,
douse them in lemon juice or strong vinegar, both natural antiseptics.
The theory that your body can gradually build up immunity to the
local strains of disease is wishful thinking. For a start, you cannot
protect yourself in this way against cholera, amoebic dysentery and all
the other more serious diseases, so why abandon precautions? Moreover, while it's true that your body will eventually come to terms with
those bugs which cause traveller's diarrhoea (the sort that's self
limiting) there are an awful lot of them so the process of gradual
adjustment would have to last a whole trip. It's more sensible to stick
to the basic rules.

Water

The most potent source of infection in water is human faeces. Human
faeces can contaminate drinking water wherever sanitation is poor. In
19th-century Europe epidemics of cholera and typhoid were commonplace. They were stopped not by the discovery of new wonder
drugs but by a tremendous investment in improved sanitation.

Elsewhere in the world many countries still do not have adequate
sewage disposal systems which can ensure that contamination of

drinking water does not take place. Too few water treatment plants, inadequate plumbing or drainage can all cause problems, whilst in the tropics the monsoon season puts water supplies at risk. UNLESS YOU KNOW THE WATER SUPPLY IS SAFE YOU MUST TAKE ADEQUATE PRECAUTIONS TO PROTECT YOUR-SELF. How can you do this? The best ways of purifying drinking water are to boil it (which will kill the germs) or to chemically treat it. Water must be boiled for at least five minutes. As most travellers won't have the means to do this you must follow these rules:

1. *Always carry your own supply of purified water*. This means having a water bottle and a means of chemically treating the water. Iodine is the best stuff. You can use it as a tincture (add five drops to a litre of water, double the amount if the water is cloudy) or in tablet form. If you are buying iodine as a liquid, ask for 2% iodine or 'first aid iodine'. You can also use chlorine tablets or a chlorine based bleach (three drops per litre), though chlorine is less efficient than iodine. Once you've added the chemical wait half an hour before drinking the water. Using this system, fill and sterilise the bottle when water is available rather than waiting till you want a drink. Both iodine and chlorine will make the water taste. Make it more palatable by adding a squeeze of lemon or lime juice or some fruit juice powder.

2. *Think before you drink*. Always take care of what you drink. Even teeth water should be purified. Don't let yourself be persuaded into drinking water you're not sure is safe. One of our contributors spent three months living and working in an Indian village, scrupulously purifying her water. Feeling increasingly uneasy about appearing over-cautious and fanatical to her fellow villagers as she consistently refused their offers of shared drinks, she eventually accepted an offer of water, and became ill.

3. *Know what else is safe*. There are alternatives to fresh water which can be safely drunk. Hot drinks such as teas and coffee will be fine as the water will have been boiled in their preparation. Bottled mineral waters coming from a reputable source will be fine. Stick to the fizzy ones if you're uncertain. Carbonated bottled drinks — cokes etc. — are another alternative. Pure fruit juices which have not been diluted with water are also fine.

You must be absolutely scrupulous about keeping to these rules wherever you're not absolutely sure of the quality of the water. When you are dealing with cooked food there's at least a chance that any harmful organisms will have been killed by heating; when you're dealing with raw water there's no chance at all and that water is far more likely to be carrying dangerous and unpleasant organisms.

What about ice in drinks? Ice won't be any safer than the water it's been made from — freezing does not kill germs, it just stops them from multiplying. But sometimes it's difficult to stop ice being added to your drink. The yoghurt drink *lassi* is often made with it as are some fruit juices. Where you can sensibly do so, avoid ice in your drinks. Otherwise the quantities of water involved are probably small enough not to be a cause of undue concern.

Milk is safe provided it has been pasteurised or boiled. In tropical climates you're very unlikely to find raw milk as it keeps so badly. Both yoghurt and hard cheeses are made with milk which has been boiled. The lactic acid in yoghurt helps destroy bacteria. This makes it safe to eat and useful if you have an upset stomach.

Eating out

Keep the basic safety rules in mind when eating out. At market stalls choose foods being cooked there and then (see page 131). You can see what it is and whether you like the look of it (I could never quite stomach the idea of eating roast guinea-pig, a popular Andean dish, on account of their stumpy little legs sticking up in the air.) When it comes to restaurants pick those with a high turnover of local customers. They'll be popular for good reason. Besides, the more people who eat there the less likely it is that food will have been sitting around for hours, gradually cooling down as it waits to be served. If you're not sure what's what when you look at the menu, or don't have any definite ideas about the food you'd like to try, go for the set meal. It's cheaper than ordering à la carte and you'll get a range of dishes. Some places make choice easier, if they have a limited range of dishes, by allowing you into the kitchen to take a look at what's cooking. Use the opportunity to discover what's freshly cooked and hot before deciding what to have. Another way to choose is to look at what other people in the restaurant are tucking into. You're less likely to go wrong if you choose the same and you'll also have an idea of what will turn up on your plate.

It you're interested in eating good food it is worthwhile occasionally splashing out on something more expensive. Some of the regional speciality dishes mentioned in guide books may only be available at the more up-market restaurants.

If you are doubtful about the quality of a restaurant or the food, try ordering something which has to be cooked straight away like an omelette or fried eggs. Poached eggs should be absolutely safe as they won't poach if they're rotten!

How easy it is to find somewhere to eat will depend on the size of the local tourist industry, or the extent to which eating out is something local people do themselves. If there aren't very many restaurants then try hotels which may have their own dining facilities open to non-residents. Stations generally have some sort of café, if not actually right there, then nearby. They can be good places for a single woman to eat without attracting unnecessary attention. Restaurants in India sometimes provide family rooms for women and children, which you might want to use.

One of the delights of going abroad lies in being able to sample all sorts of new foods. Be prepared to experiment and try out new tastes. At market stalls pick out an unfamiliar fruit and see whether you like it. Of course if you're in South East Asia you might just get the infamous durian — a fruit which, it is rumoured, tastes divine but smells like rotting corpses: some hotels ban you from taking one onto the premises. On the other hand you could discover you're eating a delicious guava, chewing a stick of sugar cane or enjoying the taste of green coconut milk. Fruits which may already be familiar but which you normally eat after they've spent months in a refrigerated shipping container will taste infinitely better when eaten fresh. It can be like discovering a whole new taste. You may also be surprised at the number of local varieties available.

In Bolivia, for instance, you can visit banana shops which sell nothing else: there are cooking bananas, eating bananas, bananas which will never go soft, small pink bananas, all different kinds. There are as many sorts as there are apples in England.

Using your own eyes

No tourist office or guide book will tell you everything you want to know. However, by paying attention to your surroundings you can begin to work out for yourself what the set-up is and where you fit in. In many ways you are your own best resource. This is so whether you're trying to work out how and where to spend a relaxed evening or puzzling over the meaning of sights and events witnessed during the day.

Don't expect to have all the answers straight away. Learning from experience is inevitably a slow business, though there are some short cuts too. Talk to other travellers, especially women. They'll have plenty of useful advice to hand on.

> 'One of the best places I stayed in the early days of an overland trip to Asia was in an all-female dormitory. It was great to suddenly be surrounded by so many women who had so much to share, tales to swop and experiences to compare.'

Don't rush to pass judgement on what's going on around you. Take time to absorb it all. Be open and, above all, be receptive. Many, many women have travelled successfully and had fun! A self-styled OAP amongst our contributors had this to say:

> 'I have met unaccompanied travelling companions in my journeys with tremendous gratitude and enjoyment and have been regretful when they have departed. They are often of like mind to myself and prepared to make the best of any situation. Do not above all be too great a perfectionist unless you are a QE2 or Concorde type with unlimited funds at your disposal.'

6
Staying Healthy

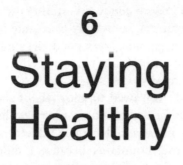

When I first went travelling I'd got only the haziest view of the health risks I might be running. Although I had read the medical tips in my guide book, the only point that really stuck in my mind was that I must avoid sleeping on possum-infested floors in darkened huts or I might pick up an incurable disease. Memorable as this advice was I never got a chance to heed the warning — the hotels I stayed in were noticeably possum-free.

Of course I wasn't totally unprepared. I'd had all the jabs my doctor had advised and left with a supply of malaria tablets, a bottle of antibiotics and some pessaries in case I got thrush. I knew what the pessaries were for, though in the event I didn't need them. I was less certain what I'd do with the antibiotics. They were simply what you took if you got really ill, weren't they? Besides, just knowing they were there made me feel safer.

On the whole I was surprisingly healthy. Apart from one or two minor stomach upsets, the only time I was actually laid up was shortly after arriving in La Paz when a combination of high altitude and a particularly nasty bout of diarrhoea kept me staggering between bedroom and loo. Some fellow Westerners staying in the hotel suggested glucose tablets, somebody else came up with heavy duty German anti-diarrhoea pills, 'very good, very powerful', and I took whatever was offered. They didn't have any effect but then, after a few days I was better anyway.

So how much do you need to know about staying healthy? It is useful to be well informed. I took some risks through ignorance: I stopped taking my malaria tablets once I'd left the tropical coastline to head up into the mountains because I didn't know why it's important to keep on taking them after you've left a malarious area. Being clearer on the reasons why the medicine is prescribed as it is might have helped. On the other hand, it is possible to worry too much when faced with a long list of tropical diseases. As with so many other aspects of travelling, it's a question of keeping things in proportion and using common sense. Know what the dangers are, the precautions you can take and how best to seek help if you need it.

BEFORE YOU GO — PRECAUTIONS

It is always better to prevent an illness occurring if you can, rather than treat it afterwards. Start your journey in good health. If you have an existing medical condition, consult your doctor about medicines you may need and any complications which may arise from your mode of travel. Get your dentist to check your teeth before you go, and have any necessary work done. It could save pain and expense later, especially as many insurance policies exclude all but emergency work.

Immunisations

Consult your doctor about the immunisations you will need a good two or even three months before you go abroad. This will leave plenty of time to organise and complete a programme of injections. You can rush through them faster if you have to but it won't give you as good protection and besides, you'll end up feeling like a pin-cushion.

Compulsory immunisations

You should check whether the countries you are visiting require you to have had any particular immunisations before they'll let you in. If they do you'll have to produce a valid certificate of immunisation signed and stamped by the doctor who gives you the jab. It's no good having the vaccination and then not bothering about the certificate. Since the eradication of smallpox, the two diseases which have been subject to such control are Yellow Fever and Cholera.

Leaflet T5, put out by the Department of Health and updated yearly, is a useful source of advice. It is generally available from your G.P. or at main post offices. The medical journal *Pulse* and the travel agents' trade magazine *ABC* also carry country-by-country lists of compulsory vaccinations. They are up-dated regularly and may reflect more accurately what will actually be asked for on the border. The *ABC* guide can be consulted via a travel agent.

Yellow fever

Yellow Fever is a serious disease which attacks the liver, producing jaundice and fever — hence its name. It is endemic in tropical forests across a wide band of Central Africa and in northern parts of South America. If you're going to these areas you'll need to have the injection.

The disease primarily infects monkeys and is transmitted amongst them by forest mosquitoes. It can spread to humans if they are bitten by a mosquito carrying the disease. Problems arise when a person who is so infected returns to their community. If they are subsequently bitten by a mosquito which preys on humans that mosquito can pick up and then transmit the disease to other members of the local population. An urban epidemic can begin. The World Health Organisation is particularly anxious to control Yellow Fever to ensure that it doesn't spread in this way from forest mosquitoes to mosquitoes which prey on humans and eventually to areas outside the endemic zones.

Immunisation is important to protect yourself but also to protect others. The injection gives complete immunity, becomes effective ten days after the jab and lasts for ten years. In the U.K. it is only available at Yellow Fever Vaccination Centres (addresses and phone numbers available from your G.P. or travel agent).

Cholera

Cholera is a severe bowel infection which causes profuse water diarrhoea followed by vomiting and muscular cramps. The greatest risk to any one who has caught the disease comes from the subsequent dehydration which, if not checked, can kill. It is a disease associated with poor sanitation. The bacteria which cause it are excreted in faeces and it's by faecal contamination of water or food that it is passed on.

In 1973 the World Health Organisation abandoned the attempt to control the spread of the disease by compulsory immunisation of those moving in and out of cholera infected areas as it seemed to be having little effect. Officially no country now requires a certificate of vaccination. However, some border officials do still ask for evidence of vaccination, especially if you've travelled through an area where there has been a recent outbreak. It may be better to play safe and have it anyway if you're going to a part of the world where cholera is prevalent. (This currently includes many countries in Asia, Africa, the Middle East and some parts of South America.) Not only will this minimise the chance of border hassle, but will also provide some protection against contracting the disease — though estimates of the vaccine's effectiveness vary between 40% and 80%. The protective effect of the injection wears off after six months.

Recommended immunisations

Depending on where you're going and how you're likely to be living whilst you're away, the other immunisations you should consider having are Typhoid Fever, Poliomyelitis, Tetanus and Hepatitis A.

Typhoid fever

Like Cholera, Typhoid is spread by faecal contamination of water or food. The bacteria which cause it are part of the salmonella group and the symptoms include headache, fever, constipation or diarrhoea and a rash on the chest or abdomen. The vaccination offers 70 % to 90% protection. It is useful if you are going to be travelling or living rough in an area where sanitation is poor. It can now be administered as a tablet instead of an injection. Both are equally effective.

Poliomyelitis

Polio is a serious disease that can result in permanent paralysis. It is caused by a virus which is still common in many parts of the world. Before travelling abroad you must check that you have been immunised sufficiently recently. If you haven't or you don't know then you should have a reinforcing dose. This will be in the form of drops on a sugar lump.

Tetanus

Tetanus is a bacterial infection which effects the nervous system. In its final stages it causes rigidity and muscle spasms (hence the old name 'lockjaw'). The bacteria are common in soil or animal manure and can enter the body through a cut or some other skin wound. Because you can get tetanus in this country as well as abroad you should have received an immunisation as part of your routine jabs when you were a baby. Booster doses are necessary roughly every twenty years. You, your mother or your doctor may know when you last had a booster. If you are not sure whether you are covered have one before you go.

If you do get a wound that is contaminated by soil or manure it must be thoroughly cleaned even if you are immune to tetanus.

Hepatitis

Hepatitis A is a viral disease of the liver, largely spread by faecal contamination of food and water, but also by direct contact with an infected person. You can get it in this country as well as abroad but will be most at risk if sanitation and hygiene are poor. Symptoms include nausea, loss of appetite, fever and abdominal pain followed by jaundice. A new vaccine, Havirex, is now available. You need two shots before you go, the first at least a month ahead. A third shot, 6-12 months after the second, will give 10 years' immunity. To maintain your immunity, you then need a single booster every 10 years. Havirex is much more effective than the old immunoglobulin injections.

Other immunisations

If you're travelling abroad to work as a vet, teacher, health worker or in some other specialised service and are going to live in a particularly high risk environment you would be well advised to consider immunisation against rabies, and Hepatitis B. These precautions are not necessary for the ordinary traveller. However, if you are planning to spend a long time in Asia you might consider protection against Japanese Encephalitis, a mosquito-borne illness prevalent in rural areas.

Protection against malaria

Malaria is an infection caused by microscopic parasites transmitted from one person to another by mosquito bites. The symptoms are fever, headache, vomiting and diarrhoea. There are four different strains of malaria, each caused by a different group of parasites: Plasmodium falciparum, P. vivax, P. malariae or P. ovale.

What happens is that the female mosquitoes ingest the parasites when they bite someone suffering from malaria. The parasites mature inside the mosquito and can then be passed on when the mosquito bites again. Once the parasites have entered the human bloodstream they are carried to the liver where they continue to develop. At this stage of the disease there are no symptoms

After about ten days the parasites move out from the liver back into the bloodstream. They invade the red blood cells where they will carry on multiplying until the cells burst releasing yet more parasites to attack yet more red cells. This is when fever sets in. If the parasites go unchecked the continual destruction of red cells will lead to anaemia and an enlarged spleen, as the body's defences are broken down. Of the four sorts of parasite P. falciparum is the most dangerous. If it is left unchecked it can invade the brain and the resulting fits or coma can kill. The other three are less deadly but are more difficult to eradicate completely. They can lie dormant in the liver for months or even years, periodically breaking out into the bloodstream and setting off the symptoms of fever once more.

All travellers passing through or staying in a part of the world where malaria is endemic must take precautions against contracting this serious disease. There is no vaccine available. Instead travellers should protect themselves by routinely taking drugs which will attack the parasites as soon as they enter the bloodstream and before they have a chance to establish themselves. Such drugs (called prophylactics because they prevent a disease from starting rather than curing it) must be taken regularly at the prescribed intervals if they are to work properly. If you don't do this you won't be fully protected. It is important to start taking them one week before entering a malarious region so that they can build up to the right levels, and for a full month after you've left so that they can eradicate any parasites which may still be in your system. Whilst the parasites are still lying dormant in the liver the prophylactics can't affect them.

Unfortunately some strains of malaria parasite have built up resistance to some of the prophylactics. For this reason you should always get up-to-date advice on which drugs to use where. There is no one 'right' regime, and you may find people on your travels taking different combinations of medication, especially travellers from different countries of origin. If you're going to be living in a high risk area you may be prescribed a combination of drugs to ensure adequate protection. This may be a nuisance but take them. *Never* take more than the prescribed amount. Too big a dose can have serious side effects.

Since prophylactics do not confer immunity and because of the resistance to some of the drugs, it is still possible to get malaria despite taking precautions. This is why it is essential to check out any persistent fever whether you're still travelling in a malarious region or have recently returned from one. If you're back home make sure your doctor knows where you have been. Without that information he or she might not consider the possibility of malaria, as the symptoms are the same for a number of other diseases. Late or missed diagnosis can be fatal. A blood test should reveal whether parasites are present or not.

Anyone who was brought up in a malarious area of the world or who is visiting relatives living there should be aware that any immunity local people have to the disease is the result of surviving continuous exposure to the parasites from childhood onwards. Less than a year's absence from such a region will lessen that immunity and mean that you have to take additional precautions on your return.

Homeopathy and immunisation

Travellers increasingly ask about Homeopathic alternatives to immunisation. The advice given by the Bristol Homeopathic Hospital is that there is *no* homeopathic alternative, and travellers must take the recommended vaccination.

Advice before you go

G.P.s are *general* practitioners, not experts on the far-flung corners of the world. For up-to-date specialist advice tailored to the countries you are visiting you can contact MASTA (Medical Advisory Services for Travellers Abroad Ltd) on their Travellers Health Line. A similar service is provided by the Travel Clinic Health Line run from the Hospital for Tropical Diseases. (For further details, see page 278.)

COMMON COMPLAINTS EN ROUTE

Getting the right jabs before you go and assembling your own medical kit (see page 166) are necessary steps to take before leaving home. They do not mean that you'll stay healthy all the time you're away. The level of risk you run depends partly on how and where you are travelling.

Endsleigh Insurance, who deal particularly with low budget, long distance travellers, reckon that about half of the medical claims made on their travel insurance policies are a result of minor accidents, that is injuries arising from being knocked down or falling over. They say this is as true for those travelling in developing countries as it is for those travelling in Europe. The next largest category is stomach problems of one sort or another, followed by insect bites and allergic reactions.

V.S.O., who are responsible for posting volunteers abroad for two whole years, mainly in Africa and Asia, reckon the most common complaints are malaria, diarrhoea, skin infections and flu, whilst the greatest chance of actually dying comes from having a motor bike accident.

Information gathered by the Communicable Disease Surveillance Centre on all infections brought back into the U.K. suggests that gastrointestinal infections are still common amongst travellers visiting developing countries, whilst the number of travellers returning to this country with malaria caused by P. falciparum is rising, particularly amongst those who have visited West or East Africa.

As far as our own contributors go, diarrhoea was by far the most frequently mentioned complaint, with vaginal infections and cystitis next on the list.

Each of these sources offers only a partial view but they do give some idea of what to watch out for. Besides being immunised and taking malaria prophylactics, the most important precautions any traveller can take whilst away are to be very careful about food, water and personal hygiene (see chapter 5, page 129). Most of the diseases that you run the risk of catching are transmitted via food and water, from diarrhoea and dysentery to the much more serious infections listed above such as cholera, hepatitis and polio.

Taking some responsibility for your own health from the beginning of a trip can help you avoid serious illness later. Often half the battle is just thinking ahead.

'Taking responsibility for the first time for my own health care was something I found really challenging and exciting.'

Africa

The most common complaints are not the most serious ones so just because you're ill don't assume you've picked up a deadly disease. You'll be able to treat most of them quite easily yourself, following the advice below.

Diarrhoea

Diarrhoea in the traveller is almost invariably caused by eating or drinking contaminated food or water. The most important preventive measures are therefore to follow the rules laid down in Chapter 5. If you get diarrhoea you should think carefully about what you've been eating and drinking and consider how you could change your habits in the future.

The commonest forms of diarrhoea are self-limiting. That is to say they will clear themselves up without the need for medical treatment, probably within three days.

Your best course of action is to eat nothing for 24 hours to give your bowel a chance of recuperating on its own, and drink plenty of fluids: weak tea, herbal teas, clear soup, fruit juices and pure water are all good. Rice water and green coconut water are excellent. If the diarrhoea is very severe then you will need to increase your intake of fluids to prevent dehydration and should make certain that the liquids contain sufficient salts to replace those your body will be losing. The easiest way to do this is to mix half a level teaspoonful of salt and eight level teaspoonfuls of sugar in a litre of water (1.8 pints). Drink at least a glassful every hour, more if you feel thirsty. Sipping rather than gulping will help you to keep the fluid down if you're also vomiting.

An alternative to making your own preparation of salt and sugar is to buy Oral Rehydration Solution (Dioralyte) if you can get it, from a chemist. This is a more precise combination of minerals and glucose which can be mixed up and used in the same way as the homemade version. This method of dealing with diarrhoea by increasing the fluid and salt intake is known as Oral Rehydration Therapy.

After 24 hours you can try to eat something. Start with plain foods: boiled rice, yoghurt, bananas, bread and toast or dry biscuits, for instance. Avoid foods with a high fat content. Exactly what you choose will depend on the circumstances:

> **'Look at the food you have in mind. Your stomach will tell you if you can manage it. When in doubt, don't.'**
>
> *Turkey*

By the end of the fourth day you will need to make a decision about what to do. Ask yourself if you're still eating and drinking poor food and water. Did you really starve yourself for 24 hours? If you're sure you've been sensible but nothing has improved, or if the diarrhoea is accompanied by fever or blood in the stools you are suffering from something more serious and need to seek medical advice.

If you're smitten with the runs at a time when you really can't follow this let-your-body-clear-itself approach (in the middle of a long train or coach journey, for instance) you may want to take something which will alleviate the symptoms. Imodium is generally considered the most effective treatment in these circumstances. Take two capsules initially, then one with each loose stool. This will control the diarrhoea and lessen stomach cramps.

However, in themselves these kinds of drugs will do nothing to cure you, just make the experience somewhat less unpleasant. They may even slow down your recovery and in rare cases can make the symptoms worse. Don't take them as a routine medicine just because you've got diarrhoea.

Antibiotics and diarrhoea

By and large there is little point in using antibiotics to deal with travellers' diarrhoea. This is not just because by doing so you run the risk of creating antibiotic resistant strains of bugs. There are other less altruistic reasons too. First antibiotics won't just select the bugs that are irritating your gut to get to work on, they'll wipe out everything. This means that at the end of a course of treatment your bowel will be faced once again with the problem of establishing a balance in numbers of competing micro-organisms, and will be less able to deal with the local strains of bug than it was before you got ill. You may have saved yourself some unpleasantness this time, but will have done nothing to diminish your chances of getting a second attack.

Secondly, by alleviating symptoms a course of antibiotics may end up masking the fact that you are actually suffering from a much more serious condition than travellers' diarrhoea. This could prevent you from recognising that you need medical help fast.

If you have compelling reasons for staying diarrhoea-free for a short period of time — let's imagine that you're an athlete off training to an exotic clime; or a business woman about to clinch a deal in some far-off country; a representative at a conference or some such — then a doctor might suggest using the antibiotics Streptotriad or Septrin prophylactically. They will both offer protection, but should never be used for more than two weeks.

Bacillary dysentery   Blood and mucus in the stools are a sign of dysentery. There are two kinds of dysentery, which require different sorts of treatment so it is important to establish exactly which sort you have. Bacillary dysentery is caused by the presence in the gut of bacteria belonging to the Shigella group. It can vary in its intensity but is generally marked by its sudden onset, the presence of blood and mucus in the stools and an accompanying high temperature. You're likely to feel really ill with nausea and headache, diarrhoea is frequent and there may be sharp abdominal pains. Oral rehydration therapy is the best treatment. Antibiotics are unlikely to be effective unless prescribed by a doctor following a specimen test.

Amoebic dysentery   This is caused by the presence of microscopic parasites in the large intestine. The parasites are spread by contaminated food or drinking water. The symptoms may not be so strikingly obvious as in the case of bacillary dysentery. There is often no fever and only moderate diarrhoea, or you may feel constipated and generally unwell with headaches and stomach pains. Symptoms fluctuate and may cease altogether for a time, to return later. This makes the disease hard to diagnose without proper stool examination.

To find out whether or not you have the disease you will need to present a fresh specimen for examination as the amoebae soon die once outside the body. If you think you may have amoebic dysentery it is important to get it CHECKED OUT as, if the disease goes untreated, it can lead to an abcess of the liver which, if it ruptures, can kill.

Treatment includes oral rehydration therapy to prevent dehydration, whilst metronidazole (Flagyl) is used to clear the system of amoebae. (The dosage is 400 mg three times daily for seven days.)

Giardiasis   This infection is caused by microscopic parasites moving into the small intestine via contaminated food or drinking water. The symptoms can include diarrhoea with pale frothy stools, an unpleasant smell and abdominal pain. Treatment is with metronidazole (Flagyl). (The dosage is 400 mg three times daily for seven days.)

There are several other infections which provoke diarrhoea. Even malaria can be responsible. If you have a stomach upset and it doesn't clear up within three days, there is blood or mucus in the stools, or you feel feverish and have cramping pains in the abdomen, you need to do something about it. Get medical advice.

Constipation

A change in the diet, little exercise and unaccustomed sweating can lead to constipation. So can the lack of a handy toilet or just the thought of being faced by dirty and unpleasant ones. Your body will probably sort itself out. In the meantime eat plenty of fruit and vegetables and drink a lot. It is better to deal with this by changing your diet than by swallowing laxatives. If things are desperate then a local chemist would be able to sell you a remedy such as lactulose which is reasonably gentle and naturally acting.

Insect bites and stings

These can be a nuisance even if the insect is not actively transmitting disease in its bite. Midge and mosquito bites can be horribly itchy and in some people will provoke an allergic reaction.

Remember, you may need to protect yourself against mosquitoes and midges in Northern Europe during the summer months as well as further south. Even the Arctic is not insect free — whilst if you're travelling in the tropics you should be avoiding mosquitoes anyway to minimise the risks of getting malaria.

Protecting yourself means covering up bare arms and legs in the evening when mosquitoes are most active and using an insect repellant containing diethyl toluamide or dimethyl phthalate. (See page 32 for advice on buying repellents.) The trouble with these sorts of repellents is that, no matter how strong, their effectiveness wears out after a while. Spraying onto clothes rather than your skin will help them last longer.

If you suffer from a severe allergic reaction you might want to start taking vitamin B12 about a week before setting off on your travels and continue ingesting small amounts whilst you're away. Apparently it will make your skin smell yeasty which deters mosquitoes from biting you. Cream of tartar can be used in the same way.

To soothe irritable bites once they've happened apply calamine lotion, an antihistamine cream, or a dressing of a teaspoon of starch mixed with a little water. If the bites are particularly unpleasant take antihistamine tablets, such as Piriton. Do try not to scratch them as this makes the bites more likely to become infected.

Cuts and grazes

The rapid healing of small cuts and grazes is something we tend to take for granted in the West. If you're travelling in a tropical climate you really do have to take extra care. If you don't keep them properly cleaned and protected they will turn septic and refuse to heal.

Wash the wound with soap and clean water. Wherever possible, use an antiseptic solution such as mercurochrome, hydrogen peroxide or diluted iodine. Cover the wound with an elastoplast or sterile gauze to keep it clean until a scab forms. Paraffin gauze as a dressing has the added advantage of not sticking to the wound so any healing won't be disturbed when you change the dressing. Don't use antiseptic creams except on tiny scratches. Because they are greasy they keep the wound moist and sticky and delay healing.

With deeper wounds the immediate problem may be how to stop the bleeding. Apply pressure directly to the injured part whilst squeezing the sides of the wound together. Use a sterile gauze pad if you have one. When the bleeding has stopped wash the wound with clean water and the surrounding area of skin with soap and water. Then cover with a sterile gauze pad held in place with a bandage. If bleeding continues apply more dressings but don't remove the original. This may only disturb any clots which have already formed. If the wound is on an arm or leg, then holding the limb up in the air above the level of the rest of the body will help to stop bleeding. One convenient way of closing wounds is to use a butterfly dressing or Steristrip. These are very thin strips of adhesive strapping which are designed to cross the wound, binding its two edges close together. They can be useful if a minor cut is deep enough to otherwise warrant stitching. Some casualty departments make use of them in this way. If you don't have any butterfly dressings you can make your own by taking an ordinary piece of plaster and cutting two half moon shapes back to back opposite each other leaving only a thin piece of material in between.

If the wound is quite long use more than one butterfly dressing to bring the gaping edges together. You should only do this if the cut is clean. You may need a tetanus booster injection if the wound is likely to have been contaminated, and you're uncertain whether your protection is up-to-date.

Feet

If you're going to be doing much walking make sure you take shoes which are already worn in and comfortable. Francis Galton in *The Art of Travel* (1877) recommends breaking a raw egg into your boot before putting it on to soften the shoe leather, whilst Christina Dodwell adds that soap on the inside of your socks will help prevent blisters. Less drastic measures are to pad the parts of the shoe which rub with sheep's wool or foam rubber, or cover the tender part of the foot with moleskin or a conventional plaster. Change your socks daily.

Blisters can be treated by puncturing them, applying an antiseptic solution and then covering with a plaster.

You can harden up soft skin on heels and toes by rubbing the skin with surgical spirit two or three times a day for a few days before you set off.

Athlete's Foot and other fungal skin infections All fungal infections thrive in warm and moist conditions and are therefore most likely to occur between the toes, in the armpit or in the groin. They are particularly easy to pick up in tropical climates. Probably athlete's foot is the most familiar (an infection which spreads between the toes and on to the foot) though there are others, including ringworm and dhobi itch (which affects the groin). What they have in common is a scaly, flaking surface with reddening skin underneath. They all itch.

Frequent washing and careful drying will help prevent them occurring, and as far as athlete's foot goes, one way of avoiding it is to wear flip-flops in the sorts of places where others go barefoot e.g. bathrooms and showers. Clothing should be light and airy, and underwear and socks should be changed daily. Use medicated talc after you've washed and dried on areas of the skin which seem particularly vulnerable. If the infection has already started before you get round to doing this then use Canesten cream to eradicate it.

Prickly heat

If you're spending a lot of time feeling hot and sweaty in a humid climate you may end up suffering from prickly heat. This is the name given to the rash of red spots which may occur if sweat is unable to evaporate from the skin and the ducts of the sweat glands get blocked. The rash will probably be found at any point where clothing is too tight or rubs against the skin.

The easiest way to prevent it is to keep cool: wear loose fitting clothing preferably made of cotton. A dress may be more comfortable than a skirt, especially if the latter has an elasticated waistband. You can also get prickly heat in the groin. Pretty uncomfortable, so take cotton underwear.

Bra elastic is the other area to watch out for. You may need to take the measures suggested below.

If you get a bad case of prickly heat then try to avoid any strenuous activity which makes you sweat even more. Wash often with cold water and without soap. Towel yourself dry gently and then dust with a medicated talcum powder. This should reduce the itching. If you can, spend some time (overnight, for instance) in air conditioning — just giving your skin a chance to stop sweating and dry itself out for a while will help. Calamine lotion will offer some relief.

Sunburn

Sunburn can be extremely painful and should be treated with care — the skin is being *burnt* by the sun's radiation after all. At the first signs of discomfort it is sensible to cover up. You may find that, even so, you want to keep out of direct sunlight. The sun's ultra-violet rays can penetrate thin clothing. Bathing with cold water will provide some relief, as will calamine lotion. You might want to apply a compress soaked in vinegar and water (1 tablespoon of vinegar to half a litre of cool, safe, boiled water), or you could use yoghurt.

Other useful tips

There are a variety of other minor complaints which you might want to know how to deal with.

Bee and wasp stings   Wasp stings can be soothed by applying vinegar, bee stings by dilute ammonia, or they can be dressed with papaya (paw paw) skins. These latter are said to be very effective with all sorts of stings from those of hornets to jelly fish.

Fleas, lice and bed bugs   Fleas can be dealt with by flea powder, or simply washing yourself and all the clothes you are wearing at the same time may do the trick. Head lice can be deterred by regular brushing, combing and washing of hair. In the event of an infestation use flea powder or a lotion containing carbaryl or malathion.

If you buy insect powders abroad, check the contents carefully — some contain DDT or other unpleasant insecticides you might not want to sprinkle on your skin.

Bed bugs can be deterred where necessary by moving your bed away from the wall and sleeping with the light on.

Ticks   These are pretty unpleasant creatures intent on sucking blood. In the process they may pass on infections. They're mainly on the look out for animals but sometimes take a fancy to humans. In a tick infested area, protect yourself from them by using insect repellant or wearing the sort of clothes which cover you up.

If a tick has burrowed its way into your skin you will need to remove it carefully, making sure the head comes away with the body. Don't pull straightaway. Persuade it to let go by smothering it with grease or a drop of paraffin or by holding a lighted cigarette very close. Apply an antiseptic to the bite. Leeches deserve the same sort of treatment: use salt to persuade them to let go.

Roundworms and threadworms   Both these infections can be caught anywhere where hygiene is poor. Children are particularly prone to threadworms. They are ingested from the fingers or contaminated food. Prevention is simply a matter of hygiene: washing hands after going to the loo and before eating or preparing food; making sure that food has been thoroughly cooked before eating, or if raw, that it has been peeled or properly washed. Piperazine tablets will clear the infection.

Burns   The best means of dealing with minor burns is to immerse the affected part in cold water for at least ten minutes, probably longer. The cold water will take the heat back out from the skin and stop it doing so much damage. Otherwise the heat will keep on chasing round the skin cells harming tissues. Stop the treatment when the injured part no longer feels painful once out of the water. Don't apply any ointments or grease. If blisters form, leave them alone. If necessary cover the burn with a sterile, non-adherent dressing such as Bactigras, Jelonet or Melolin.

Conjunctivitis   Conjunctivitis is the name given to an inflammation of the eyes when they become pink and feel gritty. Those who wear contact lenses may find themselves particularly susceptible to the infection when travelling in a tropical climate. There are a variety of causes including irritation of the eye by dust or smoke. But conjunctivitis can also be transmitted from person to person by eye/hand contact, for instance, or via shared towels or cameras and binoculars which are passed around. If you have conjunctivitis make sure you don't spread the infection. Antibiotic eye drops, or ointment such as sulphacetamide or tetracycline should clear it.

EXOTIC DISEASES

There are a whole host of diseases mainly associated with the tropics: Dengue Fever, Scrub Fever; sleeping sickness; Filiarsis — even the names sound impressive enough, never mind the details. Fortunately you don't need to know much about them, except how to avoid them and in most cases that's straightforward enough, barring mishaps. All the above are transmitted by insect bites of one sort or another but present far less of a hazard under normal circumstances than malaria transmitting mosquitoes.

If you are using insect repellants, mosquito nets and the other suggestions for keeping mosquitoes at bay you should be all right.

Bowel parasites

There are two other diseases, rare in the traveller but endemic in various parts of the tropics, which are worth mentioning, both caused by bowel parasites: schistosomiasis and hook worm. They are rare only because travellers take the necessary precautions to avoid contracting them.

Schistosomiasis or bilharzia

The parasites which cause this disease live in veins in the human abdomen and their eggs are passed out of the body in urine or faeces. If they get into river or lake water the eggs hatch out and larvae then invade certain species of freshwater snail. Several weeks later the parasites leave the snail and re-enter the water. They are now ready to penetrate human skin and establish themselves in the host body where they will develop into mature egg-producing worms and so the whole process will continue. Anyone swimming or bathing in water where the snails and parasites live, or drinking it, can catch the disease. Once inside the body the real damage is done by the eggs which force their way through body tissue to the bowel or bladder and are then excreted. Symptoms include itching and a rash on the skin, followed later by fever and later still by bloodstained stools or urine.

In parts of the world where schistosomiasis is endemic contact with infected water should be avoided. In practice in much of Africa that means not washing or swimming in rivers or lakes, particularly if the water is slow moving or stagnant, or overhung by vegetation. Sea water is safe as snails don't live in it.

Some protection against the parasites can be gained by using insect repellant, whilst if you do accidentally come into contact with contaminated water it is important to towel yourself thoroughly dry as soon as possible. This can prevent the parasite from penetrating.

To render the water safe it should be boiled. If you store water for three days in a snail-free container all the parasites will die, so the water will then be safe.

It is important to diagnose schistosomiasis early as the damage the parasites do is cumulative. It can be effectively treated.

Hookworm

As with schistosomiasis, the eggs of the hookworm are present in the excreta of a carrier. Walking barefoot on contaminated soil gives the parasites the chance to penetrate the skin. Hookworm infection is therefore best avoided by always wearing sandals or shoes.

Jigger fleas

In West Africa and Central America these fleas can be found living in sand. The female of the species will burrow under the skin near the toes to lay her eggs. You can avoid encountering this problem by wearing shoes.

Rabies

Rabies is another potentially very dangerous disease. There are very few countries in the world where it is not endemic: Britain, Australia, New Zealand, Iceland and Sweden are amongst them. However it is only transmitted to humans if they are bitten or scratched by a rabid animal, or if a cut or graze is licked. Any mammals can carry the disease, from dogs to foxes, monkeys, bats and members of the cat family. You would be well advised never to stroke or play with animals in countries where rabies is endemic. Once rabies has established itself it cannot be cured but fortunately in humans there is a lengthy incubation period (between 30 and 60 days) during which time the disease can be safely eradicated by a series of post-exposure vaccinations, but you *must* get to a doctor as soon as possible.

Unprovoked aggression from a dog or excessive saliva round its mouth may be signs that it is rabid. In all events it is sensible to be wary of stray dogs.

If you are bitten, the wound should be thoroughly washed as soon as possible with plenty of soap and water to flush out the virus. Don't rub. Apply an antiseptic solution such as iodine or mercurochrome. Don't attempt to close up the wound. If there's no water available, use any sterile liquid — tea or bottled drinks would do. If you can find out who the animal belongs to, so much the better. If it doesn't die within ten days then it hasn't got rabies and you'll be all right. Whatever the circumstances, get to a doctor as soon as possible. The doctor should advise you whether to start the necessary course of injections or not.

Those who are likely to be handling animals abroad should think about having a rabies vaccine before they go.

Snakes, scorpions and spiders

These don't transmit disease in their bite though any poison they may inject can have an unpleasant effect. However, even snake venom is rarely fatal and besides if you take sensible precautions you're unlikely to be bitten anyway.

Snakes   Most snakes aren't poisonous, moreover no snake is particularly keen on being found by humans. If you give them enough warning of your approach they will move off out of the way. This is why when moving through the undergrowth in an area where there are known to be snakes it is sensible to use a stick to thump on the ground as you go — any snakes in the vicinity get plenty of warning of your arrival and will disappear.

In the unlikely event of getting bitten by a snake, don't panic. The chances are that even if it's the venomous kind it won't have injected any poison into you. You may not develop any symptoms at all, and even if you do you're extremely unlikely to die. Stay calm and keep the bitten part still. This will slow down the spread of the poison. Don't cut or suck the wound. There's no point in going in for those sorts of heroics, which are unlikely to have any effect. Instead wash the wound with water, tie a tourniquet above it (releasing it for one minute in every 15) and keep the limb cool. Apply ice or place the limb in cold water. Get to a doctor.

Snakes are most likely to be out and about at night. To protect yourself, wear long trousers, proper lace-up shoes and socks if you're going out walking.

Scorpions and spiders   Yes, all spiders can bite, though on the whole they don't and in the U.K. you probably wouldn't notice much even if they did. In the tropics both spider and scorpion bites may be painful. Avoid getting bitten by turning your shoes upside down and knocking them out before putting them on. Spiders and scorpions like dark corners and may consider your shoes an ideal hiding place. They won't appreciate getting squashed and will bite defensively first.

Aspirin or paracetamol should reduce the pain and you could also try applying ice.

TROUBLES WITH TRAVEL

The way you travel, and the climate you move into can affect your health. Not everybody responds in the same way and what can be trying circumstances for one person may pass unnoticed by someone else. The following advice aims to minimise the hassle.

Travel sickness

If you know you're particularly prone to air-sickness or sea-sickness then travel with a supply of antihistamine tablets. You should take one every hour or so before you set out. If you find you feel queasy when travelling by road one way of coping is to fix your eyes on one particular landmark some distance away and then keep looking at it for as long as you can. When you pass it choose another. This is a particularly useful tactic if you're driving down a bendy road. Remember that sitting in the back of a car or bus is worse than sitting in the front.

Many travellers swear by sea bands — a stretchy bracelet with a pressure stud which you wear round your wrist. They are available from chemists and outdoor suppliers. Some people recommend eating crystallised ginger for sea-sickness. You can also now buy ginger sea-sickness pills.

Remember antihistamines may make you drowsy and impair your ability to drive. On the other hand driving in itself may make you feel less sick, so think twice about choosing to cure car-sickness with a pill.

Heat exhaustion

Heat exhaustion can set in if you are not drinking enough liquids or eating enough salt to replace what your body is losing through sweat. Symptoms include light-headedness, headache, tiredness and nausea. It is particularly important to take preventive measures during the first two weeks of a stay in a hot climate, while your body is adjusting to the increased demands made on it. You should also watch out if you're undertaking any strenuous physical activity: you may need far more water and salt than you anticipate.

> 'Don't be surprised at the amount of liquid it's possible to consume. I was getting through well over a gallon a day when cycling.'
>
> *Sri Lanka*

To treat the symptoms, lie down somewhere cool and drink plenty of slightly salted water or fruit juice. To avoid getting in this state in the first place make sure you are drinking plenty of fluids when you can. If you've been stuck on a bus and unable to drink much during the day, have lots to drink in the evening. At meal times salt your food to taste in the expectation that you will need more than normal. Your body will know how much: if you're lacking in salt you won't be able to taste it.

Hypothermia

Every year walkers are brought off the hills in Britain suffering from exposure, as hypothermia is more commonly called. It is worth bearing this in mind when setting out for a day's walking in the mountains; you don't need to be travelling in sub-arctic conditions to be at risk — being badly equipped or just getting lost may be enough. Hypothermia occurs when the body's temperature falls below 95°F/ 35°C. First signs include feeling tired and apathetic, shivering, stumbling and behaving in a generally odd manner (though the person with hypothermia is usually unaware of their symptoms). Anyone in this condition needs shelter and warmth. If you're out on the hillside, look for a spot well out of the wind, put on as many extra clothes as you can or, if you're carrying one, get into a sleeping bag or survival bag. Have something to eat. If you can make one, have a hot drink   don't take any alcohol — by dilating the blood vessels it encourages heat loss. If you're with others get them to warm you by holding and hugging you.

Mountain sickness

Anybody moving rapidly from a low to a high altitude (10,000 feet or more) may experience some breathlessness on arrival, as the higher you go the less easy it is to absorb the oxygen you need into the bloodstream. To compensate for this difficulty your body will have to produce more red blood cells. Whilst you are acclimatising in this way, you may find yourself unable to maintain your normal level of physical activity and perhaps feel lightheaded. These symptoms can be prevented by making a gradual ascent though, even so, you may well notice the difference once you get over 12,000 feet. At this sort of height it may help to go no more than 1,000 feet further up in a day. If you're trekking in the high mountains another way of coping is to climb 300 or 400 feet higher than your stopping place and then return to sleep. This may help you rest more comfortably.

Despite these precautions, a few women may develop acute mountain sickness particularly at heights of 15,000 feet and above. In its mild form the symptoms include headache, nausea, difficulty in sleeping and a general sensation of weakness. Rest at your current altitude. However, be on the look out. This condition can intensify into pulmonary or cerebral oedema, which can both be fatal. Watch for any of these symptoms: little urine, a persistent headache, lips which look blue, 'bubbly' breathing which may be accompanied by a cough producing frothy phlegm. The sufferer may feel very drowsy and confused or breathless when resting. Anyone who has these symptoms must take action *at once* and rapidly return to a lower altitude, or their life could be in danger.

LOCAL HEALTH CARE

The range of health care services on offer and their standard varies terrifically around the world. Westernised countries may have more and better medical facilities but they are often private and there can be a heavy price to pay for using them. In countries where there is a choice between public and private facilities, find out which is better. As a visitor you may well have to pay for both anyway so assuming your medical insurance will cover you in either case (it certainly should, see Chapter 4) you should choose on the quality of the service. In the U.K., Denmark or New Zealand, for instance, public facilities are of a high standard, whereas in Greece they are few and far between and it might be easier to go private. Leaflet T5, issued by the Department of Health and available from main post offices or your G.P. gives details of free or subsidised medical treatment available for U.K. citizens in some other countries and includes some information on the standard of health care you can expect.

Developing countries don't inevitably have third rate medical services, though finding where the best hospitals or doctors are may take time. In some cases they can offer the traveller excellent facilities for treating the particular infections they are prone to. If a country seems to have poor facilities, you may find that a mission hospital is better equipped (though this is by no means always the case), or that a large teaching hospital has more doctors who speak English. Even when the service seems rudimentary, remember the doctors will all have had considerable experience at spotting and dealing with what for us are considered exotic diseases.

If you need to seek medical advice your best first step is to get to the nearest hospital out-patients department. Failing that, if the complaint is minor then find a doctor. Fellow travellers, expatriates or a reputable hotel are all potential sources of information on this score. If you're more seriously ill in a developing country then try to get to the capital and either go to the main hospital, or ask the consulate or embassy to recommend someone.

It may well be possible to ask to be seen by a woman doctor — you certainly shouldn't assume that there won't be any — particularly in

Moslem countries where medicine may be one of the few careers open to women.

> 'The National Health Service is of a good standard and free (though you may have to queue). There are a high proportion of women doctors if you prefer to go to one.'
>
> *Sri Lanka*

If you can't find a woman doctor and need a gynaecological examination, take a friend along as a chaperone, or insist on a nurse being present.

Those who subscribe to a belt and braces approach to life might want to know exactly where to find an English speaking doctor should they become ill. The International Association for Medical Assistance to Travellers (IAMAT) issue a list of English speaking doctors working in most parts of the world. The information will be provided free if you write to them at the address mentioned on page 278. As they are funded by donation, contributions would be welcome. Obtain receipts for all medical treatment you receive so that you can claim for it on your insurance policy.

It is worth remembering that most chemists are extremely well trained and knowledgeable. Seek their advice first if you cannot easily find a doctor.

Alternative medicine

Whilst some alternatives to Western medicine such as acupuncture have become well known to many of us, others have remained obscure, yet they may be part of as extensive a tradition. Ayurvedic medicine for instance, is an Indian herbal medicine whose history goes back centuries. It takes a holistic approach to disease, and sees sickness as symptomatic of the bodily system being out of balance. The practitioners' task is to restore the balance by prescribing particular herbs. There are Ayurvedic pharmacies, hospitals and training colleges as well as practising doctors in many Indian cities. Unani is another equally widely practised form of medicine in India which uses knowledge first systematised by the ancient Greeks.

Elsewhere, traditional herbal medicine may be practised in a much less formalised way — often available at market stalls alongside charms (dried monkey, peacock feathers, live lizards etc.) or spells (not recommended). We're only just beginning to tap the knowledge of plants and herbs known to traditional healers in developing countries. However, whilst some can speak from their own experience of dramatic results using these methods, most of us probably wouldn't want to risk an experiment if we had something seriously wrong. There's also the problem of communication — athlete's foot might be easy enough to explain, but what about thrush? You might want to try herbal remedies if you're suffering from travellers' diarrhoea, muscular aches and pains or some other minor ailments.

Don't use herbal medicine if you're pregnant — some herbs act as very powerful drugs — nor should you use them to cure eye problems.

Self medication

In some countries it is possible to buy almost any drugs you might want over the counter without a prescription. This is particularly true in developing countries. This means if you know the generic name of the drug you want you may be able to get hold of it quite easily (brand names often vary). However, knowing which sorts of drugs treat which sorts of diseases is not the same thing as being able to diagnose a complaint accurately. For this reason if there is a possibility that you may be seriously ill we have recommended that you seek expert advice rather than rely on your own judgement.

In the case of more minor complaints before buying any drugs or medicines, check the expiry dates carefully. Many drugs deteriorate in strong sunlight. Bear this in mind when choosing which chemist to buy from. If you can, choose stock which has been kept refrigerated.

A few developing countries run an essential drugs list. That is to say the Government restricts the number of drugs which can be imported for sale. It is one way of preventing a country from spending enormous amounts of hard currency reserves on expensive drugs for which there are cheaper alternatives. Despite a lack of choice you should still be able to find what you really need.

If you get ill while you are travelling in remote areas and go down with something you can clearly identify as a chest infection, cystitis, earache or a cut beginning to turn septic it is appropriate to begin taking a course of antibiotics rather than waiting for treatment until you return to the big city. You must, however, take the full course once you've started. That means carrying on for five whole days. No matter if you feel better sooner, don't stop taking the drugs. That's the way antibiotic resistant strains of infection get going. Remember you can't take any old antibiotic for any ailment. Cotrimoxazole (Septrin) and clavulanate-amoxycillin (Augmentin), which we recommend you take with you (see page 167), are both broad spectrum antibiotics which will clear up the sorts of infection listed above.

One final point, if you've been prescribed an injection for any reason in a developing country where you're not sure of the standard of the medical facilities, make sure you buy your own needle, and if in doubt, sterilise it yourself. HIV and Hepatitis B are just two of the nasty diseases you risk picking up from contaminated needles. Depending on where you are travelling to, it may make more sense to take disposable needles and syringes with you. These are available as part of emergency medical travel kits. See below.

MEDICAL KIT

Just a few items can be used to deal with quite a range of complaints if you choose carefully. There's probably not much point in carrying an extensive list of supplies with you anyway unless you're heading into really remote areas for long periods of time and have the knowledge to use a wide variety of drugs. The items recommended below are those which you might have most cause to use. Add to them any medication you need for complaints you're particularly prone to or which you take regularly.

Pack your medical supplies into a plastic container with a close-fitting lid (a sandwich box, for instance). This keeps everything together and also provides additional protection against spillage. Label the medicines clearly, saying what they are and with directions for their use. Cover the labels with sellotape or sticky plastic to ensure they don't come adrift from the bottle and that the directions remain legible. If you're travelling with children you will need to have the reduced doses written down as well. Dressings, sachets or anything in powdered form should be placed inside a sealed plastic bag.

Painkillers

Take either aspirin or paracetamol. They can be used for headaches and period pains. Aspirin brings a temperature down. Soluble aspirin can be sucked to ease a sore throat.

Anti-diarrhoea

If you're going to the tropics, take an oral rehydration powder such as Dioralyte. Imodium will temporarily control the symptoms of diarrhoea.

Anti-fungal

Clotrimazole can be used as a cream to deal with athlete's foot and other fungal infections including mild thrush. Apply three times daily for 10–14 days.

Antiseptic

Antiseptic solutions are more useful than creams. There are several to choose from: Cetrimide can be bought in sachet form (Savlon concentrate); Mercurochrome Aq. 5% will dry out a cut and help prevent infection. Apply daily. Iodine can also be used.

Antibiotics

These are not a cure-all. Specific antibiotics are needed to treat specific complaints which is why under ideal conditions you should seek a doctor's advice before taking them. Take a broad spectrum antibiotic such as cotrimoxazole (Septrin, Bactrim) or amoxycillin, for use as indicated above (see page 165).

Antihistamines

Take Piriton for widespread and itchy bites or severe prickly heat.

Anti-malaria drugs

You must take these if you're going to a malarial area.

Dressings

Take some ordinary plasters for small cuts and blisters, Steristrips or butterfly dressings to close larger cuts and a selection of gauze dressings.

Make sure you've packed insect repellants and water sterilisers.

The following are further suggestions you might want to consider:
- eye drops or eye ointment — to cure minor eye infections,

- lactulose — for constipation,

- calamine lotion — for sunburn and insect bites,

- surgical spirit — to harden feet,

- Pripsen (piperazine) — to clear round and threadworm infections,

- sunscreen,

- disposable needles.

Emergency medical travel kits, including disposable needles and syringes, are now available from specialist travel centres and chemists. These would be well worth considering if you are going to an area where medical facilities may be poor. The items are sealed and ready for use by medical personnel.

When packing your medical kit remember to include any necessary contraception, and if you wear glasses, take a spare pair or at least a lens prescription.

If you're going to be out of easy reach of a doctor in an area where you risk infection with amoebic dysentery or giardiasis it's worth taking extra medication with you. You will need ONE course of metronidazole (see page 149).

7
Women Only

COMPLAINTS

Thrush and cystitis are familiar problems which can make travelling uncomfortable. They're also more likely to flare up in a hot and humid climate when it may be hard to keep as clean, and when your diet may be changeable. There are sensible precautions you can take to try and avoid them.

Thrush

Vaginal thrush can be a real nuisance. It produces a thick white discharge which looks rather like cottage cheese and makes the vulva extremely itchy. If you've had it before you'll know all the danger signs but it's worth explaining exactly what is happening and suggesting some simple self-help measures which can reduce the likelihood of it occurring or banish it once it has started. Basically the yeasts which cause it are always present on the skin and in the bowel. During a thrush infection they are temporarily flourishing. There can be a variety of reasons for this. For some women being on the pill may produce the right environment for the yeasts to grow in; or antibiotics, by killing off other organisms in the body, can create the space for them to thrive in; warmth and moisture help, so wearing nylon underwear or tight trousers, especially in hot weather, will encourage them; and they love sugar so a sudden increase in the amount of sugar intake in your diet may trigger them off. Whatever the reason the end result will be an alteration in the naturally acid environment of the vagina which otherwise keeps thrush at bay.

To minimise the risks of getting thrush it is sensible to wear cotton underwear and loosely fitting trousers or a skirt. Washing and wiping between your legs front to back will stop yeasts from the bowel moving into the vulva. Once you have got thrush, stop washing with soap which only seems to make matters worse. Instead use plain water or if you can get it, clean the vulva with olive oil on cotton wool.

Nystatin pessaries should clear the infection (there's now a one dose version available), or you could paint the vagina, cervix and vulva with gentian violet. They're both rather messy methods, so wear a sanitary pad during treatment. In the absence of the above use clotrimazole (Canesten) which you should have in your medical kit (see page 167). You can smear some on a tampon and then insert it, as well as using it on the vulva.

There are other ways of dealing with thrush besides knocking out the yeasts. The following methods all rely on re-establishing the natural balance of the vagina, though they work best if you can start them at the very first sign of trouble. Begin by cutting down on the amount of carbohydrates in your diet, drinking less alcohol and eating more plain yoghurt. The bacteria plain yoghurt contains will fight back against the yeasts. You can also use yoghurt externally to soothe the itching, whilst a tampon dipped in yoghurt will help the vagina.

Vinegar is another good means of restoring the balance to your system. Have a bath with enough vinegar in it to make it smell. In the absence of a bath sitting in a makeshift bidet would do, put in one tablespoon of vinegar to a quart of water, or use a tampon soaked in a solution of water and vinegar. You can use a solution of bicarbonate of soda in the same way — it works by making the vagina even more alkaline, rather than acid. Some people prefer bathing with salt water. I have found that vaginal acid jelly (Aci-jel) is the best means of curing a really bad attack. If you're liable to thrush and have a favourite remedy, take it with you.

Cystitis

Like thrush, cystitis can make travelling very uncomfortable. Where thrush affects the vagina, cystitis affects the urethra, bladder, and, if it goes unchecked, the kidneys. The most common symptoms are a burning sensation when peeing; a feeling that you have to go to the loo all the time — even though when you get there there's not much urine; pain in the lower abdomen and strongly coloured urine.

Cystitis is most commonly started by germs found in the bowel moving into the urinary system. These germs are probably a group of bacteria known as E. coli which in the right place — the bowel — work to aid the digestion. In the wrong place — the urethra — they can start an infection. The yeasts which cause thrush, if they get into the urethra, can also do damage. The best form of protection, therefore, is to try and keep such germs out. There are various ways of doing this. Clean yourself carefully and often between the legs, always wiping in the direction front to back. Use plain water rather than soap when washing. Take special care to wash before having sex and to empty your bladder afterwards, as sexual activity may increase the risk of infection.

Drink plenty of fluids: water, fruit juices or herbal teas. By making you go to the loo often it will keep your urinary system well flushed and give any lurking germs less chance to get going. It will also combat one of the effects of a hot climate: if you lose most of your fluid intake through sweat your urine becomes more concentrated and an ideal breeding ground for germs.

Ascorbic acid tablets (vitamin C) taken regularly will acidify your urine and keep germs at bay. If you're susceptible to cystitis take them to minimise your chances of getting an infection.

If you do get cystitis then your best hope of curing yourself is to do everything you can in the first three or four hours. That means drinking a pint of water to start with, then drinking half a pint of any bland, weak liquid every twenty minutes. Weak tea is a good idea as it'll encourage you to go to the loo. Take a teaspoon of bicarbonate of soda in water as soon as possible and repeat this once an hour. Every time you pee, no matter how little, rinse between your legs with plain water. If you can improvise a hot water bottle, use it between your legs or against your back to reduce any pain. Keep warm.

This treatment may banish cystitis altogether. If it doesn't work see if you can find a mixture of potassium citrate (known as Mist. Pot. Cit. in the U.K.) or look for sodium citrate. The latter can be bought in sachet form under the trade name Cymalon. Both of these work by acidifying the urine. Otherwise you will need a course of antibiotics to stop cystitis developing into a kidney infection. Cotrimoxazole is suitable. You should take two tablets twice daily at twelve hour intervals for five days.

Vaginal discharge

It is possible for an infection in the vagina to spread up to the fallopian tubes and the ovaries. If it develops into a pelvic inflammatory disease the resulting scarring of the tubes can lead to infertility. Any abnormal vaginal discharge therefore deserves investigation. Particular signs to look for are if the discharge is yellow and frothy, smells unpleasant and is accompanied by pain when you pee, or if the discharge looks like creamy pus. If the infection reaches the tubes additional symptoms may include pain in the lower abdomen and possibly fever.

Sexually transmitted diseases

In Colombia there's a myth circulating that you can catch VD by sitting on a seat whilst it's still warm from somebody else's bottom. Consequently the buses are sprinkled with people wedging themselves up against the seat backs waiting for their seat to cool down before they sit on it. The precaution is completely unnecessary.

However, Sexually Transmitted Diseases (STDs) are on the increase world-wide and the following points are worth bearing in mind.

- The only guarantee of avoiding an STD is to avoid sexual contact.

- Sexual contact with those who have had a lot of other partners is more risky than sexual contact with those who've had very few.

- The more often you have sexual contact with someone who's infected the more likely you are to acquire the infection.

- Unless you're sleeping with a stable male partner ask the man to use the sheath. If he does the risks of your becoming infected are considerably reduced.

- If *you* use the cap and a spermicide you'll be safer.

- If there's any likelihood that you may have contracted an STD you must get a medical examination. Some STDs can lead to pelvic inflammatory disease. Signs to watch for are any abnormal vaginal discharge, soreness, small ulcers or warty growths.

HIV and AIDS   The spread of HIV and Aids by travellers and tourists is now of serious concern, and the Department of Health and Health Education Authority produce a useful leaflet aimed at travellers, and available via your GP.

HIV can be passed on: through unprotected sex with an infected person; by sharing needles and other equipment with an infected person; through infected medical and dental instruments, and by a blood transfusion with HIV infected blood.

Around the world, the commonest way that HIV is transmitted is through sex between heterosexual women and men. Women travellers who have sex with a man who is not their usual partner, should ALWAYS insist that he uses a condom. And you should consider stocking up with a reputable make from home. Condoms do not have an unlimited shelf life, and may have deteriorated if stored for a very long time in hot climates.

As well as transmission via unprotected sex, HIV can be passed on through poor sterilisation of medical equipment, or via blood products.

Some countries can not reach the same standards of healthcare we take for granted in the West, and needles used in medical treatments or dentistry may not be sterilised. Again, if you want to be sure, you should take supplies with you. (And not just for emergencies; I once had a routine blood sample taken in Afghanistan — pre AIDS, I am glad to report — to diagnose flu.) Kits containing disposable needles and syringes can be bought from chemists, travel suppliers, or sometimes from your GP.

If at all possible, avoid having a blood transfusion unless the blood has been screened. If it's an emergency and you have time, take advice from the local British consulate or embassy.

Other things to avoid are: tattoos, acupuncture or having your ears etc. pierced (unless you are SURE that the needle is sterile), sharing needles or syringes and unnecessary injections.

DO have a dental check up BEFORE you go.

HIV cannot be spread through mosquito or other insect bites, through kissing, dirty crockery, swimming pools or toilet seats.

CONTRACEPTION

The various forms of contraception are widely available but take your own supplies. You may not be able to find as reliable a source locally or get exactly what you want, and making yourself understood on the subject can be embarrassing.

However, if your luggage gets stolen and with it all your pills or you have a problem with the method you are using then local hospitals, doctors or family planning agencies will be able to help. The International Planned Parenthood Federation keeps an up-to-date address list of family planning agencies, available free on request (see page 278). Given the interest in family planning in many developing countries, such agencies can be found even in remoter parts of the globe. The I.P.P.F. also issue a worldwide country-by-country guide to hormonal contraception, last revised in 1992, listing the various types of Pill available in different places, their trade names and their composition. Called *The I.P.P.F. Directory of Hormonal Contraceptives*, it currently costs £7.

The sheath, the diaphragm and spermicides

If you're using these methods of contraception you may need to know how a tropical climate will affect them. Condoms and diaphragms may both deteriorate quickly under these conditions becoming thin and sticky, so check them carefully before use. Keep them as cool as possible in a closed container. Spermicides are also affected by the heat and direct sunlight. Don't take solid spermicides such as pessaries or foaming tablets which work by being dissolved. They're particularly vulnerable and may melt in the heat. Jellies and creams do better but, like the cap and sheaths, under ideal circumstances in a hot climate they should be kept refrigerated or at least in air-conditioning, both of which conditions the long-distance back-packer will have little chance of providing. Keep them cool if you can.

It is worth adding here that if the heat is affecting the supplies you're carrying with you it will do the same to the products themselves in chemists' shops. Don't buy from chemists who keep their wares in the full rays of the sun and check expiry dates carefully.

If you do need to replace your diaphragm whilst abroad it is important to go to a reliable doctor as it needs to be fitted with care if it is to work properly. Try a family planning agency or see if you can get a recommendation from the British Consul or the British Council. The British expatriate scene can be a useful source of local knowledge.

The Pill

Because of the sorts of difficulties outlined above, many women prefer to use the Pill when travelling abroad.

> 'I took a cap with me and the rubber became thin and sticky in a short space of time. I spent ages finding a replacement which was in equally poor condition. It's better to take a supply of Pills.'
>
> *Pakistan*

Take ample supplies — you can't depend on finding your particular brand abroad — but remember it may still be worth having another form of contraception to fall back on.

If you're interested, John Guillebaud in the appendix to his book *The Pill* gives a world directory of Pill names, organised according to composition so you can check what other brands match your own.

When travelling you must continue to take the Pill regularly without leaving more than 24 hours between doses. If you are crossing time zones and consequently altering your sleeping habits bring the time at which you take the Pill *forward* so that any gap between doses is less than 24 hours, never put it back.

The progestogen-only Pill has to be taken at the same time of day to work properly. This makes travel across time zones potentially difficult. One way of dealing with this is to keep a watch or alarm clock running on home time, and to continue taking the Pill at what would be your normal hour. Only adjust the time at which you take the Pill once you are settled in a new time zone. Bring the hour at which you take the Pill *forward*.

Before you go, sit down and actually read the manufacturers' notes that are sent out with the Pill. They give some useful advice which you may need to know if you're out of reach of a doctor and become ill or have to use other drugs.

Vomiting, diarrhoea and the Pill   If you've got a stomach upset and are vomiting or have diarrhoea, even if it's only for one day, the Pill probably won't be absorbed as efficiently as normally. Depending on where you are in your cycle you could be at risk of getting pregnant. Where you are in your cycle matters because of the way the Pill works. The extra hormone intake in the Pill is designed to keep the hormonal balance of the body at a point where ovulation won't take place. During the seven days whilst you're not taking the Pill the hormonal level will begin to fall (this is why bleeding occurs) and then build up again once you've restarted. When you take the Pill regularly this slight reduction in the hormone level during your period isn't significant — you'll still be protected from ovulating — but in the days immediately before and after the end of your period when the hormonal level is at its lowest the effect of missing a Pill or not fully absorbing it will matter most.

If you have a stomach upset, observe the following guidelines: you don't have to worry if you vomit three or more hours after taking the Pill, or have diarrhoea 12 or more hours after taking it. In the case of diarrhoea, if it sets in less than 12 hours after taking the Pill, consider yourself unprotected. Keep taking the Pill regularly but use extra contraceptive measures for 14 days after you are better. In the case of vomiting, if you're on the combined Pill (containing both oestrogen and progestogen) and are sick less than three hours after taking the Pill see if you can manage to take and keep down another Pill within the next 12 hours. If so you'll still be safe. Go back to taking your Pills at the normal time. If you carry on being sick, consider yourself unprotected. Resume taking your Pills as soon as you can but use extra contraceptive measures for 14 days after you're better.

The progestogen-only Pill differs in that the time lag between when you should have taken the Pill and managing to keep one down is shorter — only three hours can elapse if you're to be properly protected.

Antibiotics and the Pill   It is now known that certain antibiotics interact with the combined Pill and reduce its effectiveness. Bear this in mind when considering which antibiotic to take. Antibiotics do not interfere with the action of the progestogen-only Pill.

Conversely, some other drugs — cotrimoxazole and metronidazole — may enhance the Pill's effect. The same is true of vitamin C, though the latter increases the absorption of oestrogen to such an extent that if you take more than 300mg daily you will end up turning a low dose oestrogen Pill into a high dose one.

Pill supplies   The Pill can be bought over the counter in many countries abroad but they may well be brands you are unfamiliar with and their composition may also be different. If you do lose all your Pills or run out of supplies before you go home and have to buy locally you should be able to check how much oestrogen any brand contains by seeing how much ethinyloestradiol or mestranol is listed. (Those are the chemical names for oestrogen.) In this country the most common amount prescribed is 30/35 micrograms per tablet (that's 0.03/0.035 milligrams), though some women may still be taking 50 micograms (0.05 milligrams). It is more difficult to work out the progestogen content as it is marketed under many different names and the amount present in different brands varies considerably. The picture is still further complicated as some Pills also contain dextronorgestrel, a substance which has no contraceptive effect.

You can simplify the process of getting what you want if you remember to keep an empty packet, or the notes which come with the Pill to show to a pharmacist. They both include details of the composition.

If you're on a low dose Pill yourself look for the lowest replacement you can find. In many developing countries only higher dose Pills are available. Short-term use of higher dose Pills is unlikely to be damaging to long-term health but may provoke unpleasant side effects such as nausea and breast tenderness.

There is no need to take extra precautions if you switch from a low to a higher dose Pill. If you move from a higher to a lower dose Pill either begin the new brand without taking a seven-day break for your period, or use additional contraceptive measures for the first 14 days.

Hepatitis   One final point: if you're on the Pill and get Hepatitis, stop taking it. Hepatitis is an infection of the liver and it is the liver which is responsible for directing the Pill into your bloodstream. Taking the Pill will have the same effect as eating fats or drinking alcohol — it provides extra work for the liver at a time when it can't cope. You will need to consult a doctor to check that your liver is functioning properly again before you start retaking the Pill.

The IUD

The coil can be a convenient form of contraception to use when travelling, however not all women take to them. If problems of expulsion, pain or severe bleeding are going to occur they are most likely to happen in the first month after the coil has been fitted. If you're going to change to the coil do so well before your trip.

One drawback to the coil is that if you do get a vaginal infection it may turn more easily into a pelvic infection. The best way of protecting yourself is to prevent the vaginal infection by being scrupulous about personal hygiene.

The morning after pill

In emergencies the following method of post-coital contraception can be used. Within 72 hours of having had unprotected sex take two pills containing 250 mg of levonorgestrel and 50 mg of ethinyloestradiol. (In the U.K. this would mean taking either two Eugynon 50 Pills or two Ovran pills and 12 hours later take another two pills.) You should then have your next period within three weeks. Unfortunately this is not a foolproof method of preventing pregnancy and should NOT be used as a normal method of contraception as the high hormone doses will disrupt your body cycles.

MENSTRUATION

Tampons and sanitary towels

It's easiest to take your own supplies of tampons or sanitary towels with you — the former take up very little space. Outside Europe and the U.S.A. tampons may be difficult to find even in large cities and will probably be expensive, whilst some locally-produced brands may be of poor quality and therefore not very absorbent.

Sanitary towels are more widely available but even so, in many developing countries only shops in large towns may stock them and again quality may be poor. In emergencies use an old T-shirt or some similarly absorbent material torn into strips.

A re-usable sponge is not to be recommended for routine use.

Depending on where and how you are travelling you can't rely on water being available to wash the sponge or yourself with, and actually keeping it clean in between periods could be difficult.

If you're travelling in areas where sanitation is poor and particularly in rural areas where the toilet may be the open field, disposing of used tampons and sanitary towels can be a problem. If there is no obvious place to leave them in the toilet, take an empty bag with you and then carry them away to a rubbish bin. Putting them down the hole may simply block up the local sewage system. If you're out in the wilds, use a pocket knife to turf a small area and then bury the evidence, if you can.

As far as cleanliness goes, the most important point to remember is that the germs which are most likely to infect the vagina live in your own bowel. Take good care to avoid transferring them across, whilst changing tampons or towels.

Irregular menstruation

Irregular menstruation is one of the most common problems facing the woman traveller.

> 'A lot of women travellers I met, and myself included, suffered from irregular periods while travelling — it seemed common to stop having periods but mine came more often: every two weeks — so I decided to go on the Pill, to regulate and reduce the flow.'
>
> *Peru*

If your periods become much less frequent or even stop altogether of their own accord, it can be very alarming, especially if you're not expecting this.

> 'When my periods stopped I began to worry. I knew I couldn't be pregnant, but couldn't think of any other explanation for what was happening. Luckily I bumped into two women nurses returning home overland who had had the same experience.

They said it was a common occurrence: it's just our bodies' way
of recognising that now would be the wrong time to get pregnant.'

India

If this happens to you it may take your body some time to readjust even
after you are back home.

Infrequent periods are not a cause for concern, and indeed if your
periods have stopped not only are you saved the bother of changing
tampons but you'll also be better protected against pelvic and vaginal
infections. The cervical mucus which helps make the vagina an acid
and inhospitable environment for germs as well as sperm, normally
thins during ovulation. If you have no periods you are not ovulating
so the cervical mucus will remain thick and hostile.

On the other hand several of the contributors to this book com-
plained that their periods were more, not less, troublesome: they were
heavier, came more often or lasted longer. This is a rather more
annoying response to the stresses of travelling. If it happens to you,
you might want to consider going on the Pill. Otherwise make sure you
keep to a balanced diet, and eat plenty of foods containing iron. Iron
can be found in green leafy vegetables, dried pulses, kidney, liver and
dried apricots and figs. If you have heavier periods remember to use
extra towels before setting out on a long bus journey where changing
can be difficult.

It is worth pointing out that there are a few medical conditions
(Pelvic Inflammatory Disease, uterinal fibroids and even, very rarely,
cervical cancer) which can also cause abnormally heavy and long
bleeding.

From the point of view of cervical cancer it might be worth setting
your mind at rest before you travel by telling your doctor you're about
to go away and asking for a smear test. The test will detect cervical
cancer at a pre-symptomatic stage *before* the cancer has developed and
when it is easy to treat. Otherwise if the bleeding is heavy or painful
enough to be of concern see if you can find a reliable doctor to examine
your cervix and womb. Anything requiring attention should be
straightforward to diagnose.

Suppressing monthy periods

It is possible to avoid having periods whilst you're travelling by taking the Pill continuously. Ask your doctor for advice on which sort you can most safely use like this.

PREGNANCY

Very few women deliberately time their travels to coincide with pregnancy but what do you do if you find that you're pregnant when you're already travelling? Return home? Carry on? And what if you have no alternative but to remain on the move, abroad, during the pregnancy? It is possible to travel safely during this time, but think carefully before you make the decision. If you've travelled before, know what the problems may be and feel confident that you can cope, then go ahead. It may be more difficult to travel successfully if it is a new experience. Just being pregnant may be strange and wonderful enough without being abroad too!

Timing

If you can choose your time then go between the 16th and 30th week. At this stage of the pregnancy you won't be troubled by sickness, you won't be uncomfortably large and you will feel most energetic. It is also the safest time: risk of miscarriage diminishes after the 14th week whilst there's little likelihood of premature labour.

On the move

Once you're on the move, don't push yourself too hard. Listen to your body and let your feelings be your guide. Remember you may tire more easily especially in the first three and last two months of pregnancy. Very long journeys which leave you exhausted won't do you any good, so take things easy. Arrange your schedule to suit how you feel. If you need a nap in the afternoon, get to a hotel by lunchtime so that you can collapse quietly. When choosing what clothes to take with you remember that you will increase in size from 20 weeks on. Think ahead when packing. Choose loose fitting clothes and comfortable roomy shoes.

On long journeys you may find that your feet and ankles swell up. It's a common feature of pregnancy which can be brought on by the heat, or simply by the increased pressure exerted on the veins in your legs by your enlarging womb. If you're travelling by plane or on a train you can help control the symptoms by walking up and down the passageways every so often; if you're on a bus then get out and stroll about when the bus stops. If you can't do this easily then simply stretching your legs out whilst you're sitting down, rotating your feet from side to side and flexing your leg muscles is a good idea.

One of the side effects of pregnancy, particularly in the early and late stages, is that you will want to pee more often. This can make travelling uncomfortable if it isn't easy to get to the loo. Bear this in mind when deciding how to travel. Booking first class on the trains could be worth it if it means being able to find a loo whose doors will shut and which isn't being used as an extra compartment in the crowded third class.

Remember that you may well need more support and reassurance. Explain this to your companions before you start out rather than once things get tough. Take a book on pregnancy with you. It can help explain what is happening to your body and stop you worrying unnecessarily.

Airlines

When you book your ticket you should tell the airline that you're pregnant. They may require a doctor's certificate saying you are fit to fly if you're travelling after the 28th week of pregnancy and will not accept you on international journeys after the end of the 35th week. Your ability to get travel insurance to cover you for air flight in the later

stages of pregnancy will depend on the airline knowing your circumstances and agreeing to take you.

Drink plenty of water or fruit juices during the flight to stop
yourself getting dehydrated.

Diet

As at home, you need a well-balanced diet with plenty of variety. Read
up on nutrition before you go so that you've some idea what the food
you are eating contains. It can be a useful and often surprising exercise.
You may already know that liver and spinach contain a lot of iron, but
did you know that lentils, dried apricots and figs, and cocoa are also
iron-rich?

In this country pregnant women are no longer routinely prescribed
iron after the 14th week, but you may still want to take supplies away
with you to top up your diet. Don't treat the pills as a substitute for
eating well, though. You'll still do best if you get what you need from
your food.

If you are not sure of finding milk or milk products abroad then take
calcium tablets along too. However, milk isn't the only source of
calcium available. You can find it in fish, especially if, like sardines,
they are small enough to be eaten whole, bones and all. Dried figs are
a good source too. It is also worth noting that, if there is a choice,
yoghurt is safer than milk in hot countries because bacteria is destroyed by the lactic acid in yoghurt.

In some parts of the world where iodine is short in local foodstuffs,
iodized salt is sold to make up the deficiency. Use it instead of ordinary
salt.

It is important to take folic acid tablets if you are using an anti-
malarial drug which contains pyrimethamine or proguanil, as the
latter will deplete the supplies of folic acid in your body and without
it you could become anaemic.

Drink as much and as often as you feel like it. It will help stop you
getting constipated — always a problem in pregnancy and more so if
you're in a hot climate. If you do get constipated try improving your
diet by eating more roughage, especially fresh fruit and vegetables,
before resorting to a laxative.

Take plenty of snack foods with you when you're travelling. A little food eaten often will stop you feeling so nauseous.

Avoid alcohol except in small quantities.

Vaccines and medication in pregnancy

Any drug which can have a harmful effect on the developing foetus will do most damage during the first 14 weeks whilst the foetus' limbs and organs are forming. Don't take any unnecessary drugs during this time.

Otherwise when taking any form of medication during pregnancy it's always a matter of balancing the risks of any drugs you might use against the risks of the particular disease. Bearing this in mind the following information provides a rough outline of the main do's and don'ts.

Immunisation   There are two sorts of vaccines available: killed, such as cholera and typhoid; or live, such as yellow fever and polio, when the latter is taken orally. Live vaccinations are best avoided during pregnancy. You can still be vaccinated against polio as it can be administered killed (Salk vaccine). Yellow fever vaccination will only be given in pregnancy if there's a high risk of your catching the disease. If this isn't your case but you are going to a country which requires a certificate of vaccination against yellow fever as a condition of entry, take a letter from your doctor, endorsed with a health authority or health board stamp, saying that inoculation is contraindicated. It is normally accepted instead.

It is perfectly safe to have a tetanus injection during pregnancy. The immunity will be passed on to the baby once it's born.

Malaria   If you are travelling in a part of the world where there's a risk of getting malaria you must take adequate precautions: the disease is highly dangerous to the foetus as well as yourself. This will mean using a drug which will protect you (a prophylactic). Of those drugs which are routinely prescribed as malaria prophylactics, chloroquine and proguanil can be used safely.

If you are going to an area where there is resistance to these drugs, Maloprim can be substituted, though if possible it should be avoided during the last two weeks of pregnancy and the first six of breast-feeding. Any risk from using Maloprim is outweighed by the risk of contracting malaria. If you're using proguanil or Maloprim remember to take folic acid tablets (see page 184).

Fansidar, which used to be prescribed as a prophylactic, is now only recommended for treating malaria after the disease has been caught. This is partly because of its side-effects. In any case it should not be used during the first three months or from the 28th week onwards until six weeks after birth. It can induce jaundice in a new born baby.

Other drugs A variety of drugs which might otherwise be recommended should not be used if you're pregnant.

Some antibiotics may not be safe. Tetracycline, an antibiotic which is prescribed for cases of cholera, if taken after the third month of pregnancy, can lead to the discolouration of the baby's first teeth. The antibiotic Streptomycin, administered in the same period, might result in damage to the nerves in the baby's ear. In general it's best to avoid the group of antibiotics known as sulphonomides in the last three months of pregnancy. This group includes cotrimoxazole (Septrin).

If you need a treatment for threadworms choose a preparation which doesn't contain either pyrantel pamoate or mebendazole.

If you haven't managed to cure constipation by the measures suggested in the diet section, stick to mild laxatives containing senna. Don't use phenolphthalein.

Paracetomol can be safely used in pregnancy. Aspirin should be avoided in the final weeks.

Using health care services

It is perfectly possible to maintain antenatal care whilst abroad. Take your antenatal card with you and get your weight, urine and blood pressure checked at monthly intervals. The best place to get these tests done is at a large hospital. Choose a mission or a teaching hospital if possible.

'In each main town we were in at monthly intervals we found the largest hospital, pointed at my obvious stomach and asked if we could use their facilities to test my blood pressure, weight and urine. We met with total cooperation in Delhi, Bangkok, Kuala Lumpur and Jakarta and so I continued full antenatal care.'

South-East Asia

Danger sign — swelling, blurred vision and headache

Ankles, feet and even hands, may all swell slightly both during pregnancy and while travelling. This is not a cause for alarm and can be partly dealt with by rest. However, if the swelling is severe and your face also begins to puff up, especially round the eyes, you should get to a hospital and ask them to test for protein in your urine. You could be suffering from eclamptic toxaemia. You will need to rest properly until you are better. If the condition goes unchecked it will lead to headaches, disturbed vision (either blurred, or troubled by flashing lights) and, in the last stages, fits. Eclamptic toxaemia is potentially fatal for you and the foetus. This is why it's particularly important that you continue to have a regular check-up including a urine test, whilst you're travelling.

Danger sign — bleeding

Don't ignore any sign of bleeding during pregnancy and where possible call a doctor. Stay where you are and rest until three days after any discharge has ceased. You may need medical advice before travelling on.

If the bleeding is slight (less than a normal period) you should go to bed and rest there.

If the bleeding is accompanied by pain in the lower abdomen (as if you'd got a period), then this is the sign of a miscarriage. Stay in bed until the bleeding stops and continue to rest there for three more days. Take things easy when you do get up.

However if at any stage the bleeding is heavy you must seek medical help urgently. This could be the sign of an incomplete abortion. Without an operation to remove any membranes remaining in the uterus, the resulting blood-loss and infection could be life-threatening.

8
Travelling 'Green'

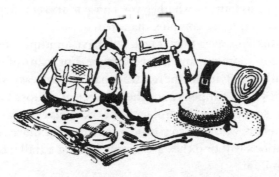

WHAT DOES GREEN TOURISM MEAN?

'Green' tourism is much talked about these days and is sometimes also described as 'alternative tourism', 'responsible tourism' or 'real holidaying'. But what exactly do these terms mean outside a brochure? What does 'green travel' mean for us, and for those whom we travel amongst ?

'Green' or 'responsible tourism' is above all about travelling on terms which RESPECT both the people and the physical environment through which we are moving.

Most of us would agree with this as an aim, especially if we think of the concrete jungles, British bars, German clubs, and all the other horrors of the Costas, along what was once an undeveloped coastline in Europe. What is much more difficult for some travellers to accept is that the growing number of beach cafés, beach bars, road side stalls and guest houses on popular travellers' beaches (Phuket, Koh Samui, Goa, Kuta etc) around the world are part and parcel of the same problem. Today some popular traveller destinations are in fact little more than Western ghettos, enshrining cherished Western leisure patterns, and reflecting *our* life styles, *our* fashions, *our* tastes, *our* music, *our* scene.

The problem is that we still cling to an old idea that is becoming increasingly difficult to justify — the idea that somehow whilst *tourists* can do no right, *independent travellers* can do no wrong.

It is easy to fall into the trap of thinking that it's how we make our travelling *arrangements* that makes all the difference. Yet what makes a good, 'green' traveller is not decided by whether or not you booked to go on a group tour, or whether you chose to travel independently; the issues are far more complex than that.

All visitors, however they travel, will have an impact on the local economy, environment, and indeed culture. For many of us, coming to terms with what is in fact the real truth has not been easy. But anyone who watches what happens once the number of visitors builds up in a particular spot can see the problems for themselves only too clearly. Those travellers who seek to escape by heading for more remote and exotic locations will find they are simply blazing a trail which others will soon follow.

Nepal

Nepal, for instance, is a country which provides a good example of some of the problems, and some of the potential solutions. Opened up to tourism by the original independent travellers ('60s hippies!), Nepal today receives tens of thousands of visitors who go trekking amid its dramatic scenery. These include *tourists* on inclusive tours (a posh phrase for a package tour) and *travellers* who prefer to make their own arrangements independently. BOTH groups are causing havoc with the natural environment as trees are cut down to build lodges for visitors, to provide firewood for heating and cooking, and for heating water for trekkers to wash in. BOTH tourists and travellers contribute to the problem of sanitation and litter (a growing trail of loo paper, discarded shampoo sachets etc) and BOTH are blamed for eroding Nepali culture. Yet there is some evidence that it is in fact easier to educate those in tour groups, once you can reach the tour operators. Finding ways of getting the message across about cultural and environmental issues to independent travellers has not proved so easy.

In the most popular trekking area of Annapurna, a local (non government) community association finally decided that something must be done to help visitors become better informed. The Annapurna Conservation Area Project (ACAP) has drawn up a Code of Conduct which sets out the issues and advises trekkers about how to respond. Simple, practical advice is given to help reduce deforestation and pollution, and guidelines are given about some of the aspects of culture clash that most bother local people. (For example visitors are asked not to give sweets or money to local children, and to respect local ideas about dress and behaviour).

Working with the organisation Tourism Concern in Britain, the ACAP Code has been redrafted as the Himalayan Tourist Code (see page 271), and is distributed to visitors through tour operators and travel agents in the UK. In order to get the same information and advice across to independent travellers, guide book writers were invited to include the main points of the Code in their guide books to the area, (see the Lonely Planet and Rough Guide series), and copies were made available to Air Nepal for visitors flying in from India.

In Nepal, being a good 'green' traveller means being prepared to recognise that there are problems of deforestation. Because of this, travellers need to use less hot water, be prepared to put on another jumper instead of lighting a fire, and understand that it makes sense to order food in groups, so that precious fuel may not be wasted on a meal for just one or two. It means understanding that because there is no sewage system, human wastes need to be buried, and panty liners left at home. It means thinking about the local culture, and being prepared to respond to one or two simple requests about how we might behave and dress.

Being a 'green' traveller is something which is open to everyone, *wherever* they go. You do not have to be visiting Nepal, (neither do you need to be part of the environmental lobby, or a signed up member of a pressure group). As we said at the start of this chapter, what is important is your willingness to travel on terms which respect both people and the physical environment. Fitting in with other cultures and adapting our usual ways of going about things has been a theme running throughout this book, and where possible we have included advice to help you to do so. Below are some guide lines for practical ways of protecting the physical environment.

Practical ways of protecting the environment

Environmental degradation on a large scale — for example, purpose-built hotel complexes, artificially created beaches, golf courses, new roadways, new airports, new concrete timeshare developments and so on — is not usually part of the traveller's scene. However, this doesn't mean that as travellers we don't have a responsibility to the physical environments through which we move.

By following some pretty straightforward do's and don'ts you can avoid the worst of the problems:

At the beach

- Do not collect shells, pieces of coral etc, and do not buy souvenirs made from these and similar items — unless you are sure you are not contributing to environmental problems.

- Take care not to damage fragile environments, especially coral reefs.

In wilderness areas

- Keep to footpaths, especially where there is obvious erosion.

- Do not uproot, damage or pick plants.

- Keep camp sites tidy.

- Carry kerosene if possible, and limit wood fires to the absolute minimum.

- Make sure any fires are put out safely.

- Do not pollute streams and rivers.

- Bury wastes, burn rubbish, and take litter home.

Wildlife

- Make sure your wildlife safari is not disturbing species by disrupting feeding, and breeding patterns. (Loggerhead turtles, whales and other species have suffered in this way.)

- Do not buy souvenirs made from materials such as tortoiseshell, ivory, snakeskin or feathers.

- Observe, but do not disturb, the wildlife you have come to see.

Leisure Pursuits

- Book with companies and organisations that make a point of including environmental pointers for those involved in leisure pursuits. Bungie jumping, white water rafting, trekking, heli-skiing, scuba diving, cruising, climbing and mountain biking can all have an impact on the environment once large numbers of visitors are involved.

- Where environmental advice is given, follow it!

'Take nothing but photos; leave nothing but footsteps; use nothing but time ... Wilderness is there to change you, not you to change it.'

Himalaya guide

FINDING OUT MORE

Many of the other issues surrounding travel and tourism are out of the scope of this book. However, many travellers come back concerned with what they have seen, and also concerned about what impact an ever increasing number of visitors is having on host nations.

There are several ways you can find out more, both before you go and on your return. Katie Wood's *The Green Tourist Guide* (see *Recommended Reading* on page 275) is a useful introduction to the issues, with details of many of the smaller independent tour operators, home stay organisations and those offering alternative holidays.

Those who want a more in-depth approach, and an opportunity to campaign for a better deal, should contact Tourism Concern (see *Useful Addresses* on page 278). Members receive a quarterly newsletter, the opportunity to join (or start!) a local group and to staff a stand at the holiday shows and exhibitions around the country, and to support campaigns.

Finally, all travellers should follow the Traveller's Code given on page 271. It is only by adopting a responsible attitude and respecting the local people, customs and environment that we can preserve places for future generations of travellers.

9
Disorientation

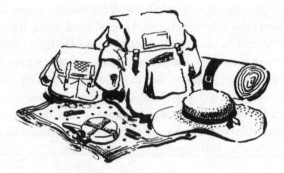

Travellers step off the plane or train looking forward to their trip with varying amounts of excitement, usually mixed with some trepidation. If you've been before, if you have somewhere booked for the first night, or if you have a friend coming to meet you, excitement may win over apprehension. But if it has been a long flight or a tiring overnight coach journey, trepidation may be temporarily winning over optimism.

Some disorientation is an inevitable part of moving into a strange culture. It means we have to rethink what we know, learn to interpret what goes on around us, adapt to new customs. Making this step, adjusting to the differences between 'them and us' can be the most rewarding aspect of the whole trip, leading us to re-evaluate what we know of others as well as what we think about ourselves. This chapter suggests ways in which we can begin the process of positively exploring and enjoying those differences, so we end up making the most of our trip.

CULTURE SHOCK

Of all the stories you will hear abroad, tales of travellers who arrive at their destination and immediately get back on the next plane suffering from 'culture shock' are the most common. Culture shock is presented to the nervous first-timer as a sort of instant disease that strikes you down as you emerge from the airport.

However the classic culture shock syndrome is in fact more likely to affect long term residents working abroad than travellers. Expatriates who may have been inadequately briefed by their companies, who may be in a country more for reasons of salary than because of any real desire to get to know the people and share their lifestyle, and who may be struggling to put the Protestant work ethic into operation in a very different context than at home often do have problems, sometimes developing a dislike of their surroundings and the people with whom they've had to mix.

> **'I remember after coming back to England we stopped at Watford, and tears coming into my eyes and thinking that Motorway Service Stations are what civilisation is all about.'**
> *Ex-patriate talking on Radio 4.*

Travellers, who are not under the pressure of work, and who have chosen their destination because of a real interest in it are far less likely to have severe difficulties in adjusting, but even so you may find you get, on occasion, unaccountably irritable and frustrated by local ways of doing things. You may feel unusually insecure and vulnerable at the start of your trip. You may find yourself worrying overmuch about theft or being 'ripped off' or becoming over obsessive about hygiene. You might be over-anxious about harmless insects like cockroaches, or develop a sudden craving for bacon and egg breakfasts with all the trimmings 'just like home'.

All these are signs of mild culture shock and certainly shouldn't lead you to think you have to get on the next plane home. Once you're aware of what's happening you can take steps to slow down, relax and take more time to explore the differences around you at your own pace.

It seems ridiculous, doesn't it, that the differences are so unnerving?

After all you've gone all that way *because* it is going to be different — that is the reason you're travelling at all. The first time you buy a railway ticket it is so bewildering — what's this queue for? Where do I go now? Is this person a guard? Who do I pay? What have I done wrong? It is not surprising we feel so confused, most of us haven't felt this uncertain about everyday procedures since childhood. Getting a meal, catching a bus, visiting a house — a whole range of skills that back home we take for granted, whole areas of knowledge that are so second nature we didn't even know we had them, are suddenly redundant. Simple, practical, everyday procedures have to be learnt afresh and often in a foreign language in which we may hardly be competent. Suddenly we have to be a lot more observant, take more time working out whatever the local systems are, and be much more prepared to ask people for help. The latter in itself may be enough to unnerve some travellers. It may be a long time since you had to rely on other people for such a simple thing as how to go about ordering a drink for example. You may feel thoroughly foolish at so obviously not knowing what to do, and further confused by what people tell you as they try to help you out.

LANGUAGE

The biggest help in dealing with everyday practical problems and indeed with all aspects of your trip, is to have some knowledge of the local language:

> 'Being able to speak Spanish was the passport to getting out of so many situations, and demanding action when it was needed...The ability of asking for what you want, to exchange compliments with the locals, and share their lives in their language is the greatest joy.'
>
> *South America*

English speakers are luckier than others, we do use the most widely understood language in the world, and you will be able to find someone with at least a smattering of English in all but the most rural areas. However there is the temptation to assume that everyone speaks English, that we can 'get by' without any effort. English speakers are notoriously lazy when it comes to learning foreign languages, unlike Europeans such as the Dutch or the Germans who are often fluent in one and sometimes two other European languages; unlike for example large numbers of Indians who are fluent in two or three languages and may be literate in two or more alphabets. In ex-colonies even today it is usual for the language of the former colonising country to be in common usage alongside the local language or languages, so in many parts of the world to be bilingual or even multi-lingual is considered unremarkable.

The confidence you will get from being able to understand at least a little of what is going on, of being able to ask for things and understand simple transactions makes *any* attempt you make at the local language worthwhile. And if your efforts don't exactly put you in the bilingual category, they'll be appreciated even so.

> **'It really is greatly appreciated if you learn some words. Japanese is not really so difficult. Learn some formal greetings. It puts people at their ease.'**
>
> *Japan*

If learning another language really is beyond you, you can still cope with everyday situations by watching other people and using them as guides to what to do. We're all quick learners and once you've been through a situation you will know what to do for the next time. People are usually happy to help and tolerant of mistakes. If all else fails, laugh at your errors. The time you mistook the gents lav for the exit makes a good tale later on even if you did feel foolish at the time.

DIRT

Most of us in the West have an overdeveloped sense of hygiene fed by the cleaning industry in our respective countries. We are constantly being encouraged to feel uneasy about possible germs, dirt, dust, unclean air etc. by the manufacturers of all sorts of cleaning appliances and products who play on fears of risks to our health.

This super-awareness of dirt is always strongest in strange surroundings. At home you may live quite comfortably with the odd crumb on the carpet, or dust on the book case but how many of us have been to visit a friend and caught ourselves wondering if it wasn't about time they got out the vacuum cleaner?

No wonder therefore on their travels, when they're hyped up to notice *everything* more clearly and have quite justifiable concerns about staying well, that some travellers become obsessive about standards of cleanliness that are different from those back home.

This is particularly true for visitors to those developing countries where mains water is a luxury, where sewage systems may be rudimentary or non-existent, where the climate makes a thin film of dust on everything inevitable, and where, even if they were available, people could not afford spray polishes and air fresheners.

Ironically the people who live in such surroundings are often personally much cleaner than the travellers they meet.

> '**Ethiopians are themselves cleaner in personal habits than we are.**'
>
> *Ethiopia*

> '**Hindus and Moslems are scrupulous about personal hygiene...**'
>
> *Asia*

We put so much emphasis on creating a clean environment that daily or twice daily baths are not really necessary for us, and a temperate climate does not necessitate a twice daily change of clothes. In poorer countries where the environment is less clean, and the climate one where clothes become quickly sticky with sweat, those who have access to clean water wash themselves and their garments *more* often than we might. Local people frequently comment on the grubby clothes of some travel-stained visitors and have as many complaints about us as we have of them.

If you do find yourself getting anxious about dirt what can you do about it?

> 'We bought a bottle of disinfectant and scrubbed out the whole bathroom and loo. The manager thought we were mad.'
>
> *Turkey*

Well, you could clean the place up yourself, but there are other solutions.

Assess whatever is worrying you in terms of the real risk to your health (see Chapter 6). Peeling paint, a dirt floor, a light layer of dust and old fashioned plumbing aren't going to finish you off, even if they are not what you're used to. You don't have to get to like dirt, open sewers, or non-existent sanitary arrangements, but you can learn to be fairly blasé by ignoring as far as possible conditions which are not a direct threat to your health, and by taking evasive action for yourself in situations which are. Remind yourself that people have got along for centuries without lemon-scented washing-up liquid or funny chemicals that you spray on the chrome bits of baths.

If you are paying for your accommodation, complain, but again, after you've assessed the situation. At the cheap end of the market you have every right to complain about a filthy toilet, but if it's dust that is bothering you, your complaint is likely to be met with incomprehension or a shrug.

The more up-market your accommodation, the cleaner and the more expensive it is going to be. It is reasonable that accommodation which is aimed at the international tourist market should also aim at international (i.e. Western) standards.

POVERTY

Coming to terms with poverty is the biggest cultural problem for most travellers and one that impinges next, after the shock of new surroundings.

Not the least of the difficulty is our confusion over what is poverty and who is poor.

Is a family, living in a simply furnished hut, eating a diet we would find monotonous, with no electricity or transport and with only a modicum of spare cash, poor?

Are the schoolchildren, who appear in smart uniforms (but with bare feet), who are carrying schoolbooks but who cluster round asking for pens, money, sweets, poor?

The taxi-drivers who mob tourists like hawks, touting for fares (and upping the prices), are they poor, or merely greedy?

And what about these beggars? There doesn't seem to be much wrong with them, as they pursue travellers down the road pleading 'baksheesh' 'baksheesh'. Are *they* the poor?

There is of course no simple answer. Up to a point poverty is relative and we come to our conclusions depending on the comparisons we draw. As we begin to 'get our eye in', we stop making the comparisons in Western terms, judging poverty by the presence or absence of washing machines, food mixers and other luxury items, and start defining the haves and havenots by their own societies' standards. It is important that we do this if our responses are going to be appropriate to the people that we meet. Paradoxically the commonest mistake that travellers make is to give over-generously to those that do not expect it, and actually to brush aside those that do need help.

All over the world there are people who live full and satisfying lives, with very few of the commodities we take for granted. Their world is physically harsher than ours with long hours of hard work in the home or in the fields. Health care may be rudimentary, money in short supply, education limited, but such families do not necessarily feel themselves to be poor. It would be foolish to be over-sentimental about this 'simple life', but it is also easy to overlook a rich cultural heritage, a secure place in a tight-knit community and lives untouched by the alarms of nuclear weapons, terrorism and violent crime that bedevil Western nations.

Often such people share common traditions of courtesy and hospitality towards strangers that we have lost in our society, and many travellers find it difficult to come to terms with the offers of food, accommodation and help that they receive from people so much 'poorer' than themselves. At home we are polite and welcoming to people we feel have some call upon us, friends, friends-of-friends, business associates, but only occasionally do we extend this to the total stranger. We probably seldom meet visitors to our own land, and we expect them to stay in the accommodation set aside for them — hotels, guesthouses etc. We expect them to enter into a contract based on money for the services they receive during their visit, and to pay for food, entertainment and hospitality.

For us to meet people from different cultures who freely offer so much, who give from a strong sense of duty, not grudgingly but happily and with pride, is disconcerting, particularly where these people have very little.

In order to even things up, we, who are often bad receivers, as well as bad givers, want to offer something in exchange. We are genuinely concerned to 'pay back' in some way to our hosts, and it is because of these feelings that travellers can make inappropriate gestures towards those who expect little other than real appreciation, in return for what they have to offer.

Where large numbers of visitors respond to local traditions of hospitality by giving sums of money, or presents that to the recipients are expensive and lavish, they create needs and expectations where once there were none. Slowly the old traditions are undermined as the younger generation comes to expect a trade-off in return for the old ways of openness and generosity.

Does this mean that you should just accept what is offered and not reciprocate at all? No, it certainly does not, but it does mean being thoughtful about how you respond. There are other ways of showing appreciation than by teaching local people, however poor, to crave for Western goods.

'Gifts should emphasise the transcendent values of friendship, knowledge and health over material wealth.'
                    Stephen Bezruchka — Trekking in Nepal

Learn to accept gracefully things that are offered. Refusal often offends by breaking local codes of politeness, or by implying that local standards aren't good enough.

Don't take other people's hospitality for granted. Even where you know you can rely on it, once you've mentally assumed a right to it, something has gone wrong.

Don't trade off every occasion with a present, thereby reducing every act of polite kindness to a business transaction. A smile which shows you genuinely appreciate your host's kindness is often enough.

Think of reciprocating in terms other than the giving of material things. Can you help with their English, teach children to count, do you play a musical instrument, juggle oranges or provide entertainment in other ways? Are you a good conversationalist (where language allows)? Can you offer a service of some kind, bandage a foot, repair a piece of machinery?

Can you limit what you accept in ways that are helpful — by turning up outside meal times so that only a cup of tea need be offered? By accepting a small portion of food only? By showing that you would like to share what is offered with your hosts as well?

Does your giving belittle your host by drawing too much attention to your relative prosperity, or vice versa?

Finally, if you promise a return service to be carried out from home, do it. Far too many of us promise to send books, photos, equipment, presents from our own country and somehow, six months later still haven't got around to it.

Inappropriate giving

Children all over the world are much less concerned than adults with the ethics of giving and receiving. Most adore presents and are far from hesitant about receiving whatever is on offer. Children are delightfully funny, pretty, picturesque, eminently spoilable and easy to please. They are also past masters at exploiting their charm for every last penny, and are quite prepared to take to daylight robbery in pursuit of sweets.

So many travellers make presents to the local kids that they quickly come to see any foreigner as a source of ready bounty. In many parts of the world previously polite and charming children now mob visitors with demands for 'baksheesh', 'one-school-pen', 'sweets', 'pennies' etc. In some places it is so automatic that I once emerged dripping from the sea clad only in a bikini to be immediately accosted by the nearest Sri Lankan child for 'one-school-pen'. He only looked mildly abashed at the absurdity of his demand when I silently turned over my wet and empty hands.

Children 'beg' whenever they think they can get away with it. Asking for sweets, biros and pennies seldom has much to do with real necessity and in any case it's easy to spot the genuinely needy amongst the opportunist cadgers. Many children have parents who still hold to traditional values and would be horrified if they knew what their offspring were up to. Apart from encouraging the local kids to turn into regular pests to the annoyance of all future travellers, indiscriminate handouts undermine local traditional hospitality. So ignore package tour operators who recommend you take sweets and pens to give away.

Keep presents for real occasions and choose ones which are small and preferably useful — biros *are* a good idea, in small numbers. Fruit is healthier than sweets. Cigarettes should be avoided, and drugs or alcohol should NEVER be offered.

You don't have to give material things. Some of your time, a chance to practise their English, a look through your binoculars are alternatives to money or sweets. Showing pictures of your country or your family and being prepared to talk about them is educational as well as fun. Moreover, a song, or sharing a game of cat's cradle lead to real contact in a way that a quick handout does not.

Serious deprivation

It is when travellers encounter people without adequate food, shelter
or clothing that the real shock of poverty hits them. Seeing for the first
time children sleeping in doorways, slum or shanty town shacks, the
pavement dwellers of India, or the poverty of parts of rural Africa can
be devastating. If you are setting off for Asia, parts of South America
or any large city in developing countries you'll probably be expecting
deprivation on this sort of scale but even where you expect it, the real
difference between the lives of many in the poorer parts of the world,
and our own comfortable lives at home is shocking.

> 'It was difficult to know how to react when confronted with
> things that weren't so much puzzling as shocking. Eating a
> meal in a cheap restaurant I noticed a small group of boys
> clustered round the door. I couldn't work out what they were up
> to, as they didn't seem to be selling anything. Then a customer
> finished his meal and left. Immediately one of the boys darted
> in and over to the table and scooped up the leftovers into his
> box. That was his meal. He'd been waiting to eat.'
>
> *Colombia*

But even the straightforwardly hungry don't upset travellers as much
as do the ill and disabled poor. In countries with no state welfare
system these may be forced to display their amputated stumps or
misshapen limbs to public gaze in the hope of collecting enough
charity to get by.

Unfortunately, as you may find, your reactions to such sad sights
are not always those of overwhelmingly pity and compassion. All too
often our reactions are of disgust towards the grotesque, coupled with
an urgent need to look the other way and walk on. Neither do we
necessarily behave any better towards the able-bodied whose livelihood comes from begging.

> 'We have all admitted that beggars just provoke feelings of
> intense annoyance. I never feel compassion.'
>
> *India*

The problem with the deformed or immobile is that the greater their needs, the more awful their deformity, the more difficult we find it to take notice. The greater our shock, the greater our own need to protect ourselves from our own unpleasant reactions by getting away as quickly as possible.

The problem with the able-bodied poor is made more complicated by our suspicion (and it may be correct) that some of them are not really as poor as they make out. Because they're able bodied they are able to approach and surround us and make demands and requests. We don't have time to stand back, to try and assess whether their need is genuine, nor to try and put ourselves in their shoes. So instead of concern or compassion, we feel 'got at', angry at being surrounded and 'picked on', guilty and confused about how to react.

Genuine poverty *is* shocking, it *is* difficult to come to terms with, and it has many causes. Floods, droughts, wars and earthquakes are all disasters which can make thousands homeless and landless; social systems can concentrate a country's wealth in the hands of a few, religious ideas can confine whole castes and classes to lifelong poverty, but one of the root causes is the huge problem of imbalance of the world's resources and the economic exploitation of the developing countries by the richest nations on earth.

The individual traveller can have little real impact on the problem of world poverty. At best we can affect the day-today needs of a handful of the people with whom we come into contact. What travellers can also do is find ways of coping with their own feelings that are positive, by doing something, rather than negative, by angrily pushing the problem aside. The recipients will feel better, *you* will feel better and ultimately you will have a happier trip if instead of trying to avoid all the guilt and confusion, you face the problem head on.

Are we saying give to the beggars you meet? Not necessarily, there are other possibilities.

You could choose to do nothing during your trip, but decide instead to find out more about the causes of world poverty and what the West can do, on your return home.

You could spend some part of your travels working for one of the many local or international aid agencies, or you could make a financial donation instead. This latter course at least relieves you of the problem of worrying about whether your help is actually reaching people who need it. Don't automatically think of Mother Theresa if you are in India. (Although grateful for volunteer support she tends to get swamped with offers, whilst other similar projects are ignored.)

You could consider, on your return, applying to one of the organisations that sends volunteer workers to developing countries.

Alternatively, if you are happier responding immediately, a good way of coping if many demands are made on you, is to set aside a sum to give each day. You will find you are likely to be totally random in your giving — one person might get the lot one day, on another it might be spread around. When the sum of money is finished, that's it, finished.

Some travellers will object that this last piece of advice is more to do with solving your own conscience than actually achieving anything. And so it is. There's nothing you can do *on your travels* to tackle poverty at any meaningful level. Not giving (and feeling bad) isn't going to affect the government. It's simply going to mean that whoever's asked you for help is going to ask someone else or do without. Solving your conscience, dealing with your own feelings might help you and one or two other people have a nicer trip.

Finally, despite what you may be told, many cultures have a strong tradition of alms-giving to the poor — Islam for example requires its adherents to give a proportion of their income. Hinduism, Sikhism, Buddhism and Shintoism all teach that alms-giving brings merit to the donor.

You will observe local people making donations to the genuinely destitute who do not solely 'prey' on tourists.

THE RIP-OFF SYNDROME

Some travellers especially in developing countries spend all their time in a state of frustrated indignation, complaining and suspecting that in every transaction they are being 'ripped off' and got the better of. This is a pity because bargaining is fun.

The trader assuring you (at six o'clock in the evening) that you are his 'Lucky' first deal of the day, 'and for you I make *special* price, truly'. Or using outrageous flattery to convince 'Madam, for a *beautiful* guest to our country, only a present' (before naming a price four times greater than the one you eventually settle on). And of course you point out that you are completely penniless (point to travel-stained clothes), at the end of your trip and spent out, and in any case you're only looking. Naturally neither of you believing a word the other one says! Unfortunately, however, some travellers take it all far too seriously, and turn a game into a contest.

The problem starts because some prices have been so inflated that traders can afford to come down quite a long way and still make a reasonable living. Naturally, although they may all have roughly the same bottom line and ceiling, individuals will let goods go at different rates. Any gathering of travellers will therefore quickly discover that some have achieved better buys than others — 'You were ripped off, we only paid ...' All too often visitors, particularly those with limited budgets, start to suspect in every transaction that the trader could come down a little more, if only they were local people, if only they'd pushed a little harder, if only they'd haggled a little longer. For some, it's a short step to believing that everyone is out to cheat them, that every transaction is a confrontation which they must win.

Spending your whole time in a state of anger over rip-offs is not what bargaining is all about, it also does little for your peace of mind if you spend part of every day convinced you've somehow been 'done down', or have 'lost out'. On the other hand not bargaining at all is foolish. It confirms local beliefs that all visitors are made of money, it pushes up local prices even further to the detriment of future travellers, and it also affects local people who buy.

Keep a sense of proportion, don't expect everything to be dirt cheap. Take enough money with you so you don't have to watch every penny. Under-budgeting is a major source of frustration which can come to undermine your whole trip.

Accept that you won't pay local prices, and where your earnings are considerably higher than those of local people, there's no reason why you should. Start by offering approximately half the asking price. If this is accepted with alacrity you've offered too much. You won't be able to do anything about it now, but will know the next time to offer one third or even a quarter of the asking price. If your offer is refused, go up *slowly*. Don't accept the first alternative price suggested, try again and then judge whether or not the vendor will come down even further. By all means tell the trader you've seen the same items at a fraction of the price down the road (he won't believe you if it isn't true) or look horrified at the 'outrageous' charges, but do it pleasantly and stay good humoured. (My most spectacular 'bargain' was a stamped metal medallion from Peshawar, the small boy left in charge of his father's jewellery shop nervously asked for 100 times the amount I eventually paid!)

There is a difference between a poor bargain and being cheated. Getting a poor bargain is where you, the buyer have agreed to pay a higher price than you might have done. No one has cheated you. You may kick yourself for not having shopped around, you may be disappointed to find later on that you could have done better, but no-one forced you to pay. Unless circumstances mean you have no option but to give the asking price, you can always say no. At the end of the day any item is worth what it's worth to *you*, no matter who says later on that you were 'ripped off'. Being cheated is another matter. Always challenge local people who cheat, even if you decide to pay up anyway. You may be buying an 'all wool' jumper that obviously is made of acrylic, or an 'antique' vase that equally obviously isn't. By all means go ahead if they are what you want and you feel the price is fair, but point out that it's not wool, not antique. Equally, don't be fobbed off with taxi-drivers with 'broken' meters, or fruit sellers that use scales for everyone else but prefer to 'guess' the weight for you.

10
Making Contact

MEETING PEOPLE

Whatever the purpose of their travels, for most travellers the contact they have with the people they meet is often the highlight of their trip:

> 'Being able to contact the women of the country was lovely. Although we didn't have much language in common there were shy smiles and glances and trust is extended. You can play with the babies and there is some real contact there without words.'
>
> *Indonesia*

> 'We found many invitations came our way: picnics, outings, drinks etc ... and this led to many adventures with local people. We were able to converse about our different cultures and traditions.'
>
> *Turkey*

> 'Indians are marvellously hospitable and extremely interested in you.'
>
> *India*

'In big cities women are getting dreams of freedom and are often excited to talk to a Western woman and find out what your lifestyle is.'

Colombia

It is these experiences that bring the differences between the cultures sharply into focus, sometimes to the bafflement of visitor and local alike. How far individual travellers let these differences in etiquette bother them varies. Some seem oblivious of all but the most glaringly obvious customs and taboos. They treat every encounter as they would back home and follow their normal practice of a handshake here, a thank-you-very-much there. If the occasional solecism renders their hosts speechless, these travellers either don't notice, or don't let it bother them too much.

At the other extreme are those so nervous of making a social blunder that they are quite unable to relax. They sit rigid with fright in case they might belch in the wrong place, or worse, not belch at all. Rather than risk offending anyone's hospitality, they risk food poisoning or dying from over-consumption instead.

Fortunately, as you will discover, people may be shocked or find your ignorance and bad manners a source of great entertainment, but provided you look as if you meant well you are unlikely to cause an international incident even if you do break local codes of behaviour. Even where you have offended people, as long as you are sensitive enough to realise that something has gone wrong and are prepared to show that you know you've made a mistake (even if you don't know what it is), allowances will be made for unpredictable Westerners, who, as all the local people know, are incomprehensible anyway.

Despite this reassurance however, most travellers will prefer to try and fit in with local people and if you can follow local practice when meeting people, visiting, sharing food etc. it will be much appreciated. The problem of course is knowing what local practice is, especially as customs can change from village to village, caste to caste, or from age-group to age-group. The best guides are local people themselves. But what should you watch out for?

your host in the considerable inconvenience, and the possible expense of ritually cleansing the area polluted by your presence. If invited to inspect shrines or altars don't touch anything, and don't do as I once did by mistake and blow out any candles, oil lamps etc., that might be there. Watch your host to see if it is permissible to turn your back on images and so on.

'Never go to the back door as this is only reserved for good friends.'

Zambia

Some parts of the house may be women's quarters, often the back area, out of sight of passersby. Western women often, but not always, find that they are treated as honorary men when it comes to their status as guests, and so may be shown to the men's area and invited to sit with male members of the household. If you can persuade your hosts that you would like to meet the women as well, you will have a much wider experience than a male travelling companion.

'A woman traveller will find herself mainly with the men ... If you can get away, you can really enjoy the women's company and conversation. Extremely funny!'

Tanzania

Many women travellers have made worthwhile contact with local women and children in this way, but local men may find your request to do so puzzling, and a marked preference on your part for the company of their wives rather insulting if local women's status is low:

'One man kindly invited us to lunch and when we asked if his wife could join us as we'd like to talk to her he said it was not the custom in his house, "I am master in my own house".'

Colombia

'The men expect you to talk to them as heads of the family. If you are offered hospitality you are honouring them.'

Tanzania

Perhaps the best time to meet the women in a household is during a large celebration (wedding, religious festival) where you are not the main guest. It is more likely that in these circumstances you will be shown into the women's room:

> 'Some women are kept in purdah, even in the most modern and sophisticated homes. It is not unusual for male guests to gather in one room while the women sit in another. As a Westerner you would be tolerated by the men if you joined them, but you would feel terribly out of place.'
>
> *Pakistan*

Wherever you are shown to, on your arrival look to see if shoes are worn inside or if they should be removed. It's easy to find out, if shoes are to be removed, you will find the family footwear in a heap by the entrance way.

Leave yours there as well if this is the case. Although a custom practised mainly in Asia, the Far East and Japan, I have been asked to remove my shoes when staying in private houses in other countries. Some families provide slippers for their guests and I was once given little mats, one for each foot to slide over a polished floor.

Once inside the house watch to see if people are very foot conscious:

> 'Don't point the soles of your feet, or toes at anyone. It is considered very rude.'
>
> *Thailand*

This is where a full-length skirt has advantages over jeans. You can tuck your feet up under the folds and sit comfortably crosslegged without offending anyone.

The real minefield for travellers when visiting people's houses, equal perhaps to wandering by mistake into a forbidden area, is that of admiring your host's possessions. This is normal politeness in our culture — a friend has bought a new rug? Of course you comment on how nice it is. Visiting a house for the first time we openly admire the owner's ornaments, paintings and taste in furnishings, particularly if they are unusual in any way. To follow this Western custom elsewhere could be disastrous for your host if etiquette demands that they immediately offer the admired item to their guest. 'You like it — take it, take it.' A sentence which has caused a sinking feeling of unease to many a traveller. Are they really supposed to walk off with someone's priceless antique vase or cherished wall hanging? Their host seems insistent — would it be ruder to accept or ruder to decline? The safest way out of the situation is to politely 'accept' by saying thank you, but at the same time taking no steps towards actually acquiring the item. Often the whole scenario has in fact become a ritualised 'offer' and 'acceptance' which satisfies everyone's sense of generosity towards guests without any action having to result. However, much better, for travellers and hosts alike is to try and avoid this arising at all.

By all means politely praise your host, but keep things general — 'What a beautiful house/room/garden you have.' 'How pleasant it is in here.' 'You have made your home very welcoming/comfortable' — are all much safer compliments than to pick on any one particular item, however much its beauty catches your eye. This warning also applies to personal items such as jewellery, so again be careful what you say.

Finally, if you are invited to someone's house for a special event or even for the first time, make an effort to dress up for the occasion. If you haven't brought a set of smart clothes (see page 63) then at least wear *clean* ones. People are quick to be hurt that affluent Westerners can't be bothered to take any trouble when visiting their homes. They certainly would if visiting yours.

Do remember you are a *guest* — it is quite all right for a local person to apparently apologetically tell you that the country's health service is poor, the schools are ill-equipped and the government inept. It is *not* all right for you to agree too fervently. Particularly be very careful to be noncommittal about politics unless you are on really safe ground with someone you know well. You don't just run the risk of putting someone's back up, you risk problems with the authorities as well.

Don't overstay your welcome. In Algeria they have a saying which is worth bearing in mind when accepting others' hospitality: 'Fish and guests keep three days.'

SHARING FOOD

It is difficult to imagine any traveller on a trip which brings them into contact with local people not being invited to share food with them, on buses, trains, in the back of trucks and during long waits in airport lounges. Wherever you are, if it coincides with mealtimes (and often if it doesn't) people will offer to share everything from pickled fish to chocolate bars. If you are invited into someone's house inevitably refreshments will be served. Depending on the circumstances you might find yourself facing a 15-course elaborate formal banquet or a meagre meal of rice and dahl that has to keep several adults and children going after a full day of heavy manual work. You may be offered delicious pastries oozing nuts and honey or dubious half raw meat that guarantees an upset stomach. Snacks can vary from roasted insects to dried mulberries, from deep-fried blistering chilli-peppers to octopus, from a familiar piece of melon to exotic rambuttan.

In all societies the sharing of food is the most fundamental form of social interaction so it is not surprising that there are many customs and taboos that surround it. At home we absorb from childhood a complicated code of 'manners' which governs everything from which way we tilt a soup bowl, to the fact that we can 'politely' eat an apple with our fingers rather than with a knife and fork. Making yourself consciously aware of what we take for granted as adults at home can help travellers know, by comparison, what to watch out for abroad. If casual callers arrive at your own house do you always offer the same sort of refreshments or does it vary according to the time of day (i.e. coffee in the morning, tea in the afternoon, alcohol after six o'clock)? Are some foods served only on festivals (birthday cake, Easter eggs)? Are some foods eaten with utensils, and if so which foods and what utensil — is there any way a foreign visitor could know this? When guests are invited to supper do men and women sit together or separately? Is there any particular order in which people are served? Are people expected to talk during a meal, or eat in silence? Should guests accept a second helping? A third helping? Should they leave a little on their plates or empty them? No wonder when faced with all this guests from abroad invited to our own houses are occasionally confused, and no wonder that travellers when faced with equally baffling 'rules' on their travels wonder what to do. Luckily of course most things become obvious from watching and copying. You may not know *what* you're eating but at least you know you're to try it with chopsticks.

One of the most obvious differences between ourselves and people in many other countries right round the world is that men and women often eat separately. Nearly always this means that the women and children eat last, of what's left.

'Men eat first, then sons, then women and daughters.'

Zambia

'Women sit behind the men whilst they eat; they themselves don't eat until later.'

Japan

'In Iran the women eat separately, after the men have had the best portions.'

Iran

How to eat

Whether you are sitting with men or with women, the next difference from the way things are at home is likely to be in the utensils provided, or lack of them.

Chopsticks as used in China and Japan are not more difficult to use than the knife and fork at which you are expert — just different. Nowadays most of us have had the opportunity to experiment at our local Chinese restaurant, and as chopsticks can be bought in most towns, travellers going to the Far East can practise before they go. If you can't find a Chinese grocery which will sell you a pair, try any good kitchenware shop, or ask at your local takeaway.

However, large numbers of people around the world manage without utensils of any kind. Although many households have a few spoons which may be offered to a guest, it is more likely that where local people eat with their fingers you will be expected to do so as well. Always eat ONLY WITH YOUR RIGHT HAND. The left hand is reserved for washing yourself so the taboo makes good hygienic sense. To use your left hand would not only be the height of rudeness and dirtiness it would make food eaten from a communal dish unfit for everyone else as well.

(This is why the Islamic punishment of cutting off an offender's right hand is so devastating. It doesn't just deprive a criminal of the use of that hand, it makes it impossible for him or her to join in a communal meal and therefore effectively turns them into a social outcast.)

Left-handed travellers are at an immediate disadvantage but unfortunately to try and explain their preferred way of doing things will not help. In most cultures where this custom exists, lefthandedness is 'cured' in childhood:

> **'A child who appears left-handed has a calabash tied to the palm of their hand so they can't pick up anything. They have to become ambidextrous and are trained never to use their left hand for food.'**
>
> *Africa*

Left-handed travellers therefore have to manage as well as possible.

Using your fingers doesn't, as some travellers might imagine, mean eating untidily. In some societies only the tips of the fingers should be used, in others the whole hand may squelch food into a ball. Nowhere do people really approve of licking the fingers during eating, instead you rinse your hand when you have finished with water provided. (Water will also be brought at the beginning of a meal, or you will be shown where to wash.)

Where food is sloppy or difficult to pick up spoons may be used but more usually food can be scooped up with bread, or mixed with rice or something similar until it has a consistency that is manageable.

Eating from a communal dish is also a widespread custom. You always eat only from the area immediately in front of you:

> **'If eating from a communal bowl, help yourself only from the**

area in front of you. Don't reach across for a tit-bit from someone else's section.'

Senegal

As you are a guest, choice bits of food will be handed over to your part of the dish where you can reach them.

There is one society where you won't be expected to eat from a common plate. Hindu culture has perhaps more food taboos to catch out the unwary than any others.

Hindus believe that food can be polluted if it is touched by anyone outside their caste or religion. As a Westerner you are considered an untouchable and sharing food from the same dish or cup with an orthodox Brahmin would be impossible. Travellers regularly horrify devout Indians by helping themselves to food from each other's plates (only wives may eat from their husband's plate) or, worse still, by passing round a water bottle and actually allowing it to touch the lips. In a typical café in Madurai, the pilgrim city that sees thousands of visitors each year, there was no cutlery and no crockery, except for cooking utensils and one beaker. Food was served on banana leaves, which apart from being cheap and disposable got round the caste system, and water stood in a pail with just one cup for the whole place. Indians learn early to pour water into their mouths without touching the container (something that looks a lot easier than it is).

Wherever you are during your travels, don't necessarily expect conversation during a meal. The sort of dinner-party talk we hope for at home, or even just family news and chat common during our own meals may be discouraged and conversation limited to polite compliments to the cook or host during the time people are actually eating:

'Maldivans don't socialise as we do. They come, they eat, they go.'

Maldives

A great deal is made to travellers about the necessity to belch to show their appreciation of the food they have eaten. In any society the showing of appreciation is what's important, not how you show it. Don't worry about belching, do smile and say thank you. Ask for recipes, compliment your host, find out about strange ingredients and unfamiliar cooking methods, show you have enjoyed and taken an interest in your meal.

Acceptance, declining and reciprocating

The above advice about how to go about tackling a meal is all very well if it's a delicious banquet and you're starving. But what do you do if you've already eaten, or if you've eaten as much as you can manage, or if you don't want what is being offered, because you're worried about a probable stomach upset?

Over and over again the women contributing to this book stress the importance of accepting what is offered:

'Don't refuse food or drink however obnoxious it may appear.'

Ethiopia

'It is almost impossible to refuse food when it is offered.'

Indonesia

Luckily it is usually possible to satisfy local people's codes of hospitality by accepting a small taste or portion only, which is particularly important if they are depriving themselves in order to share food with you.

'I was offered some unpasteurised milk, but luckily after a very small sip, when I handed back the bowl with a big smile and a thank you, nobody seemed to mind.'

Nepal

'Do accept food if offered, but you can say "I've just eaten so I'll just have a little".'

Sierra Leone

'Refuse if you don't want any — and keep refusing. Etiquette demands about three offers and three refusals.'

Egypt

It is also usual in many countries to signal that you've had enough by leaving a small amount (but this doesn't apply everywhere, so watch others to see what they do).

'Leave some food on your plate to show that you are full. Thais are very generous. I and a companion were invited out by a not well off teacher and duly emptied our plates, protesting each time as more food arrived. Our Thai host became more and more worried until we were so stuffed we could not finish what was left. We discovered later that it is polite to leave food on your plate to show you are full.'

Thailand

Vegetarians may well have problems declining meat unless they are travelling to India where vegetarianism is part of local culture and tradition:

'It is not easy to be a vegetarian unless you're self catering. If invited to eat it will be fish or meat.'

East Africa

'Being a vegetarian is a problem in rural areas. Food is scarce so people have problems understanding why anyone should deliberately choose not to eat meat.'

Zambia

Both of the last quotations came from women who had worked with V.S.O. Both agreed that all the volunteers they knew of who had started out as vegetarians had eventually started to eat meat.

Finally, the habit of offering food should apply as much to travellers as to the local people they're travelling amongst:

'Before you eat, always ask the other people at the table to share it. You say "Karibu" - "come here".'

Tanzania

PHOTOGRAPHY

'When taking photographs, respect privacy — ask permission, and use restraint.'

Himalayan Tourist Code

The confession that neither of us owns a camera might at first sight disqualify us from the rest of this section.

However, I was persuaded to borrow one on my first trip. Alas, it remained at the bottom of my rucksack virtually the whole time. I was much too paranoid about having even the cheapest of cameras stolen to risk getting it out — and when eventually I did so, I could not bring myself to move up close enough to local people to produce anything more than the most blurred and distant images.

So my first trip remains, apart from a dozen fuzzy shots, on the pages of my diary, on the back of the steady stream of postcards I sent homewards, and in my head.

I cannot in all honesty say that I miss the photos I never took. The only one I am fond of is one of myself with a family I stayed with whilst trekking the foothills around Darjeeling.

Since those days photography has become much more of an issue, particularly for local people who increasingly resent having cameras and video recorders stuck into every corner of their lives, and who end up feeling little more than 'image' fodder.

'Seven women languidly nurse their babies, gazing blankly into camera lenses... We try to ease our discomfort with conversation through a translator, but the Longneck women

(of Thailand) have heard it all before. Until last year, the Longnecks refused to allow video recording. Now if you want a video you must pay £5. Poverty cannot afford principles.'

Kristina Woolnough, Scotland on Sunday, 1993

So do you need to take a camera or video with you ? If the answer is 'Yes!' ask yourself why. Is it to prove you were there ? To whom ? Are you such a good photographer that your images are really going to provide a better visual record than one professionally shot, and already available on postcards or in books about the area ? How else might you record your impressions — in words? In sketches? In your head ? How many of your memories are going to be made up of experiences that utilise ALL your senses — Smell, Touch, Sound, Sight, and Taste ? How much of this will be relegated to the background whilst you are getting the focus right, adjusting the shutter speed, changing the film ?

On our last trip, we made a point of collecting ephemera as mementos — bus tickets, hotel bills, pressed flowers, admission tickets, locally produced (and luridly coloured) postcards and guides, a peacock feather......

There are alternatives!

VISITING RELIGIOUS SITES

It is sometimes difficult for some Western visitors to appreciate how sensitive local people can be about their religious places.

Ours, by and large is a society where religion has only a minor role, and our own important religious sites are often appreciated more from a historical or artistic point of view than because we feel they are particularly connected with a sense of a God.

In other parts of the world local people's depth of feeling can surprise unwary travellers who may unthinkingly offend them by inappropriate behaviour, insensitivity, or plain bad manners. This is a pity because where travellers show obvious respect for others they often find themselves welcomed into temples and shrines, and are shown round by local people happy to share an important part of their culture with visitors.

Whatever your own beliefs, you owe to others, if not an understanding, at least a respect for and tolerance of their religious ideas. You can best show this by being as unobtrusive as possible when visiting religious places. Aim to be virtually unnoticeable because of your quiet manner and your willingness to follow local customs when it comes to head coverings, removal of footwear etc. Don't enter if you are in shorts or holiday wear that is too revealing, especially if your upper arms and legs are bared. (Trousers or a biggish skirt with a top with sleeves, are acceptable everywhere.) Do have a scarf with you. Remain in the background particularly if prayers or ceremonies are taking place, unless invited to move forward. Taking photographs, especially with a flash is often inappropriate, if not actually forbidden (although some places, now resigned to tourists, charge for visitors with cameras).

Finally, always observe what local women do because their religious practices may be different from those of the men. Women may have separate areas where they hold their own ceremonies, or they may have their own customs. In some cultures men are forbidden to enter or take part in women's rites and vice versa.

In addition to the general suggestions above, the following is a list of guidelines for different religions. However, exact practices can still vary from region to region.

Sikh Gudwaras (temples)

Women must cover their heads and remove their shoes. Water may be provided to wash your feet. Cigarette smoking is forbidden not just in temples but usually in any adjoining buildings. Keep the soles of your bare feet pointing downwards or covered when sitting cross-legged on the ground.

Hindu temples

Hindu temples are not always open to Western visitors. Where they are there may be certain areas where non-Hindus are forbidden to enter. (In temples that get a lot of visitors you will find signs in English asking you not to go any further.)

Shoes must be removed; and local women usually keep their heads covered, but this is not essential for visitors.

On Bali special temple scarfs are worn wrapped round the waist and hips. These can be bought locally. You will find notices outside Balinese temples requesting menstruating women not to enter.

Buddhist temples

Shoes must be removed and your head uncovered. Worshippers never turn their backs to the statue of Buddha. Monks should not touch or be touched by women. Special seats may be reserved for them on buses, trains etc.

Mosques

Non-Moslems are not often allowed to enter mosques. Where it is permitted, women should cover their heads and remove their shoes. Conservative dress covering the legs and arms is *essential*. Usually an area at the back is reserved for women who may not enter other areas. Travellers should be aware that during Ramadan (annual fast) Moslems do not eat or drink from sunrise to sunset and visitors should tactfully avoid doing so publicly.

Synagogues

Traditionally women have a separate area, usually hidden from the men, behind screens, or perhaps upstairs. In modern progressive synagogues men and women worship together.

Christian churches

Even in the West, visitors should remember that these are places of worship as well as of historic or architectural interest. Traditionally, Catholic women cover their heads, shoulders and upper arms but this is rarely observed strictly today, even in strongly Catholic countries such as Ireland, Italy, or in South America.

11
Personal Safety

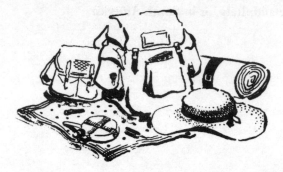

'Confidence, compromise and common sense.'

Marco Polo Travel Advisory Service

The fear of violence and rape does more to keep women 'safely at home' than anything else. Uncomfortable beds, unsanitary loos, possible illness or straightforward inconvenience I could take in my stride, but fear of being attacked, alone and in a strange country, haunted me as nothing else could. Before I set out I remember being given a lecture on safety by a concerned male acquaintance. He underlined the many risks I'd be taking (white slave trade, gang-bangs by bandits etc.), and pointed out the irresponsibility of my actions. By travelling at all I was placing an intolerable burden of responsibility on other male travellers who would doubtless have to protect me!

Of course this conversation didn't stop me going but equally it did nothing to relieve the anxieties I already had. How brave was I going to have to be? Other friends' admiration was no more reassuring: 'Wow, I'd be far too frightened. Aren't you scared?'

Talking with other women who had already travelled gave a different picture. Sure, there had been problems, but things hadn't been that bad; the majority of their horror stories were about *escape* from impossible situations. Given forethought and ordinary common sense you could travel safely, even on your own.

So I left, expecting to survive. But in the back of my head the long list of 'difficulties to be overcome' travelled with me. Possible assault, sexual harassment, being followed, the threat of violence ... I was on the lookout for danger — to survive was to avoid. And the easiest way to avoid was to melt into the background, become invisible, attract no attention. Right, that would be my strategy.

So much for forward planning! One of the first things you discover when travelling is that invisibility is the last thing you will achieve. This is so whether you are male or female. The way you dress, your looks, will inevitably mark you out from those who surround you.

> **'All oriental people stare. It is not rude. They feel sorry for us with our huge noses, awful hair and furry bodies, and are very curious about them.'**
>
> *Japan*

Even within Europe your backpack and your travel equipment stamp 'visitor' all over you no matter how much you'd like to be taken for a local:

> **'People were always asking if we were British, sometimes even before we spoke or anything. Maybe it was our poor wan faces that hadn't seen the sun.'**
>
> *Portugal*

The further you move away from the accepted tourist centres the more true this is. In many developing countries the very fact that you are travelling in the first place is something to be remarked on. For travelling for pleasure is one of the privileges of our modern Western society. In most peasant-based cultures, travel is an expensive and difficult undertaking which is usually only embarked on in a time of crisis. We, on the other hand, turn up for just a few days with no particular purpose in mind except sightseeing, to the amazement of local people.

In societies where families depend for their survival on subsistence fanning, they can only afford to release members to travel for serious reasons: a legal dispute, a family crisis involving serious illness or death, or a religious pilgrimage. Moreover, in these cases, it is usually the men who go. Women are too busy with children, with agriculture and with other domestic responsibilities to be spared, even for short periods. In any case in many of these societies women have too low a status to represent the family. All of this means that if Western travellers stand out as conspicuous oddities and privileged ones at that, women travellers stand out doubly on account of our sex.

In more urban settings and in the West the position is slightly different. Here local people accept travellers for what they are. Tourists are a familiar part of the scene and we generate interest not so much because of our strangeness but because we represent a source of income. Shoe shine boys, hoteliers, taxi-drivers, guide and souvenir sellers all depend on the traveller for their livelihoods.

For their curiosity and economic value then travellers are often the focus of more attention than they'd expect at home. At first you may find this nerve wracking. Being so obviously visible makes us jumpy. We expect attention in itself to lead to trouble. It rarely does.

INNOCENT HARASSMENT

'It took me a long time to realise that most touching, conversation, helpfulness etc. is not sexual.'

Tanzania

So much of the attention women receive in our society is sexual — men imposing their presence and reminding us of their power by wolf-whistling, leering, making offensive remarks. Behind it lies the threat that they will take what they want, that we challenge their assumptions at our own risk. Some of the attention you will meet with abroad will be of precisely this sort. I remember riding on the back of an open trailer whilst hitching in Peru with an Australian man. He was sitting at the front, waving to the passing lorry drivers who cheerfully signalled back. When we changed places and I did the same I was rewarded with lewd gestures!

But more often than not behaviour which you may begin by interpreting in this way isn't meant in the same spirit at all. Staring, touching, spoken comments are not always part of a plot to make you feel uneasy. They are more likely to be a straightforward response to your presence. The following quotations from other women travellers show that such behaviour is really innocent harrassment rather than sexual intimidation.

> 'White women are quite rare in Indonesia, excluding Bali. I encountered a lot of staring from both sexes and all ages. It was a little unnerving, but I got used to it.'
>
> *Indonesia*

> 'Touching is far more common in other countries. It's no good being offended if your bottom is patted in West Africa — it's a compliment.'
>
> *Ghana*

> 'Groups of men will shout "Adios mon amor" or "Goodbye my love" after women. It's really only a form of greeting —ignore it.'
>
> *Colombia*

However, if this sort of attention is not necessarily sexual, or threatening it can be irritating. After a tiring 15-hour bus journey in India when you feel you have been keeping all the other (local) passengers amused by doing such things as opening a rucksack (pile up in the corridor whilst everyone leans over to see what is in it), and reading a book (it is politely taken away and handed round upside down), how do you feel when you get off the self same bus in a strange town and are immediately surrounded by a fascinated crowd of both sexes and all ages who put out tentative (or not so tentative) hands to stroke hair, finger your skirt, and inquire politely 'Where are you from?' 'Where are you going?'

Learning to accept this sort of attention philosophically takes time, but you will find that consciously relaxing and reminding yourself that curiosity and hostility are not necessarily the same thing does help.

It could be said the British are probably least well prepared to cope. From our earliest days we are told 'Don't turn round', 'Don't stare!', and of course speaking to, let alone touching total strangers is completely outside our code of etiquette.

Staring in particular (because it's so widespread), is hard to bear. Under our society's rules of politeness staring is NOT DONE. A stare for us is at the least a sign of bad manners, and at the worst, a deliberately provocative act of aggression.

You may find that breaking down this famous British Reserve takes a lot of doing, but it *is* possible to do so — to accept all the attention, and even to stare or touch back! During the first part of my travels I can remember rushing nervously past scenes in the street, with the 'don't stare' message from my childhood ringing in my ears. Eventually I learnt to slow down, even to join the interested crowd round a minor family drama, or was able to reach out with a smile on a train, to touch and admire the beautiful jewellery worn by local women.

Relaxing can also help you to see the funny side of situations:

'Thais seem to find us ungainly, oversized, hairy people, very funny. Much goodwill can be created if you see the joke. At one stall men only were buying strange little glasses of liquid. A male bought me one and when I had a sip everyone dissolved into hysterical laughter. It was indicated in sign language that it was some sort of virility potion!'

Thailand

And if you do adopt a positive approach you can turn attention to your own advantage:

> **'On a trek when one is wearing clothes never seen before, and carrying personal gear twice the value of a whole farm, it would be unfair to presume your privacy is essential. Make use of the attention — you'll certainly get some lovely photos.'**
>
> *Nepal*

Apart from generally keeping calm and accepting or ignoring the strokers, starers, and commentors, there are, however one or two do's and don'ts that can help reduce unwanted attentions.

Don't, however tempted, lose your temper. Not only do you become twice as noticeable (and twice as interesting), but you run the risk of causing genuine offence, and turning innocent curiosity into real hostility.

In some parts of the world a queue will quickly form for 'snaps'. So, if you are an amateur photographer in search of a quiet life, you might find it better to wait until the train departs to take your photos rather than when you arrive at the station with two hours to kill.

It's common sense, to observe local customs as regards public behaviour. Look at local women — do they have an obvious public presence, or do they fade into the background? How do couples relate to each other in public? In many countries you will find that overt displays of affection or hostility towards your partner are reserved for private family life at home. So, if this seems the case, try to avoid much hand holding, kissing, or arguing in public.

Finally, in some places you may be tempted to give out medicines. Even if you are a trained doctor or nurse with ample supplies, think twice before you start. An aspirin handed over for a headache can start a flood of requests, particularly in rural areas, where Western drugs are few. You might be asked to cure far more serious conditions than migraines or infected cuts, and you may well be held responsible if the 'cure' doesn't work and the patient dies anyway. If a sick animal is concerned, you could be asked to pay compensation, but things could be much worse if a person dies and you are held responsible for murder.

SEXUAL HARASSMENT

Both male and female travellers experience the sort of 'innocent harassment' discussed above, however, as women, we are much more likely to be worried about unwanted hostile and sexual attentions. There is all the difference in the world between innocent curiosity from both sexes and all ages, and overtly sexually threatening behaviour from men.

So what can women travellers expect, and how can unwanted advances be minimised? Happily you should start by realising that rape and violence towards women are not *condoned* by *any* society. Despite the horror stories you may hear, in the vast majority of incidents unwanted attentions *do* stop well short of actual rape or violence. However, not necessarily before the woman or women involved have been at the least very alarmed, and, at the worst, seriously frightened.

> **'I have never heard of a woman being raped, but many stories of women thinking they were to be raped. All these stories end with the women getting out of it one way or another. There is certainly plenty of threatening behaviour — rarely does one hear of actual bodily harm of any sort.'**
>
> *Central America*

Although actual rape is usually no more likely abroad than at home (and in some countries considerably less likely), unfortunately Western women travellers, particularly on their own, often report that they are seen as fair game for local men to approach.

> **'My own worst experience was in Indonesia (it happened twice) — a group of young men would walk towards me, surround me, grab at my shoulder bag, breasts and crutch all at once. Neither time was anything stolen, but I never knew what to protect — my bag or my body. Serious intent or their idea of fun? I'm not sure.'**
>
> *Indonesia*

In my case the only real incident of sexual harassment I can remember was when I was sitting on a very crowded bus in Delhi. A man standing in the corridor and crushing up against me, started rubbing his crutch up against my shoulder. What I can chiefly recall is not a feeling of fear — it was daytime and I was surrounded by other people — but a feeling of embarrassment. Quite apart from anything else, it took me quite a while to realise that what he was doing was in fact deliberate and not just the jolting movement of the bus ride. Even then I wasn't sure what to do. Shout out? Jab out my elbow? Try and move further towards the window? In the end I turned away as far as was possible, and eventually he got off.

The reasons for this sort of behaviour are complex. Some of the most obvious factors involved in any particular situation are the status (or lack of it) of local women, and the assertion of male authority and virility. There is also the way the West is viewed politically and economically and socially, by the society in which you are travelling. But at its very simplest what underlies some of the behaviour and attitudes of some local men is the confused message they receive about us.

The free-Western-woman myth

'I was told by an educated, English-speaking Indian that ordinary people can't understand why we're travelling alone. We must have been disowned by our parents and therefore must be loose.'

India

The so-called sexual revolution that has transformed the lives and freedom of many Western women in the last 40 years is often very misunderstood in cultures outside our own. There are a lot of stereotypes of travellers, the 'drug-crazed hippy', the 'millionaire backpacker', the 'gullible tourist', and finally the 'free Western woman', willing and able to have sex with whom she pleases. This mythical figure derives from many sources — third rate Western sex films are seen in many places outside the West; copies of *Playboy* and

Mayfair can be found on the street corners of many of the world's
cities; it can be fuelled by the misunderstood descriptions of Western
life that are sent home by immigrants now settled in Europe and North
America, or by TV and videos widely seen abroad. (The stereotype is
so well developed in some cultures that I once saw an Indian film in
which mini-skirts, platform shoes and cigarettes were used to denote
the 'bad' girl, whilst the 'good' girl remained demure in sandals and
sari.)

> 'Being white and female, they do tend to think you will have
> sex.'
>
> *Thailand*

> 'We saw pictures from *Playboy* stuck up in a village hut right
> in the middle of the jungle. No wonder some men in South
> America get the wrong idea about us.'
>
> *Peru*

Unfortunately it is difficult for travellers not to add unwittingly to the
myth themselves. The topless bathers on the tourist beaches of Kenya,
Sri Lanka and Goa contribute as much as, in retrospect, I no doubt did
myself when travelling with a small mixed group of Europeans I'd met
up with in Northern Turkey. We arrived at a tiny town, well off the
beaten track and decided to share the same six-bedded guest room,
instead of splitting into groups of men and women. From a culture
where 'nice girls' are strictly chaperoned, the half-horrified, half-
delighted hoteliers came in over and over again, on pretext after
pretext, presumably to catch us in the orgy they assumed was taking
place.

This sort of confusion on the part of some local males is further
increased by the number of Western travellers they meet who are
clearly in couples, but equally clearly not married; by the number of
single women they see, travelling alone and unchaperoned; whilst the
whole bundle of misconceptions can be compounded by travellers
who have the occasional affair with local men.

The most usual problems that result for women travellers are
unwanted comments that are sexual in nature, or persistent pestering

and following. Uninvited touching up is less likely, though it does happen; and so do heavy sexual advances to sleep with the man or men concerned.

So what can women do about it all? If it's not possible to avoid sexual harassment altogether, there are a number of steps to take (and as travellers, the onus is on us) to reduce the likelihood of things getting out of hand.

Dress

Given the universality of the Western-woman myth described above, it makes sense to be aware that misconceptions and misread signals can arise from styles of dress, so choosing clothes that are relatively 'unprovocative' can help.

> 'Think carefully about how you dress — some may see you as "available", others as immodest and brazen (and therefore to be derided or ignored) if you show too much.'
>
> *India*

> 'If you are sensible about dress there are no problems.'
>
> *Peru*

It is best to avoid skimpy, figure-revealing clothes (including shorts) away from tourist areas. This doesn't have to mean choosing shapeless ankle length skirts or kaftans, which in many parts of the world are regarded as fancy dress. It is better to wear loosely-cut tops which hang over either loose trousers or fullish mid-calf skirts. Avoid revealing beachware — topless sunbathing is definitely OUT in most places, and depending on the country you are in, you may decide after observing local women, that even a modest one-piece swimsuit is better kept for a hotel swimming pool.

> 'Don't wear low cut clothes or thin shirts without a bra. One man actually stopped me to tell me I wasn't wearing one.'
>
> *Peru*

Use local women as your guides to what is and is not acceptable. Dressing to conform with what is considered 'proper' for Westerners by local people (i.e. fairly conventionally), does more than just reduce the likelihood of unwanted advances from men. You are much more likely to be able to appeal to local women for help and support should the need arise.

> 'Once we were spat at by local women for being dressed skimpily (though not by U.K. standards).'
>
> *Turkey*

Fair-haired women may find that they attract more attention than black or brown-haired travellers. Obviously novelty value has a lot to do with local reactions to blonde hair in countries where the local women are dark. I met a couple who'd returned from visiting a remote area of Bangladesh with their fair-haired toddler. The woman, who'd grown up in the area and knew the local dialect, was amused at reactions to her son's ash blond hair. Many villagers expressed concern about the way he'd prematurely gone grey.

In the context of sexual harassment unfortunately the 'sexy-blonde' stereotype is as well known abroad as in the West. Dying your hair before you go is a little extreme (and a measure only half seriously suggested to us by a couple of contributors!), however tying fair hair back and covering with a scarf can minimise attention, and in very hot countries keeps your hair in better condition anyway.

Behaviour

> 'Codes of behaviour require a lot of adapting to, but often the situation — although unpleasant, frightening, or exasperating — is often less real than imagined. We take our fears from this violent society with us.'
>
> *Peru*

'People do respond to superficial signals that may seem unimportant to Westerners, but have a different meaning to them.'
India

It is very difficult to describe the right sort of manner to aim at, confident without being pushy; assertive, but at the same time modest and demure; firm, but also polite and not over hostile:

'There is the intangible manner of bearing yourself as someone who is contained and self-possessed, giving out a certain vibe that indicates "I know where I'm going, what I'm doing and can deal with hassles", even when you're tired and lost. Hassles occur more frequently if you allow your confusion/tiredness/irritation to show.'

This advice is all very well if you feel fairly confident already. If you're still at the just-arrived, far-from-home stage of culture shock which many of us suffer from, it's not as easy as it sounds, however there are one or two tips which might help. Firstly, give yourself time to adjust — no one expects to feel perfectly sure of themselves in a new situation from the minute they arrive. Although the reward for *confidently* going out and about is a happy, hassle-free trip, there are no prizes for getting there first! Be gentle to yourself and only attempt as much as you want to.

In the early days of your trip, before leaving the hotel, plan your route. Study a street map if one is available, or get clear directions to the market or mosque etc. you want to visit. Then walk confidently to where you are going, even if it is only to the end of the street to get your bearings. Silly as it may sound, by keeping your head up, and looking ahead of you, you can avoid catching the eyes of any men that are nearing you along the street, and have time to notice what you may feel to be potential problems, such as a group of youths lounging on your side of the road. As an added bonus you actually see *more* of the local people than you do if you scuttle nervously along with your head down positively inviting attention.

> 'Street hassle may be a problem, especially in tourist areas. Avoid eye-contact and loitering about.'
>
> *Egypt*

As well as a confident but non-attention attracting manner, temporary deafness is a useful affliction to cultivate:

> 'Best to just ignore remarks, although it's hard not to laugh at the cleverer ones. Do not respond to comments/noises, this only provokes more.'
>
> *Peru*

> 'Pretend an air of bored indifference and that you can look after yourself and not get hassled.'
>
> *Morocco*

If ignoring men and just walking away doesn't work, *don't panic*, but don't just mutely acquiesce either. There is no reason to feel you have to put up with behaviour you're not happy about. In fact the Western-woman myth is sometimes helped on its way because we don't signal strongly enough that we've had enough.

By not signalling clearly enough that overtures by local men are unwelcome, you may instead be tacitly signalling that you don't mind. One friend described a time when she was on her own on a crowded beach in Egypt and was annoyed at being pestered by some local men.

When ignoring them had no results, she tried the outraged-respect-able-female tack. The 'how dare you be so disrespectful to me young man' approach worked much better. It certainly worked for me when in India I was being bothered by some youths on a local train. Egged on by his mates the man next to me put his hand on my knee and started whispering invitations in my ear. After removing his hand several times, and politely declining, I finally (and loudly) announced to his companions that 'this man is annoying me and I certainly expected better behaviour in this country!' Immediately the very friends who a moment before had been rocking with laughter, rose as one, bundled the offender out into the corridor and came back to apologise profusely for his actions!

However this method is only really effective if you're still firmly in control and are really almost acting a role. Don't wait to try it until you're actually beginning to feel a bit frightened; your own fright shows and signals that your pesterer already has the upper hand. Not only that but in genuinely losing your temper you may provoke real hostility and make things worse rather than better.

Finally, as when choosing clothing, it is important to realise that signals given out by dress or behaviour are easily misunderstood in different cultures, and indeed that this works both ways — best summed up by this quote from a woman traveller who visited Peru:

> 'A society with different values views us in a different light than which we view ourselves. Friendliness and freedom of behaviour become encouragement and availability ... The language barrier doesn't help, as implications in the words of both sides are misinterpreted and one finds that "si" means more than intended. The only advice is to try and ignore it all. Too many women let it all get on top of them so that they're frightened or unwilling to talk to *anyone*. (When visiting) a beautiful country it's a great shame when a traveller's only comment on her visit is "Oh God, the men were awful".'
>
> *Peru*

Local Allies This follows on from the previous sections about dress and behaviour. At the same time as repelling the local Romeos, most women travellers will want to remain in contact with ordinary local people, and although it is easy at times to feel that the locals only exist as single men whose life's work is to pester you, there are ordinary family groups around; perfectly responsible older men concerned for your well being and anxious that you should have a good impression of their country; and of course other women. All these are potential allies if you are being bothered, and will offer help and support if you let them know you need it.

'Always make your presence known i.e. talk to people in the village/store/bus and they will protect you if you are in trouble — you'd be amazed.'

Tanzania

'Laugh (at pesterers) if there are plenty of people around. In trucks and buses family groups are useful. Talk to women and children and the men will have less opportunity. Even better if you can turn it all into a joke with the whole bus. It can lead to a lot of fun with the whole bus joining in, and a potentially embarrassing/annoying/dangerous, situation can be defused.'

S. America

Time and place

Women travellers do tend to be more vulnerable alone and at night. In countries where the electricity supply is at best erratic, and at worst non-existent an unofficial curfew often exists, and most families are off the streets by nightfall. Not only are there therefore fewer people to call on for aid, but you stand out even more conspicuously, particularly if local women do not usually go out alone after dusk.

In the West street lighting is of course better and women have challenged the idea that somehow the night belongs to men only. But even in Europe there are some countries (Italy in particular) where you will find men dominating street life and the café scene in the evenings. Local women go out in groups or in families rather than alone. Bearing this in mind, it is worth planning journeys so you arrive in strange towns during daylight, especially if you don't have the address of somewhere to stay.

One of my more uncomfortable arrivals was in Lahore in Pakistan where most women observe Purdah. The train got in late, I didn't know the city and had no idea where the hotel area was. Even though I shared the open taxi with two European men I'd met on the train, we got hopelessly lost trying to find somewhere to stay, and ended up on the fringes of the red-light district.

All three of us got hassled, and as I was still nervous about travelling at all, I got so wound up that I left Lahore the following day, without seeing any of the things I'd meant to visit.

Once you're got your accommodation sorted out, if local people regard certain places as men-only at night, it is sensible to observe the rules, however much you feel that would go against your principles back home.

'Women are not welcome in bars and cantinas on Friday nights unless they're whores. It's a good night for a woman traveller to eat in a nice restaurant, go to a movie or stay in her hotel and write letters.'

Lynn Meisch: Travellers Guide to El Dorado and The Inca Empire

'Observing the rules may seem tedious, but as long as the horror stories persist — alongside urban congestion and high unemployment — then precautions make sense. Personal safety caution eventually becomes just tourist habit.'

Spain

Rural villages are nearly always safer than towns or cities. Everyone knows everyone else and provided you arrive in daylight, everyone knows you're around. You can even use this to your own advantage:

'We had some bother one night when we'd pitched our tent just outside a small village. Some of the local youths decided to visit us just as we were going to sleep and began to make a nuisance of themselves. Swearing at them had no effect but when my friend told them that if they didn't go away immediately she'd tell the whole village how badly they'd behaved the next day, they left without a word.'

Ireland

It is worth remembering that gun carrying is not unusual in some areas, and startling people into unpredictable behaviour might be unwise.

Deserted beaches are also places to avoid at night, and were specifically mentioned as problem areas by several of the women who contributed to this book.

Because women know that nightfall can be a problem time most of us automatically take evasive action during our travels and avoid empty streets late at night. None of the (few) women who reported actual incidents to us told us they had been harassed in these circumstances at night. The place where they had most frequently encountered problems was on crowded public transport. Once you're aware of this you can take steps to deal with it.

Try to avoid travelling when it's most crowded, but don't go to the other extreme and choose buses or train compartments where you'll be alone with one or more men. If possible reserve a seat for yourself and insist that your space is respected by local people. If you've found problems always occur in overcrowded third class try second or even first (or vice versa). Look for local allies and take advantage of areas set aside for women such as ladies-only compartments or particular seats. Where women don't have special places for themselves look for seats next to families or beside other women, and avoid places at the back or where men congregate:

'On buses I would not recommend the back seat if alone as the conductor and most men sit there and do become annoying with their inquisitiveness.'

Turkey

Always choose or reserve a seat next to your companion if you're with one. If you have to take a seat next to a strange man and have misgivings, try putting a bag between you:

'Travelling in the Arab parts of the country was often a bit of a problem — i.e. blokes squashing up next to you on the bus seat, but could be resolved by putting a bag or some object beside you so to avoid body contact.'

Israel

Although conductors and guards may sometimes hassle passengers themselves, usually they will come to your aid.

'We were very well looked after by the always male crew.'

Turkey

Fictional husbands

'People were confused by my status — asking why on earth my father or husband would allow me to travel alone.'

Bangladesh

Fictional husbands are a well tried and tested technique to keep pesterers away. They are better than boyfriends, which are misunder-stood and unfortunately, tend to fuel the free-Western-woman stereotype. 'Husbands', even fictional 'families' confer status on women in many countries and bring another party into the relation-ship between you and other men. It is annoying and I certainly felt resentful that a pesterer was more impressed by the threat of upsetting another (fictional) male than *me*, but it *is* a fact in many countries, and a useful fall-back. (In any case you'll be asked over and over again where your husband is, and it is often easier to say waiting at the next station, than to try and explain why, by your mid twenties or older you're not married.)

Many single women travellers buy wedding rings before leaving — make sure you know which finger to put it on, and don't assume everyone you meet will understand its significance without your drawing attention to it.

In addition you could also think about taking a photo of your 'husband' along.

Islamic countries

In Islamic countries Western women travelling alone or in pairs have to make much more of an adjustment to local people than elsewhere. As Moslem women are so much more restricted than ourselves in all areas of their lives — dress, behaviour, freedom of movement etc. Western women do appear very much more out of place. Not only that, but many Moslems have unfavourable views on what they consider to be 'Western decadence'.

I would recommend women intending to travel in strongly Islamic countries to do some reading about the culture they are going to visit first, and be prepared to compromise considerably about dress, behaviour and their freedom to travel about.

Undoubtedly, going with a companion who is male will go a long way towards solving harassment problems, couples are much more acceptable to local people than single women, or even women in pairs:

'I have travelled sometimes with one other woman and found that more people spoke to us. However I do feel safer travelling with a man, the assumption that you are "spoken for" because you are one of a couple can make life much easier.'

Pakistan

'Usually I would say travelling with one or more other women is ideal ... but in a Moslem society, male protection is unfortunately preferable.'

Morocco

'I would prefer to be with one or more men, as two women together are seen as prey. You can manage, but it's managing, not enjoying yourself.'

Egypt

However if you do go with a male companion, you may find your status is difficult to get used to:

'People ignored me pretty much, all transactions being conducted by men. I had less chance to talk to people as they would
automatically talk to men.'

Morocco

For Western couples, used to a partnership based on our ideas of
equality adapting to a situation where the male partner always comes
first can be a bit of a shock, to both of you. It's worth thinking about
before you go, because as many a frustrated woman traveller has found
it's not easy (or realistic) to insist on being treated in Islamic society
as you would wish to be at home. Couples are better agreeing in
advance how to ensure the women's opinions will be taken into
account, even if this means private discussion in your hotel room
before going out.

'I did feel restricted in a way I did not feel in Europe. My male
companion felt no inhibitions of this sort, although he didn't
especially enjoy the ambience of Islam. I was very taken aback
by the effect that it had on me. I hate to use the word, but I
almost felt cowed. I think I was profoundly affected by the
whole tenor of the female role in these countries. I did acclima-
tize to it — to some degree — I hadn't been out and about in a
non-European, non-Christian culture before. Obviously I had
talked to people and read about it etc., and so should have been
well prepared but curiously the reality amazed me. Very
interesting it was too!'

Algeria / Tunisia / Morocco

Provided you are happy to respect the values of the country you are in, you
will be respected in return, and there is no reason to fear violence and
assault. Many other Western women have had enjoyable, interesting and
exciting trips through Islamic countries. There is no reason to miss out.

'For a woman unable or unwilling to adapt to the attitudes of
both local men and women, travelling would be a series of
abrasive encounters or an extremely solitary affair.'

South America

THEFT

Travellers are often surprised at the honesty of many of the people they meet when travelling. Staying in a seedy part of Bogota, Colombia, I'd carefully hidden most of my money and travellers' cheques under the bottom sheet on my bed before locking my hotel room door and going out. When I returned I found that someone had come in, changed the sheets and remade the bed — carefully replacing the notes in exactly the same place.

Even when in the more vulnerable position of haggling over prices things may turn out better than you'd expect. Sitting in the train at Puno Railway station, waiting for it to leave I had bargained with a peasant women selling a jumper. Having started at 500 soles she'd dropped her price to 250, which I'd agreed on but I only had a 500 sole note and she had no change. 'Don't worry, I'll only be a minute' she said and rushed off along the platform. I was convinced that that was the last I would see of my money especially as the train was about to leave at any moment. But a few minutes later she came running back along the platform and breathlessly handed over my change.

It's easy to forget these incidents when many of the stories you hear tell a different tale. A friend of mine hitching back across Italy on her way home from North Africa was given a lift along a stretch of motorway. About ten minutes after she'd got into the car it spluttered to a halt. Something wrong with the engine, could she and her companion help push the car to start it again? They dutifully got out — whereupon the engine burst back into life, car, rucksacks and all hurtling away in the direction of Milan leaving them stranded and aghast. At least they still had their passports and money ...

What makes such stories particularly unnerving is that the methods used are often in themselves more dramatic than anything you might expect to encounter at home. Bag-slashing, for instance is common in many developing countries: a very sharp knife is used to cut through the bottom of a bag and the contents are then removed, unbeknownst to the wearer. In Italy, thieves have perfected the art of snatching bags from pedestrians' shoulders as they ride past on their motor bikes. Then there are the stories of hold-ups involving knives and machetes:

'I was well psyched up for going to Bogota — paranoia city — by being told by a friend exactly what had happened to him there. Having cashed some travellers' cheques at the bank he and his companion were returning to their hotel when they found themselves pursued by a machete-wielding gang of youths. They were attacked and lost their bags containing their passports, money, cameras and film. One of them had his glasses broken, the other received a cut on the head. All this happened in broad daylight and no-one else on the street did anything to stop it. Having heard this story we were very careful about money and left our bags in the hotel when venturing out. I didn't lose anything.'

Colombia

The chances of having everything stolen as dramatically as this are low but paying attention to such horror stories can be a useful way of learning how to be cautious. Similarly, even obviously apocryphal stories have some point. Another one from Bogota, Colombia — whose streets have the same sort of reputation for street-crime as New York — runs like this: a man is travelling on the bus in Bogota wearing a ring on his little finger. Suddenly he feels a sharp pain in his hand and yells out: a robber has hacked off his little finger with a single blow from his machete, making off with both it and the ring! Typically the moral makes more sense than the tale itself, namely that it's risky to wear jewellery in Bogota — and so it is. Use such stories not as a means of frightening yourself but as a way of planning ahead and taking precautions.

In practice most theft is opportunistic and stealthy rather than violent.

'Be realistic about the fact that particularly in public places if people notice the chance to steal something they probably will.'

India

Pick-pockets are commonplace just about everywhere. Highly skilled operators, their work will probably go unnoticed till long after they've left the scene.

'My friend had a leather wallet containing her passport and travellers' cheques stolen from a holdall by an Indonesian male pretending to read her palms. I was watching at the time and neither of us noticed a thing until later.'

Indonesia

Busy streets, market places and public transport are all ideal places for pick-pockets to work:

'Beware of pick-pockets and "hand-bag gropers" especially on service buses and in crowded places.'

China

Often thieves may be working in pairs — one distracting you whilst the other helps him or herself to the contents of your bag.

'Beware the group of three or four young men who approach you on the street — one points out "dirt" on your jeans or skirt and bends to rub it off. While you are pushing him away, his mate is going through your bag or pockets.'

Ethiopia

It's not surprising that tourists are often a target for these sorts of theft. No matter how much you dress down, how poor you feel in relation to first class tourists, thieves know that even the humblest backpacker usually carries cash, a passport, presents to take home, often a camera, not to mention that watch, pen, torch, books etc. Even the most insignificant item — a bottle of suntan lotion, a pair of tweezers, a toothbrush or a waterproof wash bag — is worth something to somebody. And this is all the truer in developing countries where the disparity in wealth between ourselves and those amongst whom we travel is at its greatest.

> 'Take care of all bags at all times. Don't leave them unattended even for a moment. People have so little in Tanzania it's understandable they are tempted if they see people who look to have so much.'
>
> *Tanzania*

However, this does not mean that everybody in poorer countries is always out to redress the balance by helping themselves to your possessions:

> 'On appearance one could get the impression that theft was a real danger faced with such real poverty. It would be easy to imagine having one's bag or camera snatched by one of the boys or young men whose escape would be easy in such a labyrinth of dark and winding streets. This, however, is not the case. Moroccans think nothing of charging you ten pounds for a bangle which isn't worth ten pence but to actually steal something from you is against their religious nature. Tangiers to me was the exception to the rule being a port. It is very rough and theft here is probably rampant, although we did not experience it personally.'
>
> *Morocco*

> 'I was pick-pocketed on a bus in Marrakesh, but the risks are much the same on the London underground.'
>
> *Morocco*

Try and keep things in perspective without feeling fatalistic, paranoid or blasé about your chances of having everything ripped off. Some countries *are* worse than others, as are some towns, some neighbourhoods, but by following the advice below and heeding the warnings it is possible to travel safely. Personally I lost nothing more than an address book whilst visiting South America and I wasn't going round in an armoured car and bulletproof vest either!

Taking precautions

Before you even pack your rucksack or think about how to hide your valuables, ask yourself how many of them you really need to take away. Obviously you have to have money and a passport, but do you need to carry jewellery with you at all, wherever you are going? Leave bracelets and chains behind. Don't take elaborate earrings. Plain studs are best. One of the perennial horror stories is of women having earrings ripped from their ears. Whilst we've yet to find anyone to whom this has actually happened it's not worth having to worry about. In fact as a general rule, don't take things you're particularly fond of. If you're sentimentally attached to your watch, leave it at home and buy a cheap alternative to travel with, the sort you could lose without much of a qualm. The same applies to clothes.

Remember the less you carry, the less you'll have to worry about, the less you care about them and the less likely you are to be upset if they do go missing.

Once abroad, if you are unlucky enough to be robbed the experience will be most devastating if you lose everything at one go. Never pack all your valuables in one place, either in your suitcase or rucksack, or in a shoulder bag. Anything you don't immediately need — travellers'cheques, the bulk of your cash, your passport — should be kept under your clothes, preferably in a money belt (see opposite), when you have to carry them with you.

Only carry the cash you need for the day in your bag or pocket. This will save you having to fumble under your clothes when all you want to do is pay for a drink. Not only will this get you some funny looks from shopkeepers it'll also reveal precisely where your valuables are to any interested bystanders. For the same reason when you are going to the bank to cash travellers' cheques separate out the bills you want to use immediately from the rest in the privacy of your hotel room. Put the latter back in your hiding place and the former in your purse.

As pockets are prime targets for picking, use those at the side or front, never at the rear of your clothes. Seal your pockets with velcro and you will hear if anyone tries to open them. Keep your camera attached to your wrist with a strong strap or in a shoulder bag which you should wear diagonally across your body so that it is in front where you can see it. This will stop it being snatched from your shoulder and means you can also keep an eye on the contents. Shoulder bags should always have a top which you can fasten shut and should preferably be made of some tough material which will be difficult to slash.

If you are staying somewhere well known for street crime, or going to be spending a morning in a crowded place where the chances of being robbed are known to be high, then try to organise things so that you leave your shoulder bag behind in your hotel room. Don't wear any jewellery or a watch. Use your money belt for your travellers' cheques and passport, if you need to have that with you. If you look less like a potential target you're less likely to have anything stolen.

Money belts   A money belt is probably the single most useful item you can take with you to help secure your valuables.

> 'Mexico is very poor with high unemployment. The Mexicans think you are fair game and they assume you can afford to lose what you have. Having lost my passport and money I would not travel without a money belt for these essential items. If you do have everything stolen you can find yourself in a jam!'
>
> *Mexico*

Don't bother buying the sort of money belt which is made out of nylon and consists of a narrow piece of webbing and a zip pocket. For one thing if you're travelling somewhere hot they'll be both sweaty and irritating if worn next to the skin. They're also very stiff and will cut into you when you bend over. Besides, they're just not large enough, even for travellers' cheques let alone a passport. Instead, make your own. Cotton is an ideal material as it is flexible, soft and absorbent. A pouch attached to a band you can tie round your waist is a convenient design. Alternatively sew extra pockets onto the inside of your clothes. A pocket hanging from the waistband of a gathered skirt works well.

> 'Sew a pocket to the inside of each of your dresses/skirts, big enough to hold passport, travellers' cheques etc. This is far more comfortable than having to wear a money belt the whole time (and is another point against jeans).'
>
> *India*

Some places provide better hiding places than others and you will need to take this into account when deciding what to do, as well as what to take. A string round the neck, for instance, will be clearly visible if you're wearing a T-shirt or collarless dress. Equally you need to take your own anatomy into account. A pocket in your bra may seem like a good idea but in practice rarely proves comfortable, and is inaccessible even to you. Whatever you decide on it's important to try the arrangement out before you set off abroad. Before I left on my travels I sewed a large pocket onto the back of one of my shirts, just the right size for a passport. It wasn't until I actually arrived in South America that I tried it out. I stowed my passport away in it, put on my jumper and then realised with horror as I looked in the horror that I'd chosen the wrong place. I'd gone all flat and angular! As a hiding place it was completely useless.

Rucksacks Part of the debate about whether you should take a rucksack away with you or not revolves around how safe it is to carry one. Doesn't it unnecessarily advertise your presence and indicate your vulnerability to every passing thief?. The answer is, surely, no more than a suitcase. The main difference between them is that whereas rucksacks are associated with budget travellers who are going to be walking to their hotel, suitcases are associated with those who can afford to take a taxi. Unless you can take the taxi as well as the suitcase, carrying the latter will not make you any less inviting a target. In fact if anything it probably increases your chances of being robbed. It is easier to snatch a suitcase from your hand than run off with a rucksack attached to your back.

Where rucksacks do present special opportunities to thieves is by virtue of the fact that they are carried behind you where you can't see what is going on. This makes exterior pockets potentially vulnerable to theft.

Take a rucksack without them, or pack the pockets with things you don't much care about losing.

Because rucksacks are made of soft material they're quite easy to slash with a knife if someone is determined to do it. If you have to carry your rucksack through an area where your guide book warns you this sort of thing might happen then carry your rucksack in front of you.

Another way of deterring this sort of crime is to line your rucksack with bulky and uninteresting articles such as towels which will be difficult to remove. Even if the rucksack is slashed the thief is unlikely to get much out of it. A few people go so far as to recommend using chicken wire for this reason.

Some people use bicycle padlocks threaded through the eyelets of their rucksack to protect their belongings. Needless to say this won't stop anyone slashing the rucksack. However, some left luggage offices insist you padlock your luggage shut before you leave it with them, presumably to prevent charges of theft being levelled against employees. Equally it might be useful if you're leaving your rucksack and most of your possessions at your hotel whilst you trek off into the mountains for a few days and want to be sure that staff won't rifle though it in your absence. The other way round this problem is to leave nothing of tempting value in your bag — if there's nothing to take you won't lose it.

> 'The only time our rucksacks were tampered with was when they'd been loaded onto the roof of the bus for the journey. Whilst we were sat inside and the bus was in motion the co-driver disappeared out the door and climbed onto the roof. When we got to our hotel later that evening we discovered that he'd spent his time rifling through them. Luckily nothing was missing; presumably he'd been looking for money or cameras, which we were carrying with us inside the bus.'
>
> *Peru*

Always keep your luggage close to you and look as if you're looking after it. A thief may well be deterred just by noticing you're noticing. The places where you're most likely to be in this predicament are of course bus and train stations. They're also the most likely places for those intent on robbery to wait for their chance. Be especially vigilant here.

GUIDES

In many countries, men will offer their services as 'guides'. Some may indeed be legitimate professionals, highly trained, knowledgeable and reliable. (In the UK, for example, guides are members of a Guild and must train and be tested on the accuracy of their information.)

At the other extreme are those hangers-on who are really acting as little more than middlemen for a shop or other business. Your 'guide' sees as his first duty getting you to part with your money, preferably in an establishment to which he is attached. To the unwary, 'guides' like these can present themselves as flatteringly interested in your trip, your opinion of their country, and play on your wishes to actually meet local people whilst you are abroad. Alas, sooner or later the truth dawns that you are being taken to visit their shop, carpet showroom, hotel or restaurant and that you are not going to get away without buying something.

> **In a small village in Morocco someone tagged on as we were going to find the bread-shop. On the way back he showed us a different route via a small ceramic workshop. It was obvious that he expected payment, so we gave him a small sum. He obviously expected a lot more and became very disgruntled, and we ended up having a shouting match...**
>
> *Morocco*

Guides can be useful. When I was in Trinidad, visiting the Botanical Gardens in the Port of Spain, an elderly man attached himself to me and my travelling companion and insisted on showing us round. He then asked for a small fee. Although this hadn't been our intention, he actually made the visit more interesting than if we'd gone on our own.

When somebody offers themselves as a guide, you should *usually expect* to pay. This may be up front as a wage, in which case you will know where you stand, and your relationship will be roughly one of employer/employee. Take local advice about how much, negotiate BEFORE you set off, and ensure that everyone is clear about what is and is not included — petrol, entrance fees to monuments, meals (for the guide) etc.

If your 'guide' offers his services as a favour to 'My friend' or 'My guest', you should anticipate that there will be an indirect payment in the form of the commission that your guide expects to get from any purchases you make during your time with him. The most likely exception to this will be local students anxious to show you around, where the 'payment' is the opportunity to practise their English.

You must be much more cautious if you are going to employ a guide to take you into unfamiliar terrain — across mountains, into the desert, up the Amazon — where you will be totally reliant upon the guide for your safety. In these circumstances, you are obviously going to be better off with a guide recruited via legitimate tourist channels, or through your hotel, than you are with a chance met individual who has imposed himself upon you. But even so, you should ask other women for their recommendations first. Otherwise, consider joining up with some other travellers for the trip. As a lone woman you should err on the side of caution, rather than end up alone and dependent on one or more males about whom you actually know very little.

DRUGS

It is almost certain that at some point during your travels you will be made aware of the drug scene — either you may be offered drugs (particularly if you are visiting places popular with low budget travellers), or you will see warning notices at every immigration point to remind you that most countries of the world today have a drugs problem.

Some cultures have a long tradition of the use of various plant derivatives which are illegal in the West. 'Bhang' (marijuana) has for years been made into special sweets and drinks bought occasionally at festival times in India; raw coca leaves are chewed by South American Indians as a mild stimulant, and the soporific and pain quelling affects of opium (also used as a treatment for diarrhoea) are well known in many countries.

The last 20 years have seen these traditions overtaken by two things — the chemical know-how that transforms opium into heroin, coca leaves into cocaine, and the growth of the huge drug industry. What started with the old hippy dream of a joint at sunset on Goa beach has got out of hand to the extent that a country like Pakistan now has a major heroin problem amongst its own population.

Travellers offered drugs by local people should not fool themselves that they are taking part in the local culture. Whilst the odd glass of 'bhang-lassi' is unlikely to do you any harm, and the traditional raw coca leaves won't either, anything else should be treated just as it would back home. You're not being offered a cultural experience, you're being offered a dubious commodity that local people have found Westerners willing to buy.

If anything the drug scene abroad is more dangerous, not less, nearer the country of origin. The drugs themselves are just as toxic and they're just as likely to be mixed with impurities as they would be down town back home. Even if they *aren't*, the strengths may be much higher than they could be in your home town.

On top of this, if you are travelling in a strange culture perhaps for the first time, drug taking can have unpredictable effects. It can for example heighten culture shock, and any anxiety you might still have about travelling in strange surroundings.

The problem is you won't know what you're getting and you won't be able to predict the results. There is also unlikely to be a safety net if you do decide to get involved but find yourself out of your depth. Unlike home there may be no army of doctors, social workers, drug-counselling organisations, or even just friends and relatives for support if things get out of hand. Instead there are the same depressingly nasty scenes in big cities and on some beaches that you might find in London, Sydney or New York. The same unhappy casualties, the same theft, illness and dirt, except that this time there is little help for anyone to turn to. (Don't expect a sympathetic hearing from the British Consulate. Only grudgingly and as a last resort will they provide support for anyone with a drugs problem — it is not their job.)

Finally, if you are not already convinced to be careful, there are the risks you run of getting involved with the local police. It is worth bearing in mind that some countries (Malaysia) still have the death penalty — and they are very tough on drug traffickers. Even where the death penalty is not in force, foreign prisons are no joke, especially for women:

'Stay away from the police, local women who get caught are often raped.'

India/Iran

'Women have a particularly nasty time as the Greek police seem to enjoy beating women up.'

N.C.P.A.

The National Council for the Welfare of Prisoners Abroad says that there are between 1,000 and 1,200 Britons in foreign gaols at any one time. Sixty per cent of their organisation's case load is made up of people detained on drugs-related charges.

Don't be tempted to experiment far from home, in strange surroundings. Even if you're travelling in other Western countries such as the United States or Australasia, you won't know the local scene.

Don't ever get involved in buying and selling. Quite apart from the risk of involvement with the police; gun carrying is usual in many parts of the world.

Don't carry drugs across borders. There is a mistaken belief that women are less likely to be searched than men, and male traffickers still try to persuade women to carry for them. Intimate body searches are unpleasant and humiliating, even if your searcher is female and not all of them are.

So don't carry packages for other people if you don't know what's in them.

Check your luggage before crossing borders to make sure no-one has added anything to your rucksack without you knowing about it.

Contact the British Consulate immediately if you are arrested and charged with an offence; and also the National Council for the Welfare of Prisoners Abroad, (see page 278) if you or a friend need help.

TERRORISM AND POLITICAL UNREST

In a few countries tourists can sometimes be targets for politically motivated dissidents, who realise how vulnerable their governments are if this part of their economy is threatened. At the time of writing, Islamic fundamentalists in Egypt, Kurds in Eastern Turkey, Kashmiri separatists in North India, and the Khymer Range, have all been in the news for kidnapping or attacking tourists to draw attention to their causes. In addition, political unrest in Afghanistan, the Middle East and parts of Africa makes some destinations dangerous to visitors.

It is extremely important that you research in advance the areas you are intending to travel to; do not take unnecessary risks.

The Foreign Office runs a Help Line for travellers and tourists (see page 278). Callers are asked for their destination(s) and any advice that has been passed to the Foreign Office from their posts abroad will be read out to you. The same information, updated regularly, is available on BBC 2 Ceefax.

12
Coming Back

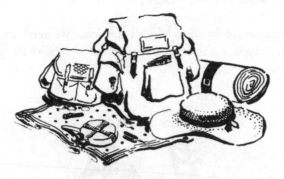

So, you're back from your travels, and you're home unpacking a rucksack of dirty clothes, gifts and precious mementos. It would be quite possible, but disappointing if the story stopped here. If you have travelled with an open mind, you will have seen and experienced things that have surprised and even bewildered you. You may well find that there is another piece of unpacking to do, that will take longer and need greater care — the unpacking of your travelling experiences.

One thing which surprised me when I came back from travelling in South America was quite how hard it was to talk about what had happened. My friends back home all wanted to hear about what it had been like but somehow they asked the wrong questions. 'Did you have a good time? Where did you go? How did you cope?' Sensible, ordinary questions to which I simply couldn't find the right answers. Yes, I had had an exciting time and I had learnt a lot but there didn't seem to be any words to describe what I felt, and trying to sum it all up by describing the places I'd visited or some of the funnier situations I'd found myself in seemed wrong. That meant tying my experience up into neat little packages, a series of verbal

263

snapshots which could be handed round and exclaimed over and I wasn't
ready to do that. Yet I was unsure what else to say. I still didn't know what
I thought about it all.

Part of the problem seems to be that whilst we expect to be puzzling
over things when we're away we often forget that half the questions we
want to ask only emerge when we get back home. In all sorts of ways
travelling can lead us to think again about ourselves, about how we
live, about the society we're part of and about our relationship to those
we've been travelling amongst.

If we are to make the most of our experience we need time to reflect
on what has happened and think about what to do with the insights we
have gained.

THINKING THINGS THROUGH

'When we returned to England after a three year gap our main
culture shock was that though we had been away for what we
considered was a long time and had visited 11 countries, hardly
anybody's life at home had changed. All our friends and
relations were all living in the same houses, all doing the same
jobs and all continuing in the same general direction. Their
lives suddenly appeared to be extremely narrow.'

Australasia and the Pacific

We're often taken aback by how little others have changed when we
return home after travelling for any length of time. Moreover, if we

have learnt to survive with the few possessions we have carried with us, learnt to cope by relying on ourselves, the lives of those we're left behind can suddenly seem overwhelmingly cluttered, even claustrophobic.

> 'Everything that all my friends were worrying about and concentrating on — jobs and mortgages and relationships — suddenly seemed amazingly small scale, just irrelevant to what I felt I'd learnt about myself and my place in the world.'
>
> *East Africa*

For some women it is important to use that difference in perspective to reassess what they're doing with their own lives:

> 'The end of a trip can be a time for change in your own life. Make the most of it. I did, even though it was hard to explain to friends exactly *how* I felt differently and I had to insist that they give me the space to be different too.'
>
> *Asia*

Others are less certain what their goals might be:

> 'Coming back home, to compensate for everything I'd left behind I felt I had two choices: invest in more consumer durables to help block out the meaninglessness of the daily grind or sell up and become a beach bum.'
>
> *Turkey*

Some can hardly wait to get travelling again whilst for many it's a question of settling back into the old familiar routines but without forgetting what has been learnt. This isn't always easy:

> 'On the two occasions I travelled alone I found it a wonderful release from a rather oppressive relationship — the bliss of being able to decide exactly what to do, the possibility of changing one's mind a thousand times without hassle, the intensity of being alone, the enormous relaxation of quiet.

I wasn't in fact able to use the time to make any changes
in my usual life — but looking back I think this was a lost
opportunity.'

Cyprus and Rhodes

Making the most of the opportunity means taking the time to sort out
what went on, how you have changed and how far what you have learnt
is appropriate to everyday life back home. Acquiring the sense of when
to bribe susceptible border officials may have limited applications, but
other insights you have gained may have a more profound impact on
your view of the world:

'Travelling does broaden the mind. It also broadens one's
attitudes to foreigners living in England. Having myself been
a stranger in a strange land I think I understand their feelings,
fears and attitudes a little better. I see a little how lost all the
women who don't speak English must feel when they arrive in
this country. I can see how they cling to their own culture for
security and how I did exactly the same things when I was
travelling. My work as a GP involves contact with Pakistani
and Bangladeshi families and though I only travelled in India
I feel my understanding of their culture, religious beliefs and
diet has helped me enormously. They certainly appreciate my
smattering of Urdu and even though I can only say a few words,
those words immediately lower one of the barriers between us
and smiles appear.'

Asia overland to Australia

One of the most lasting effects of travelling in developing countries
may be a new political awareness of and interest in development issues:

'It was painful to me to have to face up to the effects of my
country's involvement with theirs, to realise that Britain's
increasing industrialisation and material expansion has only
come about because of the exploitation of people in other
countries. I'm now aware that the lifestyle I have is supported
by the labour and sufferings of these people.'

India and Senegal

One form this awareness can take when travelling is an ambivalence and even guilt about your status as a privileged tourist. Back home you may want to think about ways of giving something back to the countries you've travelled through, whether by joining an organisation involved in fighting against poverty and injustice in developing countries or by some other means.

Whatever the conclusions you come to don't expect to know what to make of your experience or how best to use your knowledge straight away. Give yourself some time to work through what has happened. It will be worth it.

Appendix

Partly as a result of the increase in 'sex tourism' the Christian Conference of Asia conducted a programme of research on tourism in Asia. One of the results was the following Code, now translated into several languages.

THE TRAVELLERS' CODE

- Travel with a genuine desire to learn more about the people of your host country.

- Be respectful of the feelings of other people and avoid offensive behaviour on your part. This applies very much to photography and, particularly for women travellers, to styles of dress.

- Cultivate the habit of listening and observing, rather than merely hearing and seeing.

- Remember that often people in the country you visit have different time concepts from your own; this does not make them inferior, only different.

- Acquaint yourself with the local customs, people will be happy to help you.

- Cultivate the habit of asking questions (and listening to the answers).

- You are only one of a thousand travellers; do not expect special privileges.

- If you really want a 'home from home' it is foolish to waste money on travelling.

- When you are shopping, remember that the 'bargain' you obtained may only be possible because of the low wages paid to the maker.

- Do not make promises to people in your host country unless you are certain you can carry them through.

- Spend time reflecting on your daily experiences.

THE HIMALAYAN TOURIST CODE

The Himalayan Tourist Code was drawn up by Tourism Concern in Britain, and based on the Annapurna Conservation Area Project's Code of Conduct. It was produced in response to the environmental problems caused by increasing numbers of tourists visiting the Himalayas, and is widely distributed to visitors through tour operators and travel agents in the UK.

THE HIMALAYAN TOURIST CODE

By following these simple guidelines, *you* can help preserve the unique environment and ancient cultures of the Himalayas

---

Protect the natural environment

▲ **Limit deforestation - make no open fires** and discourage others from doing so on your behalf. Where water is heated by scarce firewood, use as little as possible. When possible choose accommodation that uses kerosene or fuel efficient wood stoves.

▲ **Remove litter, burn or bury paper** and carry out all non-degradable litter. Graffiti are permanent examples of environmental pollution.

▲ **Keep local water clean and avoid using pollutants** such as detergents in streams or springs. If no toilet facilities are available, make sure you are at least 30 metres away from water sources, and bury or cover wastes.

▲ **Plants should be left to flourish in their natural environment** - taking cuttings, seeds and roots is illegal in many parts of the Himalaya.

▲ **Help your guides and porters to follow conservation measures.**

The Himalayas may change you - please do not change them

Tourism Concern, Southlands College, Roehampton Institute, Wimbledon Parkside, London SW19 5NN Tel: 081-944 0464

As a guest, respect local traditions, protect local cultures, maintain local pride.

▲ **When taking photographs, respect privacy** - ask permission and use restraint.

▲ **Respect Holy places** - preserve what you have come to see, never touch or remove religious objects. Shoes should be removed when visiting temples.

▲ **Giving to children encourages begging.** A donation to a project, health centre or school is a more constructive way to help.

▲ **You will be accepted and welcomed if you follow local customs.** Use only your right hand for eating and greeting. Do not share cutlery or cups, etc. It is polite to use both hands when giving or receiving gifts.

▲ **Respect for local etiquette earns you respect** - loose, light weight clothes are preferable to revealing shorts, skimpy tops and tight fitting *action wear*. Hand holding or kissing in public are disliked by local people.

▲ **Observe standard food and bed charges** but do not condone overcharging. Remember when you're shopping that the bargains you buy may only be possible because of low income to others.

▲ **Visitors who value local traditions encourage local pride and maintain local cultures,** please help local people gain a *realistic* view of life in Western Countries.

Be patient, friendly and sensitive Remember - you are a guest

Recommended Reading

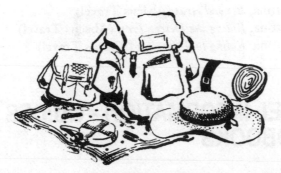

SOME TRAVEL ACCOUNTS BY WOMEN

Birkett, Dea, *Jella* (Gollancz)
Birkett, Dea, *Spinsters Abroad* (Gollancz)
Birkett, Dea, *Mary Kingsley: Imperial Adventuress* (Macmillan)
Dew, Josie, *The Wind in My Wheels* (Warner)
Dodwell, Christina, *A Traveller on Horseback* (Sceptre)
Dodwell, Christina, *Beyond Siberia* (Sceptre)
Dodwell, Christina, *In Papua New Guinea* (Sceptre)
Dodwell, Christina, *Travelling in China* (Sceptre)
Dodwell, Christina, *Travels with Pegasus* (Sceptre)
Gellhorn, Martha, *The Weather in Africa* (Eland Hippocrene)
Gellhorn, Martha, *Travels with Myself and Another* (Eland Hippocrene)
Murphy, Dervla, *Cameroon with Cuthbert* (Arrow Books, Century Travellers Series)
Murphy, Dervla, *Full Tilt* (Arrow Books, Century Travellers Series)
Murphy, Dervla, *Muddling Through Madagascar* (Arrow Books, Century Travellers Series)

Murphy, Dervla, *On a Shoe String to Coorg* (Arrow Books, Century Travellers Series)

Murphy, Dervla, *The Waiting Land* (Arrow Books, Century Travellers Series)

Murphy, Dervla, *Transylvania and Beyond* (Arrow Books, Century Travellers Series)

Murphy, Dervla, *Where the Indus is Young* (Arrow Books, Century Travellers Series)

Payne, Sheila, *Afghan Amulet* (Michael Joseph)

Selby, Bettina, *Beyond Arat* (Abacus Travel)

Selby, Bettina, *Riding the Desert Trail* (Abacus Travel)

Selby, Bettina, *Riding to Jerusalem* (Abacus Travel)

TRAVEL INFORMATION - GUIDES AND HANDBOOKS

Series

Lonely Planet Series   About 120 titles, including guides, phrase books, shoe string guides, city guides and books about travelling with children. There is an increasing number of women writers and contributors.

Rough Guides   More than 50 titles, including: *More Women Travel*, a compilation of over 70 women's travel experiences; *Nothing Ventured*, disabled travellers' accounts, and a forthcoming *World Music Guide*, and a *Gay and Lesbian Travel Guide*. A good number of women have contributed to the guides.

Smooth Ride Guides   Forthcoming guides for disabled travellers, covering Australia and New Zealand, USA and Canada (FT Publishing).

Other guides for women

Places for Women (Ferrari) — for lesbian women
City Guides for Women (Virago) — 6 titles: Amsterdam, London, New York, Paris, Rome, San Francisco.
Are You Two Together? (Virago) — for lesbian women

MEDICAL HANDBOOKS

Dawood, Richard, *Travellers' Health* (Oxford University Press)
Graber and Siegel, *Travellers' Medical Companion* (Fielding Morrow)
Schroeder, *Staying Healthy in Asia, Africa and Latin America* (Moon Publications)
Walker and Williams, *ABC of Healthy Travel* (BJM)

OTHER TITLES

Askham, Suzanne, *Adventure Unlimited* (Piccadilly)
Automobile Association *World Wheelchair Traveller* (The Automobile Association)
Graham, Scott, *Handle with Care: Responsible Travel in Developing Countries* (Noble Press)
Guillebaud, John, *The Pill* (Oxford University Press)
Wood, Katie and House, Syd, *The Good Tourist* (Mandarin)
Wood, Katie, *The Green Tourist Guide* (Mandarin)

Useful Addresses

OVERLAND TOUR OPERATORS, ADVENTURE HOLIDAYS AND GROUP TRAVEL

AITO — The Association of Independent Tour Operators has a list of the larger and most established organisations. Telephone them on: 0181-744 9280 for a list.

There are many other small independent companies, which advertise in weekend newspapers, and in specialist magazines.

Look out for: **Dragoman, Encounter Overland, Exodus, Explore, Explorasia, Guerba, Headwater, Journey Latin America, Ramblers, Sherpa and Waymark.**

Mainly for women

Lady Trek, 'Junipers', Loch Carron, Scotland IV54 8YD (Tel: 01520 2238) — Walking holidays in Scottish Highlands and Islands.

Tiger Travel, 56 Bowden Hill, Newton Abbot, Devon TQ12 1BH (Tel: 01626 62528) — Small group tours for women, visiting India, Indonesia and Egypt.

TRAVEL AGENTS

AITO (see above) have a list of independent travel agents who specialise in independent travel.

Campus Travel and STA have branches throughout the UK, Europe, Australia and the USA.

Marco Polo Travel Advisory Service, 24a Park Street, Bristol BS1 5JA (Tel: 0117 9294123) — A travel agent set up by a woman traveller who is a Fellow of the Royal Geographical Society and a member of Tourism Concern. It organises day seminars on women and travel.

Trailfinders — There are branches in Manchester, London and Bristol. Consult the telephone directory for your nearest branch.

Triangle Travel (Tel: 0114 2722990) — Gay and lesbian travel services.

MEETING LOCAL WOMEN: SOME HOME STAY ORGANISATIONS

Experiment in International Living, Otesega West Malvern Road, Malvern, Worcestershire WR14 4EN (Tel: 01684 562577)

SERVAS, (General Secretary Tel: 01943 862 965)

Women-Welcome-Women, 8a Chestnut Avenue, High Wycombe, Buckinghamshire HP11 1DJ (Tel: 01494 439481)

OTHER ADDRESSES

Foreign Office Help Line for Travellers and Tourists (Tel: 0171-270 4129/4179) — Gives up-to-date advice on areas of terrorism and political unrest.

General Register Office, PO Box 2, Southport, Merseyside PR8 2JD (Tel: 0151 471 4200) — To obtain a copy of your birth certificate.

International Association for Medical Assistance to Travellers (IAMAT), 417 Center Street, Lewiston, New York, NY 14092, USA (Tel: 0101 716 754 4883) — Issue a list of English-speaking doctors working in most parts of the world.

International Planned Parenthood Federation, Inner Circle, Regents Park, London NW1 4NS (Tel: 0171-486 0741)

Medical Advisory Services for Travellers Abroad Ltd (MASTA), (Travellers' Help Line Tel: 01891 224100)

National Council for the Welfare of Prisoners Abroad, 347a Upper Street, London N1 0PD

Royal Geographical Society's Expedition Advisory Service, 1 Kensington Gore, London SW7 2AR (Tel: 0171-581 2057) — Gives advice on outdoor cold-weather clothing and equipment.

Safariquip, The Stones, Castleton, Sheffield S30 2WX (Tel: 01433 620320) — Sells mosquito nets.

Tourism Concern, Southlands College, Roehampton Institute, Wimbledon Parkside, London SW19 5NN (Tel: 0181-944 0464) — Campaigning organisation that promotes awareness of the rights and interests of people living in the world's tourist areas.

Travel Clinic Health Line, run from the Hospital for Tropical Diseases (Tel: 01839 337733) — Gives up-to-date, specialist advice on diseases prevalent in far-flung countries of the world.

Travel Companions, 110 High Mount, Station Road, London NW4 3ST (Tel: 0181 202 8478) — A bureau service that puts would-be travel companions in touch.

Women's Travel Advisory Bureau, Lansdowne, High Street, Blockley, Gloucestershire GL56 9HF (Tel: 01386 701082) — Advice and information.

Index

279

About the Authors

Maggie and Gemma Moss are sisters. Maggie works with schools-industry links and co-runs seminars for women on travelling abroad, with a travel agent. She is a member of Tourism Concern. She has travelled widely throughout India, alone and also with a male companion. She has also spent time in Turkey, Iran, Sri Lanka, Pakistan and all over Europe. Gemma lectures at the Institute of Education at London University, and at Bristol Polytechnic. Her travelling has been most extensive throughout South America, the United States and Europe. Maggie Moss lives in Bristol and Gemma Moss lives in Southampton.